THE NEW FOLGER LIBRARY SHAKESPEARE

Designed to make Shakespeare's great plays available to all readers, the New Folger Library edition of Shakespeare's plays provides accurate texts in modern spelling and punctuation, as well as scene-by-scene action summaries, full explanatory notes, many pictures clarifying Shakespeare's language, and notes recording all significant departures from the early printed versions. Each play is prefaced by a brief introduction, by a guide to reading Shakespeare's language, and by accounts of his life and theater. Each play is followed by an annotated list of further readings and by a "Modern Perspective" written by an expert on that particular play.

Barbara A. Mowat was Director of Research *emerita* at the Folger Shakespeare Library, Consulting Editor of *Shakespeare Quarterly*, and author of *The Dramaturgy of Shakespeare's Romances* and of essays on Shakespeare's plays and their editing.

Paul Werstine is Professor of English in the Graduate School and at King's University College at Western University. He is a general editor of the New Variorum Shakespeare and author of *Early Modern Playhouse Manuscripts and the Editing of Shakespeare* and of many papers and articles on the printing and editing of Shakespeare's plays.

Folger SHAKESPEARE LIBRARY

Twelfth Night, or, What You Will

By
WILLIAM SHAKESPEARE

AN UPDATED EDITION

EDITED BY BARBARA A. MOWAT
AND PAUL WERSTINE

Simon & Schuster Paperbacks
NEW YORK LONDON TORONTO SYDNEY NEW DELHI

Simon & Schuster Paperbacks
An Imprint of Simon & Schuster, Inc.
1230 Avenue of the Americas
New York, NY 10020

This Simon & Schuster paperback edition July 2019

SIMON & SCHUSTER PAPERBACKS and colophon are registered trademarks of Simon & Schuster, Inc.

For information about special discounts for bulk purchases, please contact Simon & Schuster Special Sales at 1-866-506-1949 or business@simonandschuster.com.

The Simon & Schuster Speakers Bureau can bring authors to your live event. For more information or to book an event contact the Simon & Schuster Speakers Bureau at 1-866-248-3049 or visit our website at www.simonspeakers.com.

Manufactured in the United States of America

40 39 38 37 36 35 34 33 32

ISBN 978-0-7434-8277-6
ISBN 978-1-4767-8860-9 (ebook)

From the Director of the Folger Shakespeare Library

It is hard to imagine a world without Shakespeare. Since their composition more than four hundred years ago, Shakespeare's plays and poems have traveled the globe, inviting those who see and read his works to make them their own.

Readers of the New Folger Editions are part of this ongoing process of "taking up Shakespeare," finding our own thoughts and feelings in language that strikes us as old or unusual and, for that very reason, new. We still struggle to keep up with a writer who could think a mile a minute, whose words paint pictures that shift like clouds. These expertly edited texts, presented here with accompanying explanatory notes and up-to-date critical essays, are distinctive because of what they do: they allow readers not simply to keep up, but to engage deeply with a writer whose works invite us to think, and think again.

These New Folger Editions of Shakespeare's plays are also special because of where they come from. The Folger Shakespeare Library in Washington, D.C., where the Editions are produced, is the single greatest documentary source of Shakespeare's works. An unparalleled collection of early modern books, manuscripts, and artwork connected to Shakespeare, the Folger's holdings have been consulted extensively in the preparation of these texts. The Editions also reflect the expertise gained through the regular performance of Shakespeare's works in the Folger's Elizabethan Theater.

I want to express my deep thanks to editors Barbara Mowat and Paul Werstine for creating these indispensable editions of Shakespeare's works, which incorporate the best of textual scholarship with a richness of commentary that is both inspired and engaging. Readers who want to know more about Shakespeare and his plays can follow the paths these distinguished scholars have tread by visiting the Folger itself, where a range of physical and digital resources (available online) exist to supplement the material in these texts. I commend to you these words, and hope that they inspire.

Michael Witmore
Director, Folger Shakespeare Library

Contents

Editors' Preface

In recent years, ways of dealing with Shakespeare's texts and with the interpretation of his plays have been undergoing significant change. This edition, while retaining many of the features that have always made the Folger Shakespeare so attractive to the general reader, at the same time reflects these current ways of thinking about Shakespeare. For example, modern readers, actors, and teachers have become interested in the differences between, on the one hand, the early forms in which Shakespeare's plays were first published and, on the other hand, the forms in which editors through the centuries have presented them. In response to this interest, we have based our edition on what we consider the best early printed version of a particular play (explaining our rationale in a section called "An Introduction to This Text") and have marked our changes in the text—unobtrusively, we hope, but in such a way that the curious reader can be aware that a change has been made and can consult the "Textual Notes" to discover what appeared in the early printed version.

Current ways of looking at the plays are reflected in our brief introductions, in many of the commentary notes, in the annotated lists of "Further Reading," and especially in each play's "Modern Perspective," an essay written by an outstanding scholar who brings to the reader his or her fresh assessment of the play in the light of today's interests and concerns.

As in the Folger Library General Reader's Shakespeare, which this edition replaces, we include explanatory notes designed to help make Shakespeare's language clearer to a modern reader, and we place the notes on the page facing the text that they explain. We also follow the earlier edition in including illustrations—of objects, of clothing, of mythological figures—from books and manuscripts in the Folger Library collection. We provide fresh accounts of the life of Shakespeare, of the publishing of his plays, and of the theaters in which his plays were performed, as well as an introduction to the text itself. We also include a section called "Reading Shakespeare's Language," in which we try to help readers learn to "break the code" of Elizabethan poetic language.

For each section of each volume, we are indebted to a host of generous experts and fellow scholars. The "Reading Shakespeare's Language" sections, for example, could not have been written had not Arthur King, of Brigham Young University, and Randal Robinson, author of *Unlocking Shakespeare's Language,* led the way in untangling Shakespearean language puzzles and shared their insights and methodologies generously with us. "Shakespeare's Life" profited by the careful reading given it by S. Schoenbaum, "Shakespeare's Theater" was read and strengthened by Andrew Gurr, John Astington, and William Ingram, and "The Publication of Shakespeare's Plays" is indebted to the comments of Peter W. M. Blayney. We, as editors, take sole responsibility for any errors in our editions.

We are grateful to the authors of the "Modern Perspectives"; to Leeds Barroll and David Bevington for their generous encouragement; to the Huntington and Newberry Libraries for fellowship support; to King's University College for the grants it has provided to Paul Werstine; to the Social Sciences and Humanities Research Council of Canada, which provided him with Research Time Stipends; and to the Folger Institute's Center for Shakespeare Studies for its fortuitous sponsorship of a workshop on "Shakespeare's Texts for Students and Teachers" (funded by the National Endowment for the Humanities and led by Richard Knowles of the University of Wisconsin), a workshop from which we learned an enormous amount about what is wanted by college and high-school teachers of Shakespeare today.

In preparing this preface for the publication of *Twelfth Night* in 1993, we wrote, "Our biggest debt is to the Folger Shakespeare Library—to Werner Gundersheimer, Director of the Library, who made possible our edition; to Jean Miller, the Library's Art Curator, who combed the Library holdings for illustrations, and to Julie Ainsworth, Head of the Photography Department, who carefully photographed them; to Georgianna Ziegler, Reference Librarian, whose research skills have been invaluable; to Peggy O'Brien, Director of Education, who gave us expert advice about the needs being expressed by Shakespeare teachers and students (and to Martha Christian and other 'master teachers' who used our texts in manuscript in their classrooms); to the staff of the Academic Programs Division, especially Paul Menzer (who drafted 'Further Reading' material), Mary Tonkinson, Lena Cowen Orlin, Molly Haws, Amy Adler, and Jessica Hymowitz; to Rachel Duchak, who helped us find the 'new map'; and, finally, to the staff of the Library Reading Room, whose patience and support have been invaluable."

As we revise the play for publication in 2019, we add to the above our gratitude to Michael Witmore, Director of the Folger Shakespeare Library, who brings to our work a gratifying enthusiasm and vision; to Eric Johnson, the Folger's Director of Digital Access, who expertly manages our editions in both their paper and their many electronic forms; to Gail Kern Paster, Director of the Library from 2002 until July 2011, whose interest and support have been unfailing and whose scholarly expertise continues to be an invaluable resource; to Jonathan Evans and Alysha Bullock, our production editors at Simon & Schuster, whose expertise, attention to detail, and wisdom are essential to this project; to the Folger's Photography Department; to Deborah Curren-Aquino for continuing superb editorial assistance and for her exceptionally fine Further Reading annotations; to Alice Falk for her expert copyediting; to Michael Poston for unfailing computer support; to Jessica Roberts Frazier, Sophie Byvik, Gabrielle Linnell, and Stacey Redick; and to Rebecca Niles (whose help is crucial). Among the editions we consulted, we found Keir Elam's 2008 Arden edition especially useful. Finally, we once again express our thanks to Stephen Llano for twenty-five years of support as our invaluable production editor, to the late Jean Miller for the wonderful images she unearthed, and to the ever-supportive staff of the Library Reading Room.

Barbara A. Mowat died on Thanksgiving Day 2017. Her knowledge, wisdom, and great care of Shakespeare's texts will be sorely missed.

Paul Werstine
2019

Shakespeare's
Twelfth Night, or, What You Will

In *Twelfth Night*, Shakespeare plays with the inter-
sections of love and power. The Countess Olivia is
presented to us at the play's beginning as an independent and powerful woman. The sudden deaths of
her father and her brother have left her in charge of
her own household and have thereby given her power
over such male relatives as Sir Toby Belch. Her status
as a wealthy, aristocratic single woman makes her the
focus of male attention, and she is especially attractive
to Duke (or Count) Orsino, who, as the play begins, is
already pursuing her. There also circle about her two
other would-be suitors: the pretentious and socially
ambitious steward, Malvolio, a man whose ambi-
tions make him vulnerable to manipulation by members of Olivia's household; and the weak and foolish
Sir Andrew Aguecheek, who is altogether ignored by
Olivia but whose delusions of possible marriage to her
make him an easy victim of the flattering and swin-
dling Sir Toby.

Onto this scene arrive the well-born twins Viola and
Sebastian, and the love of power gives way to the power
of love. The twins have been shipwrecked; each thinks
the other is drowned; both are destitute. Without protection, Viola chooses to disguise herself as a page, call
herself Cesario, and enter into the service of Orsino. In
her role as the young Cesario, such is her beauty and
her command of language that she immediately wins
Orsino's complete trust; he enlists her as his envoy to
his beloved Olivia—only to have Olivia fall desperately
in love with the beautiful young messenger. Sebastian,

too, although without either power or wealth, is similarly irresistible. Antonio, for example, not only saves him from death in the sea but also risks his own life to remain in Sebastian's company.

As is usual in comedy, the play complicates these tangled relationships before it finally and wonderfully untangles them. The title of the play suggests that there is a certain urgency to the need for this disentangling. "Twelfth Night" is the twelfth night after Christmas, the last night of what used to be the extended period of celebration of the Christmas season. Thus it marks the boundary between the time for games and disguisings and the business of the workaday world. The second part of the title, "What You Will," suggests that this play gives us a world that we would all choose (or "will") to enjoy, if we but could.

After you have read the play, we invite you to read "A Modern Perspective" on *Twelfth Night* written by Professor Catherine Belsey of Cardiff University, printed at the back of this book.

Reading Shakespeare's Language: *Twelfth Night, or, What You Will*

For many people today, reading Shakespeare's language can be a problem—but it is a problem that can be solved. Those who have studied Latin (or even French or German or Spanish) and those who are used to reading poetry will have little difficulty understanding the language of Shakespeare's poetic drama. Others, though, need to develop the skills of untangling unusual sentence structures and of recognizing and understanding poetic compressions, omissions, and wordplay. And even those skilled in reading unusual sentence structures may have occasional trouble with Shakespeare's words. More than four hundred years of "static"—caused by changes in language and life—intervene between his speaking and our hearing. Most of his immense vocabulary is still in use, but a few of his words are no longer used, and many of his words now have meanings quite different from those they had in the sixteenth century. In the theater, most of these difficulties are solved for us by actors who study the language and articulate it for us so that the essential meaning is heard—or, when combined with stage action, is at least *felt*. When reading on one's own, one must do what each actor does: go over the lines (often with a dictionary close at hand) until the puzzles are solved and the lines yield up their poetry and the characters speak in words and phrases that are, suddenly, rewarding and wonderfully memorable.

are's Words

>pening scenes of a play by
>tice occasional unfamiliar
r simply because we no lon-
ing scenes of *Twelfth Night*,
he words *coistrel* (i.e., a low-
gust (i.e., taste), *an* (i.e., if),
icles or barriers), and *endue
*). Words of this kind are
xt and will become familiar
plays you read.
ll of Shakespeare's writing,
words that are still in use
t meanings. In the opening
r example, the word *valid-
rth," *pitch* is used where we
is used where we would say
where we would say "drift-
we would say "overcome,
>e explained in the notes to
>ecome familiar as you con-
language.
not because of the "static"
anguage over the past cen-
re words that Shakespeare
tic world that has its own
background mythology. In
larger world that Shake-
one set of words to create
and a second to create the
he language that constructs
ge of romantic love as seen
al terms. In this world, the
"cloistress," her tears are

called "eye-offending brine," and her lady-in-waiting is her "handmaid"; the lover, Orsino, portrays himself as the mythological figure Acteon struck down by the "fell and cruel hounds" of his desires, and he prays that his beloved be wounded by the love-god Cupid's "rich golden shaft" so that the "sovereign thrones" of her being will be filled with love for him, her "one self king."

In contrast, the language that creates the world of the Lady Olivia's estate is that of drunken uncles, foolish suitors, clever ladies-in-waiting, and self-important butlers; it is a world of "ducats," "viol-de-gamboys," "substractors," "wenches," "shrews," "buttery bars," cups of "canary," "kickshawses," "jigs," and "galliards." This second, prosaic world is transformed whenever Viola enters Olivia's estate, bringing with her Orsino's petition for Olivia's love and with it language in which love is "divinity" and its songs are "loyal cantons of contemnèd love." These language worlds together create the Illyria that Orsino, Olivia, Viola, Sebastian, and their servants and relatives inhabit. The words that create these worlds will become increasingly familiar to you as you read further into the play.

Shakespeare's Sentences

In an English sentence, meaning is quite dependent on the place given each word. "The dog bit the boy" and "The boy bit the dog" mean very different things, even though the individual words are the same. Because English places such importance on the positions of words in sentences, on the way words are arranged, unusual arrangements can puzzle a reader. Shakespeare frequently shifts his sentences away from "normal" English arrangements—often to create the rhythm he seeks, sometimes to use a line's poetic rhythm to emphasize a particular word, sometimes to give a character his or her own speech patterns or to allow the character to speak in a special way. When we attend a good performance of the play, the actors will have worked out the sentence structures and will artic-ulate the sentences so that the meaning is clear. When reading the play, we need to do as the actor does: that is, when puzzled by a character's speech, check to see if the words are being presented in an unusual sequence.

Shakespeare often places the verb before the subject (e.g., instead of "he goes" we find "goes he"). In _Twelfth Night_, we find such a construction in Orsino's "O spirit of love, how quick and fresh _art thou_," as well as in the Captain's "_Be you_ his eunuch" and in Toby's "Then _hadst thou had_ an excellent head of hair" (instead of "thou hadst had . . ."). Orsino's "That instant _was I_ turned into a hart" is another example of inverted sub-ject and verb.

Such inversions rarely cause much confusion. More problematic is Shakespeare's frequent placing of the object or the predicate adjective before the subject and verb (e.g., instead of "I hit him," we might find "him I hit," or, instead of "it is black," we might find "black it is"). Viola's "What else may hap, to time I will commit" is an example of such an inversion (the normal order would be "I will commit what else may hap [i.e., what-ever else may happen] to time"). Another example is Orsino's "So full of shapes is fancy," where the phrase serving as predicate adjective ("so full of shapes") pre-cedes the subject and verb, and where the subject and verb are themselves inverted. (The normal order would be "Fancy is so full of shapes.")

Inversions are not the only unusual sentence struc-tures in Shakespeare's language. Often in his sentences words that would normally appear together are separated from each other. (Again, this is often done to create a particular rhythm or to stress a particular word.) Take, for example, Orsino's "when liver, brain, and heart, / These sovereign thrones, are all supplied, and filled / Her sweet perfections with one self king"; here the phrase "These sovereign thrones" separates the subject ("liver, brain, and heart") from its verb ("are"), and the phrase "Her sweet perfections" interrupts the phrase "filled with." Or take the Captain's lines: "And then 'twas fresh in murmur (as, you know, / What great ones do the less will prattle of) / That he did seek the love of fair Olivia," where the normal construction "'twas fresh in murmur that he did seek the love of fair Olivia" is interrupted by the insertion of the parenthetical "as, you know, what great ones do the less will prattle of." In order to create for yourself sentences that seem more like the English of everyday speech, you may wish to rearrange the words, putting together the word clusters ("liver, brain, and heart are," "Her sweet perfections filled with," "'twas fresh in murmur that"). You will usually find that the sentence will gain in clarity but will lose its rhythm or shift its emphasis.

Locating and, if necessary, rearranging words that "belong together" is especially helpful in passages that separate basic sentence elements by long delaying or expanding interruptions. When in 1.2 the Captain tells Viola about his last sight of her brother Sebastian ("I saw your brother bind himself to a strong mast, where I saw him hold acquaintance with the waves so long as I could see"), he uses a construction that both delays the main sentence elements until subordinate material is presented and then interrupts the sentence elements with additional subordinate material:

Assure yourself, after our ship did split,
When you and those poor number saved with you
Hung on our driving boat, *I saw your brother,*
Most provident in peril, *bind himself*
(Courage and hope both teaching him the practice)
To a strong mast that lived upon the sea,
Where, like Arion on the dolphin's back,
I saw him hold acquaintance with the waves
So long as I could see.

In some of Shakespeare's plays (*Hamlet,* for instance), long interrupted sentences and sentences in which the basic sentence elements are significantly delayed are used frequently, sometimes to catch the audience up in the narrative and sometimes as a characterizing device. They appear rarely in *Twelfth Night,* where sentences tend to be structurally straightforward.

Finally, in many of Shakespeare's plays, sentences are sometimes complicated not because of unusual structures or interruptions but because Shakespeare omits words and parts of words that English sentences normally require. (In conversation, we, too, often omit words. We say "Heard from him yet?" and our hearer supplies the missing "Have you.") Frequent reading of Shakespeare—and of other poets—trains us to supply such missing words. In his later plays, Shakespeare uses omissions both of verbs and of nouns to great dramatic effect. In *Twelfth Night* omissions are rare and seem to be used to affect the tone of the speech or for the sake of speech rhythm. For example, Sir Andrew's "I'll home tomorrow" (where "go" is omitted) lends a colloquial flavor to his speech, and Orsino's "I myself am best / When least in company" (where "I am" is omitted before "least") provides a regular iambic pentameter line.

Shakespearean Wordplay

Shakespeare plays with language so often and so variously that entire books are written on the topic. Here we will mention only two kinds of wordplay, puns and metaphors. A pun is a play on words that sound the same but have different meanings (or on a single word that has more than one meaning). In the opening scene of *Twelfth Night*, a pun on the words *heart* and *hart* underlies this exchange between Orsino and Curio: "Will you go hunt, my lord?" "What, Curio?" "The hart." "Why, so I do, the noblest that I have." In a later scene Olivia, curious about the "man" who refuses to leave the gate of her estate, asks "What manner [i.e., kind] of man" he is. Malvolio's response, "Of very ill manner," puns on the word *manner*, using its meaning of "behavior." In this exchange in 1.5 between Maria and the Fool—

> FOOL   . . . I am resolved on two points.
> MARIA   That if one break, the other will hold, or if
>   both break, your gaskins fall[—]

Maria puns on the word *points*, which meant not only the "points" of an argument but also the laces that held up a man's breeches.

Because of the presence of the Fool, who makes his living by using wordplay to amuse his aristocratic patron and others in the household, *Twelfth Night* is among Shakespeare's plays that use puns frequently. The Fool's opening exchange with Olivia in 1.5—an exchange that succeeds in amusing her and thus saving the Fool's threatened position in the household—turns on his successful play on the word *Fool* (the name given the profession he follows) and *fool* (a person who behaves foolishly). Within this larger exchange, Olivia calls him a "dry [i.e., dull, not amusing] Fool" who has grown "dishonest"; his defense is a series of puns: "give the dry [i.e., dull] Fool drink, then is the Fool not dry [i.e., thirsty]. Bid the dishonest man mend [i.e., (1) reform, (2) repair] himself; if he mend [i.e., reform], he is no longer dishonest; if he cannot, let the botcher [i.e., tailor who repairs clothing] mend [i.e., repair] him." Such puns characterize the Fool's "foolery"—so much so that the language in this play, and the Fool's language in particular, needs to be listened to carefully if one is to catch all its meanings.

A metaphor is a play on words in which one object or idea is expressed as if it were something else, something with which it is said to share common features. In the opening lines of *Twelfth Night*—

> If music be the food of love, play on.
> Give me excess of it, that, surfeiting,
> The appetite may sicken and so die[—]

metaphoric language is used to express the longings of love as a physical hunger for which music is a satisfying food. As a way of saying that he wishes he were not so much in love, Orsino asks that his love be given an excessive amount of music so that love's appetite will be killed by overeating. A few lines later Orsino uses another metaphor to express the intensity of his love:

> O, when mine eyes did see Olivia first,
> . . . . .
> That instant was I turned into a hart,
> And my desires, like fell and cruel hounds,
> E'er since pursue me.

Here the lover, having seen his beloved, is pursued by his desires as a deer is by hunting dogs. (Shakespeare's audience would have recognized behind this metaphor the famous mythological account of the hunter Acteon, who, having seen the goddess Diana naked, was literally turned into a deer and destroyed by his own hounds.)

Later in the play (in 3.1) Olivia uses metaphor to express her own love pains. Having fallen in love with Cesario, she has, she thinks, earned his scorn by sending a ring to him. "What might you think?" she asks.

> Have you not set mine honor at the stake
> And baited it with all th' unmuzzled thoughts
> That tyrannous heart can think?

In this metaphor, her honor is like a bear tied to the stake and attacked by the vicious dogs of Cesario's harsh thoughts.

In *Twelfth Night* one occasionally finds metaphor used to control long stretches of dialogue. In 1.5, Viola/Cesario addresses Olivia with the claim that his message is, to Olivia's ears, divinity (i.e., something holy). Olivia responds as if "divinity" meant "theology," and asks for Cesario's "text" (i.e., the scriptural passage on which he is to expound). Olivia thus sets up a metaphor that continues for several lines of dialogue through the words *doctrine, chapter, method, the first* [chapter], and *heresy:*

VIOLA The rudeness that hath appeared in me have I learned from my entertainment. What I am and what I would are as secret as maidenhead: to your ears, divinity; to any other's, profanation.

OLIVIA Give us the place alone. We will hear this divinity. (*Maria and Attendants exit.*) Now, sir, what is your text?

VIOLA Most sweet lady—

OLIVIA A comfortable doctrine, and much may be said
of it. Where lies your text?

VIOLA In Orsino's bosom.

OLIVIA In his bosom? In what chapter of his bosom?

VIOLA To answer by the method, in the first of his
heart.

OLIVIA O, I have read it; it is heresy. Have you no more
to say?

VIOLA Good madam, let me see your face.

OLIVIA Have you any commission from your lord to
negotiate with my face? You are now out of your
text. But we will draw the curtain and show you the
picture. (*She removes her veil.*)

With Olivia's "we will draw the curtain and show you
the picture," the controlling metaphor shifts from
"love message as sermon" to "veiled face as covered
portrait," a metaphor that progresses through Olivia's
"such a one I was this present" through "'Tis in grain"
and "'Tis beauty truly blent."

In most of Shakespeare's plays, metaphors are most
often used when the idea being conveyed seems hard
to express, and the speaker is thus given language
that helps to carry the idea or the feeling to his or her
listener—and to the audience. In *Romeo and Juliet,* for
example, Romeo's metaphors of Juliet-as-saint and
Juliet-as-light employ images from the poetic tradition that seem designed to portray a lover struggling
to express the overpowering feelings that come with
being in love. In *Twelfth Night* one senses that metaphors are to be heard not so much as sincere attempts
to express deep feelings as they are a playing with language, a deliberate heightening of emotion for self-
indulgence or for display.

Implied Stage Action

Finally, in reading Shakespeare's plays we should always remember that what we are reading is a performance script. The dialogue is written to be spoken by actors who, at the same time, are moving, gesturing, picking up objects, weeping, shaking their fists. Some stage action is described in what are called "stage directions"; some is suggested within the dialogue itself. We must learn to be alert to such signals as we stage the play in our imaginations. When, in *Twelfth Night*, Sir Andrew says to Maria "Here's my hand," and a few lines later she says to him "Now I let go your hand," it is clear what stage action has occurred. Again, when, at the end of 1.3, Sir Toby says to Sir Andrew "Let me see thee caper. Ha, higher! Ha, ha, excellent!" one knows that Sir Andrew at least attempts to dance a lively dance. At several places in *Twelfth Night*, signals to the reader are not quite so clear. When, after Olivia's first meeting with Cesario, Malvolio in 2.2 says to Cesario "She returns this ring to you. . . . Receive it so. . . . you peevishly threw it to her, and her will is it should be so returned. If it be worth stooping for, there it lies . . . ," one assumes that, at some point during these speeches, Malvolio throws down the ring; one assumes, also, that Viola/Cesario picks up the ring at some point during her speech after Malvolio exits. But the precise moments for stage action in this scene are not clearly prescribed in the dialogue and must be decided upon by the actors, by the reader, or by editors who, as in the case of this edition, choose to add stage directions.

More demanding for the director and the actors (and for the reader, in imagination) is the stage action of 3.4, where many bits of stage business—both in the attempts to get Viola/Cesario and Sir Andrew to fight, and in the fight between Antonio and Sir Toby and in Antonio's arrest—may be played variously from production to production. Learning to read the language of stage action repays one many times over when one reaches a scene like that of the gulling of Malvolio (2.5) or the play's final scene, with its succession of entrances and exits climaxing in the breathtaking entrance of Sebastian.

It is immensely rewarding to work carefully with Shakespeare's language so that the words, the sentences, the wordplay, and the implied stage action all become clear—as readers for the past four centuries have discovered. It may be more pleasurable to attend a good performance of a play—though not everyone has thought so. But the joy of being able to stage one of Shakespeare's plays in one's imagination, to return to passages that continue to yield further meanings (or further questions) the more one reads them—these are pleasures that, for many, rival (or at least augment) those of the performed text, and certainly make it worth considerable effort to "break the code" of Elizabethan poetic drama and let free the remarkable language that makes up a Shakespeare text.

Shakespeare's Life

Surviving documents that give us glimpses into the life of William Shakespeare show us a playwright, poet, and actor who grew up in the market town of Stratford-upon-Avon, spent his professional life in London, and returned to Stratford a wealthy landowner. He was born in April 1564, died in April 1616, and is buried inside the chancel of Holy Trinity Church in Stratford.

We wish we could know more about the life of the world's greatest dramatist. His plays and poems are testaments to his wide reading—especially to his knowledge of Virgil, Ovid, Plutarch, Holinshed's *Chronicles*, and the Bible—and to his mastery of the English language, but we can only speculate about his education. We know that the King's New School in Stratford-upon-Avon was considered excellent. The school was one of the English "grammar schools" established to educate young men, primarily in Latin grammar and literature. As in other schools of the time, students began their studies at the age of four or five in the attached "petty school," and there learned to read and write in English, studying primarily the catechism from the Book of Common Prayer. After two years in the petty school, students entered the lower form (grade) of the grammar school, where they began the serious study of Latin grammar and Latin texts that would occupy most of the remainder of their school days. (Several Latin texts that Shakespeare used repeatedly in writing his plays and poems were texts that schoolboys memorized and recited.) Latin comedies were introduced early in the lower form; in the upper form, which the boys entered at age ten or eleven, students wrote their own Latin orations and declamations, studied Latin

Title page of a 1573 Latin and Greek catechism for children.
From Alexander Nowell, *Catechismus paruus pueris primum Latine . . .* (1573).

historians and rhetoricians, and began the study of Greek using the Greek New Testament.

Since the records of the Stratford "grammar school" do not survive, we cannot prove that William Shakespeare attended the school; however, every indication (his father's position as an alderman and bailiff of Stratford, the playwright's own knowledge of the Latin classics, scenes in the plays that recall grammar-school experiences—for example, *The Merry Wives of Windsor*, 4.1) suggests that he did. We also lack generally accepted documentation about Shakespeare's life after his schooling ended and his professional life in London began. His marriage in 1582 (at age eighteen) to Anne Hathaway and the subsequent births of his daughter Susanna (1583) and the twins Judith and Hamnet (1585) are recorded, but how he supported himself and where he lived are not known. Nor do we know when and why he left Stratford for the London theatrical world, nor how he rose to be the important figure in that world that he had become by the early 1590s.

We do know that by 1592 he had achieved some prominence in London as both an actor and a playwright. In that year was published a book by the playwright Robert Greene attacking an actor who had the audacity to write blank-verse drama and who was "in his own conceit [i.e., opinion] the only Shake-scene in a country." Since Greene's attack includes a parody of a line from one of Shakespeare's early plays, there is little doubt that it is Shakespeare to whom he refers, a "Shake-scene" who had aroused Greene's fury by successfully competing with university-educated dramatists like Greene himself. It was in 1593 that Shakespeare became a published poet. In that year he published his long narrative poem *Venus and Adonis;* in 1594, he followed it with *Lucrece.* Both poems were dedicated to the young earl of Southampton (Henry

Wriothesley), who may have become Shakespeare's patron.

It seems no coincidence that Shakespeare wrote these narrative poems at a time when the theaters were closed because of the plague, a contagious epidemic disease that devastated the population of London. When the theaters reopened in 1594, Shakespeare apparently resumed his double career of actor and playwright and began his long (and seemingly profitable) service as an acting-company shareholder. Records for December of 1594 show him to be a leading member of the Lord Chamberlain's Men. It was this company of actors, later named the King's Men, for whom he would be a principal actor, dramatist, and shareholder for the rest of his career.

So far as we can tell, that career spanned about twenty years. In the 1590s, he wrote his plays on English history as well as several comedies and at least two tragedies (*Titus Andronicus* and *Romeo and Juliet*). These histories, comedies, and tragedies are the plays credited to him in 1598 in a work, *Palladis Tamia*, that in one chapter compares English writers with "Greek, Latin, and Italian Poets." There the author, Francis Meres, claims that Shakespeare is comparable to the Latin dramatists Seneca for tragedy and Plautus for comedy, and calls him "the most excellent in both kinds for the stage." He also names him "Mellifluous and honey-tongued Shakespeare": "I say," writes Meres, "that the Muses would speak with Shakespeare's fine filed phrase, if they would speak English." Since Meres also mentions Shakespeare's "sugared sonnets among his private friends," it is assumed that many of Shakespeare's sonnets (not published until 1609) were also written in the 1590s.

In 1599, Shakespeare's company built a theater for themselves across the river from London, naming it the Globe. The plays that are considered by many to be Shakespeare's major tragedies (*Hamlet*, *Othello*, *King Lear*, and *Macbeth*) were written while the company was resident in this theater, as were such comedies as *Twelfth Night* and *Measure for Measure*. Many of Shakespeare's plays were performed at court (both for Queen Elizabeth I and, after her death in 1603, for King James I), some were presented at the Inns of Court (the residences of London's legal societies), and some were doubtless performed in other towns, at the universities, and at great houses when the King's Men went on tour; otherwise, his plays from 1599 to 1608 were, so far as we know, performed only at the Globe. Between 1608 and 1612, Shakespeare wrote several plays—among them *The Winter's Tale* and *The Tempest*—presumably for the company's new indoor Blackfriars theater, though the plays were performed also at the Globe and at court. Surviving documents describe a performance of *The Winter's Tale* in 1611 at the Globe, for example, and performances of *The Tempest* in 1611 and 1613 at the royal palace of Whitehall.

Shakespeare seems to have written very little after 1612, the year in which he probably wrote *King Henry VIII*. (It was at a performance of *Henry VIII* in 1613 that the Globe caught fire and burned to the ground.) Sometime between 1610 and 1613, according to many biographers, he returned to live in Stratford-upon-Avon, where he owned a large house and considerable property, and where his wife and his two daughters lived. (His son Hamnet had died in 1596.) However, other biographers suggest that Shakespeare did not leave London for good until much closer to the time of his death. During his professional years in London, Shakespeare had presumably derived income from the acting company's profits as well as from his own career as an actor, from the sale of his play man-

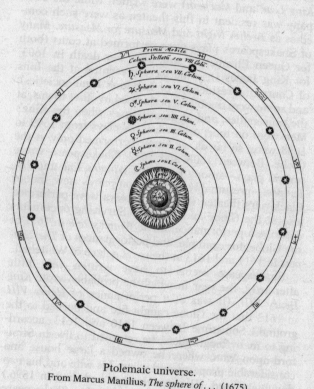

Ptolemaic universe.
From Marcus Manilius, *The sphere of . . .* (1675).

uscripts to the acting company, and, after 1599, from his shares as an owner of the Globe. It was presumably that income, carefully invested in land and other property, that made him the wealthy man that surviving documents show him to have become. It is also assumed that William Shakespeare's growing wealth and reputation played some part in inclining the Crown, in 1596, to grant John Shakespeare, William's father, the coat of arms that he had so long sought. William Shakespeare died in Stratford on April 23, 1616 (according to the epitaph carved under his bust in Holy Trinity Church) and was buried on April 25. Seven years after his death, his collected plays were published as *Mr. William Shakespeares Comedies, Histories, & Tragedies* (the work now known as the First Folio).

The years in which Shakespeare wrote were among the most exciting in English history. Intellectually, the discovery, translation, and printing of Greek and Roman classics were making available a set of works and worldviews that interacted complexly with Christian texts and beliefs. The result was a questioning, a vital intellectual ferment, that provided energy for the period's amazing dramatic and literary output and that fed directly into Shakespeare's plays. The Ghost in *Hamlet*, for example, is wonderfully complicated in part because he is a figure from Roman tragedy—the spirit of the dead returning to seek revenge—who at the same time inhabits a Christian hell (or purgatory); Hamlet's description of humankind reflects at one moment the Neoplatonic wonderment at mankind ("What a piece of work is a man!") and, at the next, the Christian view of the human condition ("And yet, to me, what is this quintessence of dust?").

As intellectual horizons expanded, so also did geographical and cosmological horizons. New worlds—

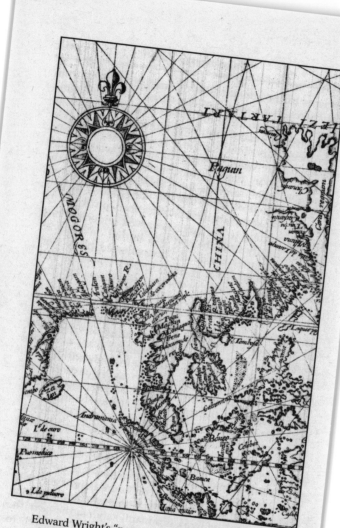

Edward Wright's "new map" of the world with "the augmentation of the Indies" (formerly attributed to E. Molyneux), reproduced from Richard Hakluyt's *Principal navigations* (1599–1600) for A. E. Nordenskiöld and included in his *Facsimile-Atlas to the Early History of Cartography* (1889).

both North and South America—were explored, and in them were found human beings who lived and worshipped in ways radically different from those of Renaissance Europeans and Englishmen. The universe during these years also seemed to shift and expand. Copernicus had earlier theorized that the Earth was not the center of the cosmos but revolved as a planet around the sun. Galileo's telescope, created in 1609, allowed scientists to see that Copernicus had been correct: the universe was not organized with the Earth at the center, nor was it so nicely circumscribed as people had, until that time, thought. In terms of expanding horizons, the impact of these discoveries on people's beliefs—religious, scientific, and philosophical—cannot be overstated.

London, too, rapidly expanded and changed during the years (from the early 1590s to 1610 or somewhat later) that Shakespeare lived there. London—the center of England's government, its economy, its royal court, its overseas trade—was, during these years, becoming an exciting metropolis, drawing to it thousands of new citizens every year. Troubled by overcrowding, by poverty, by recurring epidemics of the plague, London was also a mecca for the wealthy and the aristocratic, and for those who sought advancement at court, or power in government or finance or trade. One hears in Shakespeare's plays the voices of London—the struggles for power, the fear of venereal disease, the language of buying and selling. One hears as well the voices of Stratford-upon-Avon—references to the nearby Forest of Arden, to sheepherding, to small-town gossip, to village fairs and markets. Part of the richness of Shakespeare's work is the influence felt there of the various worlds in which he lived: the world of metropolitan London, the world of small-town and rural England, the world of the theater, and the worlds of craftsmen and shepherds.

That Shakespeare inhabited such worlds we know from surviving London and Stratford documents, as well as from the evidence of the plays and poems themselves. From such records we can sketch the dramatist's life. We know from his works that he was a voracious reader. We know from legal and business documents that he was a multifaceted theater man who became a wealthy landowner. We know a bit about his family life and a fair amount about his legal and financial dealings. Most scholars today depend upon such evidence as they draw their picture of the world's greatest playwright. Such, however, has not always been the case. Until the late eighteenth century, the William Shakespeare who lived in most biographies was the creation of legend and tradition. This was the Shakespeare who was supposedly caught poaching deer at Charlecote, the estate of Sir Thomas Lucy close by Stratford; this was the Shakespeare who fled from Sir Thomas's vengeance and made his way in London by taking care of horses outside a playhouse; this was the Shakespeare who reportedly could barely read, but whose natural gifts were extraordinary, whose father was a butcher who allowed his gifted son sometimes to help in the butcher shop, where William supposedly killed calves "in a high style," making a speech for the occasion. It was this legendary William Shakespeare whose Falstaff (in *1* and *2 Henry IV*) so pleased Queen Elizabeth that she demanded a play about Falstaff in love, and demanded that it be written in fourteen days (hence the existence of *The Merry Wives of Windsor*). It was this legendary Shakespeare who reached the top of his acting career in the roles of the Ghost in *Hamlet* and old Adam in *As You Like It*—and who died of a fever contracted by drinking too hard at "a merry meeting" with the poets Michael Drayton and Ben Jonson. This legendary Shakespeare is a rambunctious, undisciplined man, as attractively "wild" as his plays were seen by earlier generations to be. Unfortunately, there is no trace of evidence to support these wonderful stories.

Perhaps in response to the disreputable Shakespeare of legend—or perhaps in response to the fragmentary and, for some, all-too-ordinary Shakespeare documented by surviving records—some people since the mid-nineteenth century have argued that William Shakespeare could not have written the plays that bear his name. These persons have put forward some dozen names as more likely authors, among them Queen Elizabeth, Sir Francis Bacon, Edward de Vere (earl of Oxford), and Christopher Marlowe. Such attempts to find what for these people is a more believable author of the plays is a tribute to the regard in which the plays are held. Unfortunately for their claims, the documents that exist that provide evidence for the facts of Shakespeare's life tie him inextricably to the body of plays and poems that bear his name. Unlikely as it seems to those who want the works to have been written by an aristocrat, a university graduate, or an "important" person, the plays and poems seem clearly to have been produced by a man from Stratford-upon-Avon with a very good "grammar-school" education and a life of experience in London and in the world of the London theater. How this particular man produced the works that dominate the cultures of much of the world more than four hundred years after his death is one of life's mysteries—and one that will continue to tease our imaginations as we continue to delight in his plays and poems.

Shakespeare's Theater

The actors of Shakespeare's time are known to have performed plays in a great variety of locations. They played at court (that is, in the great halls of such royal residences as Whitehall, Hampton Court, and Greenwich); they played in halls at the universities of Oxford and Cambridge, and at the Inns of Court (the residences in London of the legal societies); and they also played in the private houses of great lords and civic officials. Sometimes acting companies went on tour from London into the provinces, often (but not only) when outbreaks of bubonic plague in the capital forced the closing of theaters to reduce the possibility of contagion in crowded audiences. In the provinces the actors usually staged their plays in churches (until around 1600), in guildhalls, or in the great houses of individual patrons. While surviving records show only a handful of occasions when actors played at inns while on tour, London inns were important playing places up until the 1590s.

The building of theaters in London had begun only shortly before Shakespeare wrote his first plays in the 1590s. These theaters were of two kinds: outdoor or public playhouses that could accommodate large numbers of playgoers, and indoor or private theaters for much smaller audiences. What is usually regarded as the first London outdoor public playhouse was called simply the Theatre. James Burbage—the father of Richard Burbage, who was perhaps the most famous actor in Shakespeare's company—built it in 1576 in an area north of the city of London called Shoreditch. Among the more famous of the other public playhouses that capitalized on the new fashion were the Curtain and

A stylized representation of the Globe theater.
From Claes Jansz Visscher, *Londinum florentissima Britanniae urbs* . . . [c. 1625].

the Fortune (both also built north of the city), the Rose, the Swan, the Globe, and the Hope (all located on the Bankside, a region just across the Thames south of the city of London). All these playhouses had to be built outside the jurisdiction of the city of London because many civic officials were hostile to the performance of drama and repeatedly petitioned the royal council to abolish it.

The theaters erected on the Bankside (a region under the authority of the Church of England, whose head was the monarch) shared the neighborhood with houses of prostitution and with the Paris Garden, where the blood sports of bearbaiting and bullbaiting were carried on. There may have been no clear distinction between playhouses and buildings for such sports, for we know that the Hope was used for both plays and baiting and that Philip Henslowe, owner of the Rose and, later, partner in the ownership of the Fortune, was also a partner in a monopoly on baiting. All these forms of entertainment were easily accessible to Londoners by boat across the Thames or over London Bridge.

Evidently Shakespeare's company prospered on the Bankside. They moved there in 1599. Threatened by difficulties in renewing the lease on the land where their first theater (the Theatre) had been built, Shakespeare's company took advantage of the Christmas holiday in 1598 to dismantle the Theatre and transport its timbers across the Thames to the Bankside, where, in 1599, these timbers were used in the building of the Globe. The weather in late December 1598 is recorded as having been especially harsh. It was so cold that the Thames was "nigh [nearly] frozen," and there was heavy snow. Perhaps the weather aided Shakespeare's company in eluding their landlord, the snow hiding their activity and the freezing of the Thames allowing them to slide the timbers across to the Bankside without paying tolls for repeated trips over London Bridge. Attractive as this narrative is, it remains just as likely that the heavy snow hampered transport of the timbers in wagons through the London streets to the river. It also must be remembered that the Thames was, according to report, only "nigh frozen," and therefore did not necessarily provide solid footing. Whatever the precise circumstances of this fascinating event in English theater history, Shakespeare's company was able to begin playing at their new Globe theater on the Bankside in 1599. After this theater burned down in 1613 during the staging of Shakespeare's *Henry VIII* (its thatch roof set alight by cannon fire called for in performance), Shakespeare's company immediately rebuilt on the same location. The second Globe seems to have been a grander structure than its predecessor. It remained in use until 1642, when Parliament officially closed the theaters. Soon thereafter it was pulled down.

The public theaters of Shakespeare's time were very different buildings from our theaters today. First of all, they were open-air playhouses. As recent excavations of the Rose and the Globe confirm, some were polygonal or roughly circular in shape; the Fortune, however, was square. The most recent estimates of their size put the diameter of these buildings at 72 feet (the Rose) to 100 feet (the Globe), but we know that they held vast audiences of two or three thousand, who must have been squeezed together quite tightly. Some of these spectators paid extra to sit or stand in the two or three levels of roofed galleries that extended, on the upper levels, all the way around the theater and surrounded an open space. In this space were the stage and, perhaps, the tiring house (what we would call dressing rooms), as well as the so-called yard. In the yard stood the spectators who chose to pay less, the ones whom Hamlet contemptuously called "groundlings." For a roof they had only the sky, and so they were exposed to all kinds of weather. They stood on a floor that was sometimes made of mortar and sometimes of ash mixed with the shells of hazelnuts, which, it has recently been discovered, were standard flooring material in the period.

Unlike the yard, the stage itself was covered by a roof. Its ceiling, called "the heavens," is thought to have been elaborately painted to depict the sun, moon, stars, and planets. The exact size of the stage remains hard to determine. We have a single sketch of part of the interior of the Swan. A Dutchman named Johannes de Witt visited this theater around 1596 and sent a sketch of it back to his friend, Arend van Buchel. Because van Buchel found de Witt's letter and sketch of interest, he copied both into a book. It is van Buchel's copy, adapted, it seems, to the shape and size of the page in his book, that survives. In this sketch, the stage appears to be a large rectangular platform that thrusts far out into the yard, perhaps even as far as the center of the circle formed by the surrounding galleries. This drawing, combined with the specifications for the size of the stage in the building contract for the Fortune, has led scholars to conjecture that the stage on which Shakespeare's plays were performed must have measured approximately 43 feet in width and 27 feet in depth, a vast acting area. But the digging up of a large part of the Rose by late twentieth-century archaeologists has provided evidence of a quite different stage design. The Rose stage was a platform tapered at the corners and much shallower than what seems to be depicted in the van Buchel sketch. Indeed, its measurements seem to be about 37.5 feet across at its widest point and only 15.5 feet deep. Because the surviving indications of stage size and design differ from each other so much, it is possible that the stages in other theaters, like the Theatre, the Curtain, and the Globe (the outdoor playhouses where we know that Shakespeare's plays were performed), were different from those at both the Swan and the Rose.

After about 1608 Shakespeare's plays were staged not only at the Globe but also at an indoor or private playhouse in Blackfriars. This theater had been constructed in 1596 by James Burbage in an upper hall of a former Dominican priory or monastic house. Although Henry VIII had dissolved all English monasteries in the 1530s (shortly after he had founded the Church of England), the area remained under church, rather than hostile civic, control. The hall that Burbage had purchased and renovated was a large one in which Parliament had once met. In the private theater that he constructed, the stage, lit by candles, was built across the narrow end of the hall, with boxes flanking it. The rest of the hall offered seating room only. Because there was no provision for standing room, the largest audience it could hold was less than a thousand, or about a quarter of what the Globe could accommodate. Admission to Blackfriars was correspondingly more expensive. Instead of a penny to stand in the yard at the Globe, it cost a minimum of sixpence to get into Blackfriars. The best seats at the Globe (in the Lords' Room in the gallery above and behind the stage) cost sixpence; but the boxes flanking the stage at Blackfriars were half a crown, or five times sixpence. Some spectators who were particularly interested in displaying themselves paid even more to sit on stools on the Blackfriars stage.

Whether in the outdoor or indoor playhouses, the stages of Shakespeare's time were different from ours. They were not separated from the audience by the dropping of a curtain between acts and scenes. Therefore the playwrights of the time had to find other ways of signaling to the audience that one scene (to be imagined as occurring in one location at a given time) had ended and the next (to be imagined at perhaps a different location at a later time) had begun. The customary way used by Shakespeare and many of his contemporaries was to have everyone on stage exit at the end of one scene and have one or more different characters enter to begin the next. In a few cases, where characters remain onstage from one scene to another, the dialogue or stage action makes the change of location clear, and the characters are generally to be imagined as having moved from one place to another. For example, in *Romeo and Juliet*, Romeo and his friends remain onstage in Act 1 from scene 4 to scene 5, but they are represented as having moved between scenes from the street that leads to Capulet's house into Capulet's house itself. The new location is signaled in part by the appearance onstage of Capulet's servingmen carrying table napkins, something they would not take into the streets. Playwrights had to be quite resourceful in the use of hand properties, like the napkin, or in the use of dialogue to specify where the action was taking place in their plays because, in contrast to most of today's theaters, the playhouses of Shakespeare's time did not fill the stage with scenery to make the setting precise. A consequence of this difference was that the playwrights of Shakespeare's time did not have to specify exactly where the action of their plays was set when they did not choose to do so, and much of the action of their plays is tied to no specific place.

Usually Shakespeare's stage is referred to as a "bare stage," to distinguish it from the stages of the last two or three centuries with their elaborate sets. But the stage in Shakespeare's time was not completely bare. Philip Henslowe, owner of the Rose, lists in his inventory of stage properties a rock, three tombs, and two mossy banks. Stage directions in plays of the time also call for such things as thrones (or "states"), banquets (presumably tables with plaster replicas of food on them), and beds and tombs to be pushed onto the stage. Thus the stage often held more than the actors.

The actors did not limit their performing to the stage alone. Occasionally they went beneath the stage, as the Ghost appears to do in the first act of *Hamlet*. From there they could emerge onto the stage through a trapdoor. They could retire behind the hanging across the back of the stage, as, for example, the actor playing Polonius does when he hides behind the arras. Sometimes the hangings could be drawn back during a performance to "discover" one or more actors behind them. When performance required that an actor appear "above," as when Juliet is imagined to stand at the window of her chamber in the famous and misnamed "balcony scene," then the actor probably climbed the stairs to the gallery over the back of the stage and temporarily shared it with some of the spectators. The stage was also provided with ropes and winches so that actors could descend from, and reascend to, the "heavens."

Perhaps the greatest difference between dramatic performances in Shakespeare's time and ours was that in Shakespeare's England the roles of women were played by boys. (Some of these boys grew up to take male roles in their maturity.) There were no women in the acting companies. It was not so in Europe, and it had not always been so in the history of the English stage. There are records of women on English stages in the thirteenth and fourteenth centuries, two hundred years before Shakespeare's plays were performed. After the accession of James I in 1603, the queen of England and her ladies took part in entertainments at court called masques, and with the reopening of the theaters in 1660 at the restoration of Charles II, women again took their place on the public stage.

The chief competitors of such acting companies as the one to which Shakespeare belonged and for which he wrote were companies of exclusively boy actors. The competition was most intense in the early 1600s. There were then two principal children's companies: the Children of Paul's (the choirboys from St. Paul's Cathedral, whose private playhouse was near the cathedral), and the Children of the Chapel Royal (the choirboys from the monarch's private chapel, who performed at the Blackfriars theater built by Burbage in 1596). In *Hamlet* Shakespeare writes of "an aerie [nest] of children, little eyases [hawks], that cry out on the top of question and are most tyrannically clapped for 't. These are now the fashion and . . . berattle the common stages [attack the public theaters]." In the long run, the adult actors prevailed. The Children of Paul's dissolved around 1606. By about 1608 the Children of the Chapel Royal had been forced to stop playing at the Blackfriars theater, which was then taken over by the King's Men, Shakespeare's own troupe.

Acting companies and theaters of Shakespeare's time seem to have been organized in various ways. For example, with the building of the Globe, Shakespeare's company apparently managed itself, with the principal actors, Shakespeare among them, having the status of "sharers" and the right to a share in the takings, as well as the responsibility for a part of the expenses. Five of the sharers, including Shakespeare, owned the Globe. As actor, as sharer in an acting company and in ownership of theaters, and as playwright, Shakespeare was about as involved in the theatrical industry as one could imagine. Although Shakespeare and his fellows prospered, their status under the law was conditional upon the protection of powerful patrons. "Common players"—those who did not have patrons or masters—were classed in the language of the law with "vagabonds and sturdy beggars." So the actors had to secure for themselves the official rank of servants of patrons. Among the patrons under whose protection Shakespeare's company worked were the lord chamberlain and, after the accession of King James in 1603, the king himself.

In the early 1990s we began to learn a great deal more about the theaters in which Shakespeare and his contemporaries performed—or, at least, began to open up new questions about them. At that time about 70 percent of the Rose had been excavated, as had about 10 percent of the second Globe, the one built in 1614. Excavation was halted at that point, but London has come to value the sites of its early playhouses, and takes what opportunities it can to explore them more deeply, both on the Bankside and in Shoreditch. Information about the playhouses of Shakespeare's London is therefore a constantly changing resource.

The Publication of Shakespeare's Plays

Eighteen of Shakespeare's plays found their way into print during the playwright's lifetime, but there is nothing to suggest that he took any interest in their publication. These eighteen appeared separately in editions in quarto or, in the case of *Henry VI, Part 3*, octavo format. The quarto pages are not much larger than a modern mass-market paperback book, and the octavo pages are even smaller; these little books were sold unbound for a few pence. The earliest of the quartos that still survive were printed in 1594, the year that both *Titus Andronicus* and a version of the play now called *Henry VI, Part 2* became available. While almost every one of these early quartos displays on its title page the name of the acting company that performed the play, only about half provide the name of the playwright, Shakespeare. The first quarto edition to bear the name Shakespeare on its title page is *Love's Labor's Lost* of 1598. A few of the quartos were popular with the book-buying public of Shakespeare's lifetime; for example, quarto *Richard II* went through five editions between 1597 and 1615. But most of the quartos were far from best sellers; *Love's Labor's Lost* (1598), for instance, was not reprinted in quarto until 1631. After Shakespeare's death, two more of his plays appeared in quarto format: *Othello* in 1622 and *The Two Noble Kinsmen*, coauthored with John Fletcher, in 1634.

In 1623, seven years after Shakespeare's death, *Mr. William Shakespeares Comedies, Histories, & Tragedies* was published. This printing offered readers in a single book thirty-six of the thirty-eight plays now thought to have been written by Shakespeare, including eighteen that had never been printed before. And it offered them in a style that was then reserved for serious literature and scholarship. The plays were arranged in double columns on pages nearly a foot high. This large page size is called "folio," as opposed to the smaller "quarto," and the 1623 volume is usually called the Shakespeare First Folio. It is reputed to have sold for the lordly price of a pound. (One copy at the Folger Shakespeare Library is marked fifteen shillings—that is, three-quarters of a pound.)

In a preface to the First Folio titled "To the great Variety of Readers," two of Shakespeare's former fellow actors in the King's Men, John Heminge and Henry Condell, wrote that they themselves had collected their dead companion's plays. They suggested that they had seen his own papers: "we have scarce received from him a blot in his papers." The title page of the Folio declared that the plays within it had been printed "according to the True Original Copies." Comparing the Folio to the quartos, Heminge and Condell disparaged the quartos, advising their readers that "before you were abused with divers stolen and surreptitious copies, maimed, and deformed by the frauds and stealths of injurious impostors." Many Shakespeareans of the eighteenth and nineteenth centuries believed Heminge and Condell and regarded the Folio plays as superior to anything in the quartos.

Once we begin to examine the Folio plays in detail, it becomes less easy to take at face value the word of Heminge and Condell about the superiority of the Folio texts. For example, of the first nine plays in the Folio (one-quarter of the entire collection), four were essentially reprinted from earlier quarto printings that Heminge and Condell had disparaged, and four have now been identified as printed from copies written in the hand of a professional scribe of the 1620s named Ralph Crane; the ninth, *The Comedy of Errors*, was apparently also printed from a manuscript, but one whose origin cannot be readily identified. Evidently, then, eight of the first nine plays in the First Folio were not printed, in spite of what the Folio title page announces, "according to the True Original Copies," or Shakespeare's own papers, and the source of the ninth is unknown. Since today's editors have been forced to treat Heminge and Condell's pronouncements with skepticism, they must choose whether to base their own editions upon quartos or the Folio on grounds other than Heminge and Condell's story of where the quarto and Folio versions originated.

Editors have often fashioned their own narratives to explain what lies behind the quartos and Folio. They have said that Heminge and Condell meant to criticize only a few of the early quartos, the ones that offer much shorter and sometimes quite different, often garbled, versions of plays. Among the examples of these are the 1600 quarto of *Henry V* (the Folio offers a much fuller version) or the 1603 *Hamlet* quarto. (In 1604 a different, much longer form of the play got into print as a quarto.) Early twentieth-century editors and some scholars in the present century have speculated that these questionable texts were produced when someone in the audience took notes from the plays' dialogue during performances and then employed "hack poets" to fill out the notes. The poor results were then sold to a publisher and presented in print as Shakespeare's plays. For much of the twentieth century this story gave way to another in which the shorter versions are said to be re-creations from memory of Shakespeare's plays by actors who wanted to stage them in the provinces but lacked manuscript copies. Most of the quartos offer much better texts than these so-called bad quartos. Indeed, in most of the quartos we find texts that are at least equal to or better than what is printed in the Folio. Many Shakespeare enthusiasts persuaded themselves that most of the quartos were set into type directly from Shakespeare's own papers, although there is nothing on which to base this conclusion except the desire for it to be true. Thus speculation continues about how the Shakespeare plays got to be printed. All that we have are the printed texts.

The book collector who was most successful in bringing together copies of the quartos and the First Folio was Henry Clay Folger, founder of the Folger Shakespeare Library in Washington, D.C. While it is estimated that there survive around the world only about 230 copies of the First Folio, Mr. Folger was able to acquire more than seventy-five copies, as well as a large number of fragments, for the library that bears his name. He also amassed a substantial number of quartos. For example, only fourteen copies of the First Quarto of *Love's Labor's Lost* are known to exist, and three are at the Folger Shakespeare Library. As a consequence of Mr. Folger's labors, scholars visiting the Folger Shakespeare Library have been able to learn a great deal about sixteenth- and seventeenth-century printing and, particularly, about the printing of Shakespeare's plays. And Mr. Folger did not stop at the First Folio, but collected many copies of later editions of Shakespeare, beginning with the Second Folio (1632), the Third (1663–64), and the Fourth (1685). Each of these later folios was based on its immediate predecessor and was edited anonymously. The first editor of Shakespeare whose name we know was Nicholas Rowe, whose first edition came out in 1709. Mr. Folger collected this edition and many, many more by Rowe's successors, and the collecting and scholarship continue.

An Introduction to This Text

Twelfth Night, or, What You Will was first printed in the 1623 collection of Shakespeare's plays now known as the First Folio. The present edition is based directly upon the First Folio version.* For the convenience of the reader, we have modernized the punctuation and the spelling of the Folio. Sometimes we go so far as to modernize certain old forms of words; for example, when *a* means "he," we change it to *he;* we change *mo* to *more,* and *ye* to *you.* But it is not our practice in editing any of the plays to modernize words that sound distinctly different from modern forms. For example, when the early printed texts read *sith* or *apricocks* or *porpentine,* we have not modernized to *since, apricots, porcupine.* When the forms *an, and,* or *and if* appear instead of the modern form *if,* we have reduced *and* to *an* but have not changed any of these forms to their modern equivalent, *if.* We also modernize and, where necessary, correct passages in foreign languages, unless an error in the early printed text can be reasonably explained as a joke.

Whenever we change the wording of the First Folio or add anything to its stage directions, we mark the change by enclosing it in superior half-brackets (⌈ ⌉). We want our readers to be immediately aware when we have intervened. (Only when we correct an obvious typographical error in the First Folio does the change not get marked.) Whenever we change the First Folio's wording or its punctuation so that the meaning

---

*We have also consulted the computerized text of the First Folio provided by the Text Archive of the Oxford University Computing Centre, to which we are grateful.

lii

changes, we list the change in the textual notes at the back of the book, even if all we have done is fix an obvious error.

We regularize a number of the proper names, as is the usual practice in editions of the play. For example, although the character Viola enters once under the name "Violenta" in the First Folio, in our edition she is always designated "Viola."

This edition differs from many earlier ones in its efforts to aid the reader in imagining the play as a performance. Thus stage directions are written with reference to the stage. For example, when, in 2.2, Viola refuses to take the ring offered to her by Malvolio, he throws it before her. If we were representing the play as pure fiction, our stage direction would read *"He throws the ring to the ground,"* but because we are representing the play as a stage action, our stage direction reads, instead, *"He throws down the ring."* Whenever it is reasonably certain, in our view, that a speech is accompanied by a particular action, we provide a stage direction describing the action. (Occasional exceptions to this rule occur when the action is so obvious that to add a stage direction would insult the reader.) Stage directions for the entrance of characters in mid-scene are, with rare exceptions, placed so that they immediately precede the characters' participation in the scene, even though these entrances may appear somewhat earlier in the early printed texts. Whenever we move a stage direction, we record this change in the textual notes. Latin stage directions (e.g., *Exeunt*) are translated into English (e.g., *They exit*).

We expand the often severely abbreviated forms of names used as speech headings in early printed texts into the full names of the characters. We also regularize the speakers' names in speech headings, using only a single designation for each character, even though the early printed texts sometimes use a variety of designations. Variations in the speech headings of the early printed texts are recorded in the textual notes.

In the present edition, as well, we mark with a dash any change of address within a speech, unless a stage direction intervenes. When the *-ed* ending of a word is to be pronounced, we mark it with an accent. Like editors for the last two centuries, we print metrically linked lines in the following way:

> VIOLA
> I think not so, my lord.
> ORSINO   Dear lad, believe it.

However, when there are a number of short verse-lines that can be linked in more than one way, we do not, with rare exceptions, indent any of them.

The Explanatory Notes

The notes that appear on the pages facing the text are designed to provide readers with the help that they may need to enjoy the play. Whenever the meaning of a word in the text is not readily accessible in a good contemporary dictionary, we offer the meaning in a note. Sometimes we provide a note even when the relevant meaning is to be found in the dictionary but when the word has acquired since Shakespeare's time other potentially confusing meanings. In our notes, we try to offer modern synonyms for Shakespeare's words. We also try to indicate to the reader the connection between the word in the play and the modern synonym. For example, Shakespeare sometimes uses the word *head* to mean "source," but, for modern readers, there may be no connection evident between these two words. We provide the connection by explaining Shakespeare's usage as follows: "**head**: fountainhead, source." On some occasions, a whole phrase or clause needs explanation. Then, if space allows, we rephrase in our own words the difficult passage, and add at the end synonyms for individual words in the passage. When scholars have been unable to determine the meaning of a word or phrase, we acknowledge the uncertainty. Unless otherwise noted, biblical quotations are from the Geneva Bible (1560), with spelling modernized.

TWELFTH NIGHT,

OR,

WHAT

YOU WILL

Characters in the Play

VIOLA, a lady of Messaline shipwrecked on the coast of Illyria (later disguised as CESARIO)

OLIVIA, an Illyrian countess
MARIA, her waiting-gentlewoman
SIR TOBY BELCH, Olivia's kinsman
SIR ANDREW AGUECHEEK, Sir Toby's companion
MALVOLIO, steward in Olivia's household
FOOL, Olivia's jester, named Feste
FABIAN, a gentleman in Olivia's household

ORSINO, duke (or count) of Illyria
VALENTINE }
CURIO } gentlemen serving Orsino

SEBASTIAN, Viola's brother
ANTONIO, friend to Sebastian

CAPTAIN
PRIEST
TWO OFFICERS

Lords, Sailors, Musicians, and other Attendants

TWELFTH NIGHT,

OR,

WHAT YOU WILL

ACT 1

1.1 At his court, Orsino, sick with love for the Lady Olivia, learns from his messenger that she is grieving for her dead brother and refuses to be seen for seven years.

---

0 SD. **Illyria:** an ancient country in southern Europe, on the Adriatic Sea

2–3. **that ... appetite:** i.e., so that my passion, glutted

3. **die:** See longer note, page 191.

4. **fall:** cadence (i.e., a sequence of chords ending the strain of music)

9–14. **O spirit ... minute:** Love is described here as so hungry that it can devour everything and destroy the value of even the most precious things. **quick and fresh:** keen and eager (to devour) **validity:** worth **pitch:** i.e., excellence (The pitch is the highest point in a falcon's flight.) See picture, page 42.

14–15. **fancy, high fantastical: Fancy** is both "love" and "imagination"; **high fantastical** carries the sense both of "highly imaginative, most able to create powerful images," and "extremely passionate." Orsino seems to be playing with the double meanings of these related words as he tries to describe the intensity of his lovesickness. **alone:** exclusively

18. **hart:** stag (Orsino, in the following line, plays on the fact that *hart* sounds like *heart*.)

ACT 1

Scene 1
Enter Orsino, Duke of Illyria, Curio, and other Lords, ⌜*with Musicians playing.*⌝

ORSINO
If music be the food of love, play on.
Give me excess of it, that, surfeiting,
The appetite may sicken and so die.
That strain again! It had a dying fall.
O, it came o'er my ear like the sweet sound   5
That breathes upon a bank of violets,
Stealing and giving odor. Enough; no more.
'Tis not so sweet now as it was before.
O spirit of love, how quick and fresh art thou,
That, notwithstanding thy capacity   10
Receiveth as the sea, naught enters there,
Of what validity and pitch soe'er,
But falls into abatement and low price
Even in a minute. So full of shapes is fancy
That it alone is high fantastical.   15
CURIO
Will you go hunt, my lord?
ORSINO   What, Curio?
CURIO   The hart.
ORSINO
Why, so I do, the noblest that I have.
O, when mine eyes did see Olivia first,   20

7

21. **Methought:** it seemed to me; **purged...pestilence:** i.e., purified **the air** of everything infectious

22–24. **That instant . . . pursue me:** Orsino compares himself to the mythological figure Acteon, who, having seen the goddess Diana bathing, was **turned into a hart** and destroyed by his own hounds. (See picture, page 44.) **fell:** fierce, deadly

26. **So please my lord:** a polite phrase addressed to one's superior; **might not be:** i.e., was not

28. **element itself:** i.e., the very sky; **seven years' heat:** i.e., until **seven** summers have passed

30. **cloistress:** a nun in a cloister

32. **eye-offending brine:** i.e., tears; **season:** embalm (**Brine** is salt water also used to keep food fresh.)

33. **brother's . . . love:** i.e., **love** for her **dead** brother

36. **but to a:** i.e., **to a** mere

37. **golden shaft:** In the mythology of romantic love, anyone struck by Cupid's arrow with the golden head falls desperately in love. (See picture, page 100.)

38. **affections else:** other feelings or desires

40. **thrones:** The **liver** was considered the seat of the passions, the **brain** the seat of reason, and the **heart** the seat of feeling.

40–41. **and . . . perfections:** i.e., and **her sweet perfections filled**

41. **one self king:** a single monarch

1.2 On the Adriatic seacoast, Viola, who has been saved from a shipwreck in which her brother may
(continued)

Methought she purged the air of pestilence.
That instant was I turned into a hart,
And my desires, like fell and cruel hounds,
E'er since pursue me.

Enter Valentine.

How now, what news from her?   25

VALENTINE
So please my lord, I might not be admitted,
But from her handmaid do return this answer:
The element itself, till seven years' heat,
Shall not behold her face at ample view,
But like a cloistress she will veilèd walk,   30
And water once a day her chamber round
With eye-offending brine—all this to season
A brother's dead love, which she would keep fresh
And lasting in her sad remembrance.

ORSINO
O, she that hath a heart of that fine frame   35
To pay this debt of love but to a brother,
How will she love when the rich golden shaft
Hath killed the flock of all affections else
That live in her; when liver, brain, and heart,
These sovereign thrones, are all supplied, and filled   40
Her sweet perfections with one self king!
Away before me to sweet beds of flowers!
Love thoughts lie rich when canopied with bowers.

They exit.

Scene 2
Enter Viola, a Captain, and Sailors.

VIOLA   What country, friends, is this?
CAPTAIN   This is Illyria, lady.
VIOLA
And what should I do in Illyria?

have drowned, hears about Orsino and Olivia. She wishes to join Olivia's household, but is told that Olivia will admit no one into her presence. Viola decides to disguise herself as a boy so that she can join Orsino's male retinue.

---

4. **Elysium:** in Greek mythology, where the blessed go after death

5. **Perchance:** perhaps, possibly

7, 8. **perchance:** i.e., by chance, through luck

9. **chance:** possibility

12. **driving:** i.e., drifting

13. **provident:** forward-looking

14. **practice:** method

15. **lived:** i.e., floated

16. **Arion . . . back: Arion,** a Greek poet and musician, so charmed the dolphins with his music that one saved him from drowning. (See picture, page 188.)

20–22. **Mine . . . him:** i.e., my **escape** makes me hope that my brother escaped too, and your **speech** authorizes that hope

28. **Orsino:** The Orsini were a noble Italian family.

31. **late:** recently

My brother he is in Elysium.
Perchance he is not drowned.—What think you,   5
  sailors?

CAPTAIN
It is perchance that you yourself were saved.

VIOLA
O, my poor brother! And so perchance may he be.

CAPTAIN
True, madam. And to comfort you with chance,
Assure yourself, after our ship did split,   10
When you and those poor number saved with you
Hung on our driving boat, I saw your brother,
Most provident in peril, bind himself
(Courage and hope both teaching him the practice)
To a strong mast that lived upon the sea,   15
Where, like ⌜Arion⌝ on the dolphin's back,
I saw him hold acquaintance with the waves
So long as I could see.

VIOLA, ⌜*giving him money*⌝   For saying so, there's gold.
Mine own escape unfoldeth to my hope,   20
Whereto thy speech serves for authority,
The like of him. Know'st thou this country?

CAPTAIN
Ay, madam, well, for I was bred and born
Not three hours' travel from this very place.

VIOLA   Who governs here?   25

CAPTAIN
A noble duke, in nature as in name.

VIOLA   What is his name?

CAPTAIN   Orsino.

VIOLA
Orsino. I have heard my father name him.
He was a bachelor then.   30

CAPTAIN
And so is now, or was so very late;
For but a month ago I went from hence,

33. **murmur:** rumor
34. **the less:** i.e., those of lower rank
35. **fair:** beautiful
37. **maid:** unmarried woman
38. **some twelvemonth since:** i.e., about a year ago
41. **abjured:** renounced
44. **delivered:** revealed
45. **mellow:** ripe
46. **estate:** social rank, position
47. **compass:** achieve, accomplish
48. **admit:** allow; **suit:** petition, courtship
50. **fair:** attractive
51–52. **though . . . pollution:** i.e., although natural beauty often hides inner corruption
53–54. **suits / With:** corresponds with, matches
54. **character:** i.e., personal appearance and behavior
56. **Conceal me:** i.e., **conceal,** keep secret
57. **become:** be suitable to
59. **eunuch:** a male soprano or castrato
62. **allow . . . worth:** i.e., commend me as worthy to be in
64. **wit:** plan
65. **mute:** a servant deprived of the power of speech and attending a Turkish sultan, who also employed eunuchs (The sultan's servants would be blinded if they disclosed the secrets of his harem.)

And then 'twas fresh in murmur (as, you know,
What great ones do the less will prattle of)
That he did seek the love of fair Olivia.   35

VIOLA   What's she?

CAPTAIN

A virtuous maid, the daughter of a count
That died some twelvemonth since, then leaving her
In the protection of his son, her brother,
Who shortly also died, for whose dear love,   40
They say, she hath abjured the sight
And company of men.

VIOLA   O, that I served that lady,
And might not be delivered to the world
Till I had made mine own occasion mellow,   45
What my estate is.

CAPTAIN   That were hard to compass
Because she will admit no kind of suit,
No, not the Duke's.

VIOLA

There is a fair behavior in thee, captain,   50
And though that nature with a beauteous wall
Doth oft close in pollution, yet of thee
I will believe thou hast a mind that suits
With this thy fair and outward character.
I prithee—and I'll pay thee bounteously—   55
Conceal me what I am, and be my aid
For such disguise as haply shall become
The form of my intent. I'll serve this duke.
Thou shalt present me as an eunuch to him.
It may be worth thy pains, for I can sing   60
And speak to him in many sorts of music
That will allow me very worth his service.
What else may hap, to time I will commit.
Only shape thou thy silence to my wit.

CAPTAIN

Be you his eunuch, and your mute I'll be.   65

1.3 At the estate of Lady Olivia, Sir Toby Belch, Olivia's kinsman, has brought in Sir Andrew Aguecheek to be her suitor. Maria, Olivia's lady-in-waiting, says that Andrew is a fool, and Andrew himself doubts his ability to win Olivia, but Toby encourages him to woo her.

1, 5. **niece, cousin:** Both of these terms indicate close kinship; neither was as specific as it is today.

2. **care:** sorrow

4. **By my troth:** a mild oath

5. **o' nights:** i.e., at night

7. **let . . . excepted: Let her** object to me **before** I object to her. Toby adapts the legal phrase *exceptis excipiendis* ("excepting those things that must be excepted").

9. **modest:** moderate

10. **confine myself:** i.e., dress myself

12. **An:** if

14. **quaffing:** heavy drinking; **undo you:** ruin you; cause your downfall

20. **tall:** brave (Maria takes the word in its usual sense.)

22. **has . . . ducats:** i.e., **has** an income of **three thousand** gold coins

23. **have . . . ducats:** i.e., spend all his inheritance in a single year

24. **a very:** i.e., an utter; **prodigal:** wastrel, spendthrift

25–26. **viol-de-gamboys:** viola da gamba, predecessor of the modern cello (See picture, page 60.)

27. **without book:** i.e., from memory

When my tongue blabs, then let mine eyes not see.

VIOLA I thank thee. Lead me on.

They exit.

Scene 3
Enter Sir Toby and Maria.

TOBY What a plague means my niece to take the death
    of her brother thus? I am sure care's an enemy to
    life.

MARIA By my troth, Sir Toby, you must come in earlier
    o' nights. Your cousin, my lady, takes great excep- 5
    tions to your ill hours.

TOBY Why, let her except before excepted!

MARIA Ay, but you must confine yourself within the
    modest limits of order.

TOBY Confine? I'll confine myself no finer than I am. 10
    These clothes are good enough to drink in, and so
    be these boots too. An they be not, let them hang
    themselves in their own straps!

MARIA That quaffing and drinking will undo you. I
    heard my lady talk of it yesterday, and of a foolish 15
    knight that you brought in one night here to be her
    wooer.

TOBY Who, Sir Andrew Aguecheek?

MARIA Ay, he.

TOBY He's as tall a man as any 's in Illyria. 20

MARIA What's that to th' purpose?

TOBY Why, he has three thousand ducats a year!

MARIA Ay, but he'll have but a year in all these ducats.
    He's a very fool and a prodigal.

TOBY Fie, that you'll say so! He plays o' th' viol-de- 25
    gamboys and speaks three or four languages word
    for word without book, and hath all the good gifts of
    nature.

29. **almost natural:** i.e., "all most **natural** or half-witted" and "nearly **natural**" (Elam)

30. **but that:** except for the fact that

31–32. **gust . . . in:** i.e., taste . . . for

34–35. **substractors:** i.e., detractors, slanderers

40. **coistrel:** lowborn contemptible fellow

41–42. **brains . . . toe:** i.e., head spins (Elam)

42. **parish top:** a large public whipping-top (See picture, page 186.) **Castiliano vulgo:** The meaning of this Italian-sounding phrase (if it had one) is lost.

43. **Agueface:** This misnaming of Sir Andrew calls attention to the meaning of "Aguecheek," i.e., the pale, thin cheek (or face) of someone suffering from a fever or ague.

46. **shrew:** Andrew may be alluding to Maria's size (the shrew is among the smallest of mammals); however, **shrew** referred to a scolding or brawling woman.

48. **Accost:** i.e., approach her, **woo her** (line 56) (In nautical terms, one ship accosts another by going alongside. The nautical language continues in **front**—i.e., confront—and **board** [line 55] and perhaps in **undertake** [line 57].)

60. **An . . . so:** i.e., if you let her leave so unceremoniously

MARIA   He hath indeed, almost natural, for, besides
that he's a fool, he's a great quarreler, and, but that   30
he hath the gift of a coward to allay the gust he hath
in quarreling, 'tis thought among the prudent he
would quickly have the gift of a grave.

TOBY   By this hand, they are scoundrels and substractors that say so of him. Who are they?   35

MARIA   They that add, moreover, he's drunk nightly in
your company.

TOBY   With drinking healths to my niece. I'll drink to
her as long as there is a passage in my throat and
drink in Illyria. He's a coward and a coistrel that   40
will not drink to my niece till his brains turn o' th'
toe like a parish top. What, wench! *Castiliano vulgo*,
for here comes Sir Andrew Agueface.

Enter Sir Andrew.

ANDREW   Sir Toby Belch! How now, Sir Toby Belch?

TOBY   Sweet Sir Andrew!   45

ANDREW, ⌜*to Maria*⌝   Bless you, fair shrew.

MARIA   And you too, sir.

TOBY   Accost, Sir Andrew, accost!

ANDREW   What's that?

TOBY   My niece's chambermaid.   50

⌜ANDREW⌝   Good Mistress Accost, I desire better acquaintance.

MARIA   My name is Mary, sir.

ANDREW   Good Mistress Mary Accost—

TOBY   You mistake, knight. "Accost" is front her, board   55
her, woo her, assail her.

ANDREW   By my troth, I would not undertake her in
this company. Is that the meaning of "accost"?

MARIA   Fare you well, gentlemen.   ⌜*She begins to exit.*⌝

TOBY   An thou let part so, Sir Andrew, would thou   60
mightst never draw sword again.

ANDREW   An you part so, mistress, I would I might

64. **have fools in hand:** i.e., are dealing with **fools**

66. **Marry:** a mild oath, meaning "truly" or "indeed" (originally, an oath "by the Virgin Mary")

68. **thought is free:** a proverbial response to the question "Do you think I'm a fool?"

69. **butt'ry bar:** the ledge on top of the half door to the buttery, the storeroom for food and drink

71. **Wherefore:** i.e., why

73. **dry:** withered (indicating Andrew's lack of vigor, with a probable pun on **dry** as "thirsty")

76. **dry jest:** sarcastic or ironic joke

79. **barren:** i.e., no longer full of jests

80. **canary:** sweet wine

81. **put down:** snubbed, silenced

83. **put me down:** i.e., lay me out

84. **Christian:** often used, as here, to mean an ordinary human being

90. **Pourquoi:** French for "why"

92. **tongues:** i.e., foreign languages (Toby chooses to understand **tongues** to mean tongs for curling hair.)

93. **bearbaiting:** a blood sport in which dogs attack a bear chained to a stake (See picture, page 98.)

never draw sword again. Fair lady, do you think you
have fools in hand?

MARIA   Sir, I have not you by th' hand.   65

ANDREW   Marry, but you shall have, and here's my
hand.   ⌐*He offers his hand.*⌐

MARIA, ⌐*taking his hand*⌐ Now, sir, thought is free. I
pray you, bring your hand to th' butt'ry bar and let
it drink.   70

ANDREW   Wherefore, sweetheart? What's your metaphor?

MARIA   It's dry, sir.

ANDREW   Why, I think so. I am not such an ass but I
can keep my hand dry. But what's your jest?   75

MARIA   A dry jest, sir.

ANDREW   Are you full of them?

MARIA   Ay, sir, I have them at my fingers' ends. Marry,
now I let go your hand, I am barren.   *Maria exits.*

TOBY   O knight, thou lack'st a cup of canary! When did   80
I see thee so put down?

ANDREW   Never in your life, I think, unless you see
canary put me down. Methinks sometimes I have
no more wit than a Christian or an ordinary man
has. But I am a great eater of beef, and I believe that   85
does harm to my wit.

TOBY   No question.

ANDREW   An I thought that, I'd forswear it. I'll ride
home tomorrow, Sir Toby.

TOBY   *Pourquoi*, my dear knight?   90

ANDREW   What is *"pourquoi"*? Do, or not do? I would I
had bestowed that time in the tongues that I have in
fencing, dancing, and bearbaiting. O, had I but
followed the arts!

TOBY   Then hadst thou had an excellent head of hair.   95

ANDREW   Why, would that have mended my hair?

TOBY   Past question, for thou seest it will not ⌐curl by⌐
nature.

100. **flax:** long, thin yellow-colored fibers; **distaff:** staff used in spinning thread (See picture, page 166.)

101. **huswife:** housewife (**Huswife,** pronounced "hussif," also had the sense of "hussy.")

103. **Faith:** a mild oath

105. **Count:** i.e., Orsino, referred to as a duke in the first two scenes, but referred to hereafter in the dialogue as a **count; hard by:** nearby

108. **degree:** rank; **estate:** fortune; **wit:** intelligence

111–12. **masques and revels:** merrymaking, plays, dances

113. **kickshawses:** kickshaws, trifles (French: *quelques choses*)

117. **galliard:** a leaping dance (See picture, page 156.)

118. **caper:** leap (A **caper** is also a condiment used in sauces. Toby plays on this sense when he mentions **mutton.**)

120. **back-trick:** probably, a backward leap

123. **like:** i.e., likely

124. **take . . . picture:** i.e., get dusty, and therefore need a curtain to protect them (It is unclear who "Mistress Mall" might be.)

126–27. **coranto, jig, sink-a-pace:** names for various dances

128. **virtues:** abilities

130. **star of a galliard:** a dancing **star;** or, a **star** propitious for dancing

132. **dun-colored stock:** dull brown-colored stocking

ANDREW But it becomes ⌈me⌉ well enough, does 't not?

TOBY Excellent! It hangs like flax on a distaff, and I   100
hope to see a huswife take thee between her legs
and spin it off.

ANDREW Faith, I'll home tomorrow, Sir Toby. Your
niece will not be seen, or if she be, it's four to one
she'll none of me. The Count himself here hard by   105
woos her.

TOBY She'll none o' th' Count. She'll not match above
her degree, neither in estate, years, nor wit. I have
heard her swear 't. Tut, there's life in 't, man.

ANDREW I'll stay a month longer. I am a fellow o' th'   110
strangest mind i' th' world. I delight in masques
and revels sometimes altogether.

TOBY Art thou good at these kickshawses, knight?

ANDREW As any man in Illyria, whatsoever he be,
under the degree of my betters, and yet I will not   115
compare with an old man.

TOBY What is thy excellence in a galliard, knight?

ANDREW Faith, I can cut a caper.

TOBY And I can cut the mutton to 't.

ANDREW And I think I have the back-trick simply as   120
strong as any man in Illyria.

TOBY Wherefore are these things hid? Wherefore have
these gifts a curtain before 'em? Are they like to
take dust, like Mistress Mall's picture? Why dost
thou not go to church in a galliard and come home   125
in a coranto? My very walk should be a jig. I would
not so much as make water but in a sink-a-pace.
What dost thou mean? Is it a world to hide virtues
in? I did think, by the excellent constitution of thy
leg, it was formed under the star of a galliard.   130

ANDREW Ay, 'tis strong, and it does indifferent well in a
⌈dun-colored⌉ stock. Shall we ⌈set⌉ about some
revels?

135. **Taurus:** one of the twelve signs of the zodiac, which, at least according to Chaucer, governed the neck and the throat (See pictures, pages 64 and 136.)

1.4 At Orsino's court, Viola, disguised as a page and calling herself Cesario, has gained the trust of Orsino, who decides to send her to woo Olivia for him. Viola confides to the audience that she loves Orsino herself.

———————

2. **Cesario:** the name chosen by Viola for her male disguise, which she will wear for the rest of the play; **be much advanced:** i.e., achieve promotion

5. **either . . . negligence:** i.e., are concerned either that he is whimsical or that I cannot serve him well **fear:** distrust, suspect **humor:** disposition, whim

12. **On your attendance:** i.e., at your service

13. **aloof:** i.e., aside, apart

16. **address . . . unto:** i.e., go to

18. **them:** i.e., Olivia's servants; **grow:** i.e., fasten itself

19. **have audience:** i.e., are admitted to her

TOBY   What shall we do else? Were we not born under
   Taurus?   135
ANDREW   Taurus? ⌜That's⌝ sides and heart.
TOBY   No, sir, it is legs and thighs. Let me see thee
   caper. ⌜*Sir Andrew dances.*⌝ Ha, higher! Ha, ha,
   excellent!

                                                             They exit.

                              Scene 4
Enter Valentine, and Viola in man's attire ⌜as Cesario.⌝

VALENTINE   If the Duke continue these favors towards
   you, Cesario, you are like to be much advanced. He
   hath known you but three days, and already you
   are no stranger.
VIOLA   You either fear his humor or my negligence, that   5
   you call in question the continuance of his love. Is
   he inconstant, sir, in his favors?
VALENTINE   No, believe me.
VIOLA   I thank you.

          Enter ⌜Orsino,⌝ Curio, and Attendants.

   Here comes the Count.   10
ORSINO   Who saw Cesario, ho?
VIOLA   On your attendance, my lord, here.
ORSINO, ⌜*to Curio and Attendants*⌝
   Stand you awhile aloof.—Cesario,
   Thou know'st no less but all. I have unclasped
   To thee the book even of my secret soul.   15
   Therefore, good youth, address thy gait unto her.
   Be not denied access. Stand at her doors
   And tell them, there thy fixèd foot shall grow
   Till thou have audience.
VIOLA   Sure, my noble lord,   20
   If she be so abandoned to her sorrow
   As it is spoke, she never will admit me.

23. **leap . . . bounds:** i.e., become rude

24. **unprofited:** i.e., unsuccessful

26. **unfold:** reveal, disclose

27. **Surprise:** overcome, capture (a military term); **faith:** fidelity

28. **become thee well:** be appropriate for you

29. **attend:** pay attention to

30. **nuncio's:** messenger's; **more grave aspect:** i.e., older or more serious face

33. **belie:** misrepresent

34. **Diana:** the virgin goddess, here the personification of youth and beauty (See picture, page 34.)

35. **rubious:** ruby red; **pipe:** i.e., voice

36. **organ:** i.e., voice; **sound:** i.e., not cracked

37. **is semblative . . . part:** i.e., is like a woman (**Part** may be a theatrical term. In Shakespeare's theater, boys played women's parts.)

38. **thy constellation:** i.e., the stars that govern your success (or, that have shaped you)

39. **attend:** i.e., go along with

42. **as freely as:** without servitude like

45. **barful strife:** i.e., an undertaking full of obstacles or "bars" (barriers)

1.5 Viola, disguised as Cesario, appears at Olivia's estate. Olivia allows Cesario to speak with her privately about Orsino's love. As Cesario presents Orsino's love-suit, Olivia falls in love with Cesario. She sends her steward, Malvolio, after Cesario with a ring.

---

0 SD. **Feste, the Fool:** See longer note, page 191.

ORSINO
  Be clamorous and leap all civil bounds
  Rather than make unprofited return.

VIOLA
  Say I do speak with her, my lord, what then?   25

ORSINO
  O, then unfold the passion of my love.
  Surprise her with discourse of my dear faith.
  It shall become thee well to act my woes.
  She will attend it better in thy youth
  Than in a nuncio's of more grave aspect.   30

VIOLA
  I think not so, my lord.

ORSINO   Dear lad, believe it;
  For they shall yet belie thy happy years
  That say thou art a man. Diana's lip
  Is not more smooth and rubious, thy small pipe   35
  Is as the maiden's organ, shrill and sound,
  And all is semblative a woman's part.
  I know thy constellation is right apt
  For this affair.—Some four or five attend him,
  All, if you will, for I myself am best   40
  When least in company.—Prosper well in this
  And thou shalt live as freely as thy lord,
  To call his fortunes thine.

VIOLA   I'll do my best
  To woo your lady. ⌜*Aside.*⌝ Yet a barful strife!   45
  Whoe'er I woo, myself would be his wife.

                                They exit.

Scene 5
Enter Maria and ⌜*Feste, the Fool.*⌝

MARIA   Nay, either tell me where thou hast been, or I
    will not open my lips so wide as a bristle may enter

3. **in . . . excuse:** i.e., to defend you

6. **fear no colors:** proverbial for "**fear** nothing"

7. **Make . . . good:** i.e., prove that; explain that

9. **Lenten:** i.e., weak, poor (good enough only for Lent, a time of fasting)

10. **was born:** originated

12. **In the wars:** Military flags were called **colors.**

13. **foolery:** See longer note to 1.5.0 SD, page 191.

14. **have:** Logically the word should be "lack." Thus the Fool offers a paradox.

15. **talents:** perhaps with a pun on "talons" or claws

17. **turned away:** i.e., dismissed

20. **for:** i.e., as for; **let . . . out:** i.e., may the warm weather of **summer** make it bearable

23. **if one break:** Maria plays on **points** as meaning the laces that hold up a man's breeches.

24. **gaskins:** wide, loose breeches or hose

27. **piece of Eve's flesh:** i.e., woman

29. **you were best:** We would say, "If you know what's good for you."

30. **Wit:** i.e., intelligence, brain; **an 't:** i.e., if it

31. **wits:** clever people

33. **Quinapalus:** a classical authority invented by Feste

34. **witty:** clever

in way of thy excuse. My lady will hang thee for thy
absence.

FOOL   Let her hang me. He that is well hanged in this   5
   world needs to fear no colors.

MARIA   Make that good.

FOOL   He shall see none to fear.

MARIA   A good Lenten answer. I can tell thee where
   that saying was born, of "I fear no colors."   10

FOOL   Where, good Mistress Mary?

MARIA   In the wars; and that may you be bold to say in
   your foolery.

FOOL   Well, God give them wisdom that have it, and
   those that are Fools, let them use their talents.   15

MARIA   Yet you will be hanged for being so long absent.
   Or to be turned away, is not that as good as a
   hanging to you?

FOOL   Many a good hanging prevents a bad marriage,
   and, for turning away, let summer bear it out.   20

MARIA   You are resolute, then?

FOOL   Not so, neither, but I am resolved on two points.

MARIA   That if one break, the other will hold, or if both
   break, your gaskins fall.

FOOL   Apt, in good faith, very apt. Well, go thy way. If Sir   25
   Toby would leave drinking, thou wert as witty a
   piece of Eve's flesh as any in Illyria.

MARIA   Peace, you rogue. No more o' that. Here comes
   my lady. Make your excuse wisely, you were best.
                                    ⌜*She exits.*⌝

Enter Lady Olivia with Malvolio ⌜*and Attendants.*⌝

FOOL   ⌜*aside*⌝ Wit, an 't be thy will, put me into good   30
   fooling! Those wits that think they have thee do very
   oft prove fools, and I that am sure I lack thee may
   pass for a wise man. For what says Quinapalus?
   "Better a witty Fool than a foolish wit."—God bless
   thee, lady!   35

38. **Go to:** an expression of impatience; **dry:** i.e., dull, not amusing

39. **dishonest:** dishonorable (i.e., unreliable)

40. **madonna:** my lady, madam (an Italian form of address, literally *mia donna*)

42. **dry:** thirsty; **mend:** (1) reform; (2) repair

44. **botcher:** a tailor who repairs clothing

45. **is but:** is merely

46. **amends:** reforms

47. **If that:** i.e., **if**

48. **what remedy:** i.e., there is no **remedy**

49. **cuckold:** a man whose wife is unfaithful; **calamity:** misery

50. **bade:** commanded (**Bade** is the past tense of "bid.")

53. **Misprision**: a mistake, an error

53–54. **cucullus . . . monachum:** Proverbial: "A cowl does not make a monk."

54. **to say:** as **to say**

55. **motley:** multicolored patched garments worn by professional fools

58. **Dexteriously:** i.e., dexterously, cleverly

60. **catechize:** question rigorously

60–61. **Good . . . virtue:** i.e., my **good,** virtuous **mouse** (as if addressed to a young girl being catechized by the priest)

62. **want . . . idleness:** lack of other pastime; **bide:** wait for

72. **mend:** improve

OLIVIA Take the Fool away.

FOOL Do you not hear, fellows? Take away the Lady.

OLIVIA Go to, you're a dry Fool. I'll no more of you. Besides, you grow dishonest.

FOOL Two faults, madonna, that drink and good coun- 40
sel will amend. For give the dry Fool drink, then is
the Fool not dry. Bid the dishonest man mend
himself; if he mend, he is no longer dishonest; if he
cannot, let the botcher mend him. Anything that's
mended is but patched; virtue that transgresses is 45
but patched with sin, and sin that amends is but
patched with virtue. If that this simple syllogism
will serve, so; if it will not, what remedy? As there is
no true cuckold but calamity, so beauty's a flower.
The Lady bade take away the Fool. Therefore, I say 50
again, take her away.

OLIVIA Sir, I bade them take away you.

FOOL Misprison in the highest degree! Lady, *cucullus
non facit monachum.* That's as much to say as, I
wear not motley in my brain. Good madonna, give 55
me leave to prove you a fool.

OLIVIA Can you do it?

FOOL Dexteriously, good madonna.

OLIVIA Make your proof.

FOOL I must catechize you for it, madonna. Good my 60
mouse of virtue, answer me.

OLIVIA Well, sir, for want of other idleness, I'll bide
your proof.

FOOL Good madonna, why mourn'st thou?

OLIVIA Good Fool, for my brother's death. 65

FOOL I think his soul is in hell, madonna.

OLIVIA I know his soul is in heaven, Fool.

FOOL The more fool, madonna, to mourn for your
brother's soul, being in heaven. Take away the fool,
gentlemen. 70

OLIVIA What think you of this Fool, Malvolio? Doth he
not mend?

74. **Infirmity:** old age, weakness

78. **no fox:** i.e., not clever

78–79. **pass . . . twopence:** i.e., bet tuppence

82. **barren:** witless

82–83. **put down . . . with:** i.e., defeated (in a battle of wits) by

83. **ordinary fool:** perhaps, a simpleton; or, perhaps, a Fool without an aristocratic patron

84. **out of his guard:** defenseless, without an answer (a fencing metaphor)

85–86. **minister . . . him:** give him opportunities

87. **crow:** cry out in pleasure; **set . . . Fools:** i.e., professional fools   **set:** deliberate, unspontaneous

88. **zanies:** (1) subordinate fools in comedies, whose function is to imitate the main comic character; (2) assistants, flatterers

90. **distempered:** diseased, disturbed; **generous:** high-minded

91. **free:** magnanimous

92. **bird-bolts:** blunt arrows

93. **allowed Fool:** i.e., a **Fool** who has been given permission always to speak freely

94. **rail:** rant; jest

94–95. **known discreet man:** i.e., a **man** known to be judicious, wise

96. **Mercury . . . leasing:** i.e., may **Mercury,** god of trickery, endow you with the gift of lying (See picture, page 72.)

102. **well attended:** with several attendants

106. **madman:** i.e., nonsense

107. **suit:** love-plea

MALVOLIO Yes, and shall do till the pangs of death
   shake him. Infirmity, that decays the wise, doth
   ever make the better Fool.   75
FOOL God send you, sir, a speedy infirmity, for the
   better increasing your folly! Sir Toby will be sworn
   that I am no fox, but he will not pass his word for
   twopence that you are no fool.
OLIVIA How say you to that, Malvolio?   80
MALVOLIO I marvel your Ladyship takes delight in
   such a barren rascal. I saw him put down the other
   day with an ordinary fool that has no more brain
   than a stone. Look you now, he's out of his guard
   already. Unless you laugh and minister occasion to   85
   him, he is gagged. I protest I take these wise men
   that crow so at these set kind of Fools no better than
   the Fools' zanies.
OLIVIA O, you are sick of self-love, Malvolio, and taste
   with a distempered appetite. To be generous, guilt-   90
   less, and of free disposition is to take those things
   for bird-bolts that you deem cannon bullets. There
   is no slander in an allowed Fool, though he do
   nothing but rail; nor no railing in a known discreet
   man, though he do nothing but reprove.   95
FOOL Now Mercury endue thee with leasing, for thou
   speak'st well of Fools!

Enter Maria.

MARIA Madam, there is at the gate a young gentleman
   much desires to speak with you.
OLIVIA From the Count Orsino, is it?   100
MARIA I know not, madam. 'Tis a fair young man, and
   well attended.
OLIVIA Who of my people hold him in delay?
MARIA Sir Toby, madam, your kinsman.
OLIVIA Fetch him off, I pray you. He speaks nothing   105
   but madman. Fie on him! ⌐*Maria exits.*⌐ Go you,
   Malvolio. If it be a suit from the Count, I am sick,

112. **Jove:** king of the Roman gods, pictured below

114. **pia mater:** i.e., brain

115. **What:** i.e., who

119–20. **a plague . . . herring:** perhaps Toby's explanation for his having belched or hiccoughed

120. **sot:** fool; drunkard

126. **an he will:** if he wants to

127. **it's all one:** i.e., it doesn't matter

130. **draught:** i.e., cup of wine; **above heat:** Wine was thought to warm the liver.

132. **crowner:** i.e., coroner; **sit o':** i.e., hold an inquest on

Jove. (1.5.112)
From Vincenzo Cartari, *Le vere e noue imagini . . .* (1615).

or not at home; what you will, to dismiss it. (*Malvolio exits.*) Now you see, sir, how your fooling grows old, and people dislike it. 110

FOOL Thou hast spoke for us, madonna, as if thy eldest son should be a Fool, whose skull Jove cram with brains, for—here he comes—one of thy kin has a most weak *pia mater*.

Enter Sir Toby.

OLIVIA By mine honor, half drunk!—What is he at the 115 gate, cousin?

TOBY A gentleman.

OLIVIA A gentleman? What gentleman?

TOBY 'Tis a gentleman here—a plague o' these pickle herring!—How now, sot? 120

FOOL Good Sir Toby.

OLIVIA Cousin, cousin, how have you come so early by this lethargy?

TOBY Lechery? I defy lechery. There's one at the gate.

OLIVIA Ay, marry, what is he? 125

TOBY Let him be the devil an he will, I care not. Give me faith, say I. Well, it's all one. *He exits.*

OLIVIA What's a drunken man like, Fool?

FOOL Like a drowned man, a fool, and a madman. One draught above heat makes him a fool, the second 130 mads him, and a third drowns him.

OLIVIA Go thou and seek the crowner and let him sit o' my coz, for he's in the third degree of drink: he's drowned. Go look after him.

FOOL He is but mad yet, madonna, and the Fool shall 135 look to the madman. ⌜*He exits.*⌝

Enter Malvolio.

MALVOLIO Madam, yond young fellow swears he will speak with you. I told him you were sick; he takes

146. **Has:** i.e., he **has**

147. **sheriff's post:** marker set up by a **sheriff's** door

147–48. **the . . . bench:** i.e., a bench-support

151. **manner:** kind

153. **will . . . no:** i.e., whether you want to or not

154. **personage:** appearance

156. **squash:** unripe **peascod** (pea pod)

157. **codling:** unripe apple

158. **in standing . . . man:** i.e., halfway **between boy and man,** like a tide between ebb and flow

159. **well-favored:** good-looking

159–60. **shrewishly:** i.e., shrilly

Diana. (1.4.34)
From Robert Whitcombe, *Janua divorum* (1678).

on him to understand so much, and therefore
comes to speak with you. I told him you were   140
asleep; he seems to have a foreknowledge of that
too, and therefore comes to speak with you. What is
to be said to him, lady? He's fortified against any
denial.

OLIVIA   Tell him he shall not speak with me.   145

MALVOLIO   Has been told so, and he says he'll stand at
your door like a sheriff's post and be the supporter
to a bench, but he'll speak with you.

OLIVIA   What kind o' man is he?

MALVOLIO   Why, of mankind.   150

OLIVIA   What manner of man?

MALVOLIO   Of very ill manner. He'll speak with you,
will you or no.

OLIVIA   Of what personage and years is he?

MALVOLIO   Not yet old enough for a man, nor young   155
enough for a boy—as a squash is before 'tis a
peascod, or a codling when 'tis almost an apple. 'Tis
with him in standing water, between boy and man.
He is very well-favored, and he speaks very shrewishly. One would think his mother's milk were   160
scarce out of him.

OLIVIA
Let him approach. Call in my gentlewoman.

MALVOLIO   Gentlewoman, my lady calls.   *He exits.*

Enter Maria.

OLIVIA
Give me my veil. Come, throw it o'er my face.
                              ⌜*Olivia veils.*⌝
We'll once more hear Orsino's embassy.   165

Enter ⌜*Viola.*⌝

VIOLA   The honorable lady of the house, which is she?

167. **Your will?:** i.e., what do you want?

172. **con:** memorize

173–74. **comptible . . . usage:** sensitive **to even the** smallest slight

177. **part:** role; **gentle:** noble

178. **modest:** moderate

180. **comedian:** actor

182. **that I play:** i.e., **that** which **I** act

184. **usurp:** supplant (a joke)

185–86. **usurp yourself:** i.e., wrongfully hold possession of **yourself** (in that you are refusing to marry and reproduce)

187. **reserve:** keep for yourself; **from:** i.e., not part of

190. **forgive you:** i.e., excuse you from reciting

194. **like:** i.e., likely

197. **be not mad:** This odd phrase may represent a scribal or printing error. Some editors omit the word **not;** others interpret "not" to mean "not entirely."

198. **'Tis . . . me:** i.e., I am not myself lunatic—under the influence of Luna, the moon (See picture, page 134.)

199. **make one:** i.e., take part; **skipping:** i.e., incoherent

201. **swabber:** a sailor who swabs the decks; **hull:** remain at anchor with furled sails

OLIVIA   Speak to me. I shall answer for her. Your will?

VIOLA   Most radiant, exquisite, and unmatchable
beauty—I pray you, tell me if this be the lady of the
house, for I never saw her. I would be loath to cast   170
away my speech, for, besides that it is excellently
well penned, I have taken great pains to con it. Good
beauties, let me sustain no scorn. I am very comptible even to the least sinister usage.

OLIVIA   Whence came you, sir?   175

VIOLA   I can say little more than I have studied, and
that question's out of my part. Good gentle one,
give me modest assurance if you be the lady of the
house, that I may proceed in my speech.

OLIVIA   Are you a comedian?   180

VIOLA   No, my profound heart. And yet by the very
fangs of malice I swear I am not that I play. Are
you the lady of the house?

OLIVIA   If I do not usurp myself, I am.

VIOLA   Most certain, if you are she, you do usurp   185
yourself, for what is yours to bestow is not yours to
reserve. But this is from my commission. I will on
with my speech in your praise and then show you
the heart of my message.

OLIVIA   Come to what is important in 't. I forgive you   190
the praise.

VIOLA   Alas, I took great pains to study it, and 'tis
poetical.

OLIVIA   It is the more like to be feigned. I pray you,
keep it in. I heard you were saucy at my gates, and   195
allowed your approach rather to wonder at you than
to hear you. If you be not mad, begone; if you have
reason, be brief. 'Tis not that time of moon with me
to make one in so skipping a dialogue.

MARIA   Will you hoist sail, sir? Here lies your way.   200

VIOLA   No, good swabber, I am to hull here a little

202. **giant:** a sarcastic reference to Maria's size

207. **courtesy:** formality; **fearful:** frightening

208. **office:** i.e., what you have been ordered to say

209. **alone . . . ear:** i.e., concerns no one but you

210. **taxation of:** i.e., demand that you pay; **olive:** olive branch, a symbol of peace and goodwill

215. **my entertainment:** the way I was received

217. **divinity:** i.e., religious truth, theology; **profanation:** a violation of something sacred

220. **text:** passage from Scripture, which is divided into chapters

222. **comfortable:** comforting

226. **by the method:** according to your scheme

233–34. **such . . . present:** i.e., this is a portrait of me as I am at this moment

236. **in grain:** indelible (**Grain** was a "fast" or permanent dye.)

"I hold the olive in my hand." (1.5.210–11)
From Gilles Corrozet, *Hecatongraphie . . .* (1543).

longer.—Some mollification for your giant, sweet
lady.

⌜OLIVIA⌝ Tell me your mind.

⌜VIOLA⌝ I am a messenger.   205

OLIVIA Sure you have some hideous matter to deliver
when the courtesy of it is so fearful. Speak your
office.

VIOLA It alone concerns your ear. I bring no overture
of war, no taxation of homage. I hold the olive in   210
my hand. My words are as full of peace as matter.

OLIVIA Yet you began rudely. What are you? What
would you?

VIOLA The rudeness that hath appeared in me have I
learned from my entertainment. What I am and   215
what I would are as secret as maidenhead: to your
ears, divinity; to any other's, profanation.

OLIVIA Give us the place alone. We will hear this
divinity. ⌜*Maria and Attendants exit.*⌝ Now, sir, what
is your text?   220

VIOLA Most sweet lady—

OLIVIA A comfortable doctrine, and much may be said
of it. Where lies your text?

VIOLA In Orsino's bosom.

OLIVIA In his bosom? In what chapter of his bosom?   225

VIOLA To answer by the method, in the first of his heart.

OLIVIA O, I have read it; it is heresy. Have you no more
to say?

VIOLA Good madam, let me see your face.

OLIVIA Have you any commission from your lord to   230
negotiate with my face? You are now out of your
text. But we will draw the curtain and show you the
picture. ⌜*She removes her veil.*⌝ Look you, sir, such a
one I was this present. Is 't not well done?

VIOLA Excellently done, if God did all.   235

OLIVIA 'Tis in grain, sir; 'twill endure wind and
weather.

238. **blent:** blended

239. **cunning:** expert

240. **she:** woman

241. **graces:** beauties

242. **copy:** i.e., child (Olivia responds as if **copy** here meant a written record.)

244. **divers schedules:** various lists

245. **utensil:** i.e., part of my body; **labeled:** described on paper and attached as a codicil

246. **item:** Latin for "likewise" (used to introduce each article in a formal inventory)

248. **praise:** perhaps, appraise

251. **if:** i.e., even **if; the devil:** Lucifer (Proverbial: "As proud as Lucifer.") **fair:** beautiful

253. **but recompensed:** i.e., no more than returned on equal terms

255. **The nonpareil of beauty:** i.e., a **beauty** without equal

257. **fertile:** abundant

261. **estate:** fortune, status

262. **voices:** public opinion; **divulged:** spoken of; **free:** noble

263. **in dimension . . . nature:** i.e., in his physical **shape**

264. **A gracious:** an attractive

265. **took:** taken

266. **in . . . flame:** with . . . passion

267. **deadly:** death-like

VIOLA
'Tis beauty truly blent, whose red and white
Nature's own sweet and cunning hand laid on.
Lady, you are the cruel'st she alive   240
If you will lead these graces to the grave
And leave the world no copy.

OLIVIA O, sir, I will not be so hard-hearted! I will give
    out divers schedules of my beauty. It shall be
    inventoried and every particle and utensil labeled 245
    to my will: as, *item*, two lips indifferent red; *item*,
    two gray eyes with lids to them; *item*, one neck, one
    chin, and so forth. Were you sent hither to praise
    me?

VIOLA
I see you what you are. You are too proud.   250
But if you were the devil you are fair.
My lord and master loves you. O, such love
Could be but recompensed though you were
   crowned
The nonpareil of beauty.   255

OLIVIA   How does he love me?

VIOLA With adorations, fertile tears,
With groans that thunder love, with sighs of fire.

OLIVIA
Your lord does know my mind. I cannot love him.
Yet I suppose him virtuous, know him noble,   260
Of great estate, of fresh and stainless youth;
In voices well divulged, free, learned, and valiant,
And in dimension and the shape of nature
A gracious person. But yet I cannot love him.
He might have took his answer long ago.   265

VIOLA
If I did love you in my master's flame,
With such a suff'ring, such a deadly life,
In your denial I would find no sense.
I would not understand it.

271. **willow cabin:** shelter made of **willow** branches (The **willow** is the symbol of unrequited love.)

272. **call . . . house:** i.e., **call** out to Olivia

273. **cantons:** i.e., cantos, ballads; **contemnèd:** disdained, viewed with contempt

275. **Hallow:** shout; **reverberate:** echoing

276. **the babbling . . . air:** i.e., Echo (the nymph who, in Greek mythology, pined away for love until only her voice was left to "babble")

279. **But . . . me:** i.e., unless **you** took **pity** on **me**

282. **fortunes:** (current) situation; **state:** rank

289. **fee'd post:** hired messenger

291. **Love:** i.e., may the god of love (Cupid); **make . . . flint:** i.e., turn . . . into **flint; that . . . love:** i.e., the man **you** will one day **love**

292. **fervor:** passion

298. **give . . . blazon:** i.e., proclaim your high rank five times over (A **blazon** is a coat of arms.); **Soft:** an exclamation meaning "wait a minute"

300. **man:** i.e., servant

"Pitch" (the highest point in a falcon's flight). (1.1.12.)
George Turberville, *The booke of faulconrie . . .* (1575).

OLIVIA   Why, what would you?   270

VIOLA
Make me a willow cabin at your gate
And call upon my soul within the house,
Write loyal cantons of contemnèd love
And sing them loud even in the dead of night,
Hallow your name to the reverberate hills   275
And make the babbling gossip of the air
Cry out "Olivia!" O, you should not rest
Between the elements of air and earth
But you should pity me.

OLIVIA   You might do much.   280
What is your parentage?

VIOLA
Above my fortunes, yet my state is well.
I am a gentleman.

OLIVIA   Get you to your lord.
I cannot love him. Let him send no more—   285
Unless perchance you come to me again
To tell me how he takes it. Fare you well.
I thank you for your pains. Spend this for me.
                    ⌜*She offers money.*⌝

VIOLA
I am no fee'd post, lady. Keep your purse.
My master, not myself, lacks recompense.   290
Love make his heart of flint that you shall love,
And let your fervor, like my master's, be
Placed in contempt. Farewell, fair cruelty.   *She exits.*

OLIVIA   "What is your parentage?"
"Above my fortunes, yet my state is well.   295
I am a gentleman." I'll be sworn thou art.
Thy tongue, thy face, thy limbs, actions, and spirit
Do give thee fivefold blazon. Not too fast! Soft,
        soft!
Unless the master were the man. How now?   300
Even so quickly may one catch the plague?

302. **Methinks:** it seems

304. **at mine eyes:** Proverbial: "Love comes by looking in at the eyes."

308. **County's man:** count's servant

309. **Would I:** i.e., whether I wanted it

310. **flatter with:** i.e., encourage

313. **Hie thee:** hurry

317. **owe:** own

Acteon. (1.1.22–24)
From Ovid, *Le metamorphosi . . .* (1538).

Methinks I feel this youth's perfections
With an invisible and subtle stealth
To creep in at mine eyes. Well, let it be.—
What ho, Malvolio!   305

Enter Malvolio.

MALVOLIO   Here, madam, at your service.
OLIVIA
Run after that same peevish messenger,
The County's man. He left this ring behind him,
Would I or not. Tell him I'll none of it.

⌜*She hands him a ring.*⌝

Desire him not to flatter with his lord,   310
Nor hold him up with hopes. I am not for him.
If that the youth will come this way tomorrow,
I'll give him reasons for 't. Hie thee, Malvolio.
MALVOLIO   Madam, I will.   *He exits.*
OLIVIA
I do I know not what, and fear to find   315
Mine eye too great a flatterer for my mind.
Fate, show thy force. Ourselves we do not owe.
What is decreed must be, and be this so.
                                    ⌜*She exits.*⌝

TWELFTH NIGHT,
OR,
WHAT
YOU WILL

ACT 2

2.1 A young gentleman named Sebastian, who has recently been saved from a shipwreck in which his sister has been lost, sets off for Orsino's court. Antonio, the sailor who saved him, follows him, even though Antonio risks his own life to do so.

---

1. **will you not:** i.e., do **you not** wish

3. **By your patience:** a polite phrase, "with your permission"; **darkly:** ominously

4. **malignancy:** evil influence (astrological term, carried also in the preceding phrase, "My stars shine darkly over me.")

5. **distemper:** sicken, damage

6. **evils:** misfortunes

10. **sooth:** i.e., truly; **My . . . voyage:** the journey I've set for myself

11. **mere extravagancy:** no more than wandering

12. **modesty:** reserve, lack of presumption

13. **what . . . keep in:** i.e., **what I** wish to hide

13–14. **it . . . manners:** i.e., courtesy compels me

14. **the rather:** all the more

19. **in an:** i.e., within the same

21. **some hour:** i.e., not long

22. **breach of the sea:** i.e., the breaking waves

ACT 2

Scene 1
Enter Antonio and Sebastian.

ANTONIO   Will you stay no longer? Nor will you not that
I go with you?

SEBASTIAN   By your patience, no. My stars shine darkly
over me. The malignancy of my fate might perhaps
distemper yours. Therefore I shall crave of you your   5
leave that I may bear my evils alone. It were a bad
recompense for your love to lay any of them on you.

ANTONIO   Let me yet know of you whither you are
bound.

SEBASTIAN   No, sooth, sir. My determinate voyage is   10
mere extravagancy. But I perceive in you so excellent a touch of modesty that you will not extort
from me what I am willing to keep in. Therefore it
charges me in manners the rather to express myself. You must know of me, then, Antonio, my name   15
is Sebastian, which I called Roderigo. My father was
that Sebastian of Messaline whom I know you have
heard of. He left behind him myself and a sister,
both born in an hour. If the heavens had been
pleased, would we had so ended! But you, sir,   20
altered that, for some hour before you took me
from the breach of the sea was my sister drowned.

ANTONIO   Alas the day!

26–27. **with . . . that:** i.e., believe too much in this admiring judgment of my sister's beauty

28. **publish:** proclaim

28–29. **that envy . . . fair:** i.e., **that** even the envious must **call** beautiful

32. **entertainment:** reception as my guest

34. **murder me for my love:** i.e., destroy me (1) in exchange **for my love,** or (2) because I care so much about you

37. **recovered:** rescued

39–40. **so near . . . mother:** i.e., so close to behaving like a woman

41. **will . . . me:** will weep, thus revealing my feelings

43. **gentleness:** kindliness

45. **Else:** otherwise

2.2 Malvolio finds the disguised Viola and "returns" the ring. Viola, alone, realizes that Olivia has fallen in love with Cesario and understands that Orsino, Olivia, and Viola/Cesario are now in a love triangle that she is helpless to resolve.

---

0 SD. **at several doors:** i.e., through separate stage entrances

3. **On:** i.e., at

4. **arrived but hither:** i.e., just reached this place

SEBASTIAN   A lady, sir, though it was said she much
  resembled me, was yet of many accounted beauti-   25
  ful. But though I could not with such estimable
  wonder overfar believe that, yet thus far I will boldly
  publish her: she bore a mind that envy could not but
  call fair. She is drowned already, sir, with salt water,
  though I seem to drown her remembrance again   30
  with more.

ANTONIO   Pardon me, sir, your bad entertainment.

SEBASTIAN   O good Antonio, forgive me your trouble.

ANTONIO   If you will not murder me for my love, let me
  be your servant.   35

SEBASTIAN   If you will not undo what you have done—
  that is, kill him whom you have recovered—desire
  it not. Fare you well at once. My bosom is full of
  kindness, and I am yet so near the manners of my
  mother that, upon the least occasion more, mine   40
  eyes will tell tales of me. I am bound to the Count
  Orsino's court. Farewell.   *He exits.*

ANTONIO
  The gentleness of all the gods go with thee!
  I have many enemies in Orsino's court,
  Else would I very shortly see thee there.   45
  But come what may, I do adore thee so
  That danger shall seem sport, and I will go.

                    He exits.

Scene 2
Enter Viola and Malvolio, at several doors.

MALVOLIO   Were not you even now with the Countess
  Olivia?

VIOLA   Even now, sir. On a moderate pace I have since
  arrived but hither.

MALVOLIO   She returns this ring to you, sir. You might   5

8. **a . . . assurance:** a certainty that offers him no hope

8–9. **will none of:** i.e., will not have

10. **hardy:** rashly bold; **in . . . affairs:** on . . . business

11. **this:** i.e., this message of rejection; **Receive it so:** i.e., take the ring with this understanding

12. **She . . . it:** This response seems to be a resourceful lie by Viola.

19. **made . . . me:** i.e., looked at me intently

20. **had lost:** i.e., had made her lose

22. **cunning:** craftiness

23. **Invites:** encourages, tempts

24. **None of:** i.e., she will not have (See above, lines 8–9.)

25. **the man:** i.e., the one she loves

28. **the pregnant enemy:** i.e., the devil, who uses such deceits as **disguise** in his wicked practices **pregnant:** resourceful

29. **the proper false:** those who are unfaithful but handsome

30. **In . . . forms:** i.e., to imprint their images **in women's** impressionable **hearts**

31–32. **our . . . be:** Proverbial: "Women are the weaker vessels."

33. **fadge:** i.e., work out, fit together

34. **monster:** i.e., a man/woman; **fond . . . on:** just as infatuated with

37. **My . . . for:** i.e., it is impossible that I should win

have saved me my pains to have taken it away
yourself. She adds, moreover, that you should put
your lord into a desperate assurance she will none
of him. And one thing more, that you be never so
hardy to come again in his affairs unless it be to   10
report your lord's taking of this. Receive it so.

VIOLA   She took the ring of me. I'll none of it.

MALVOLIO   Come, sir, you peevishly threw it to her, and
her will is it should be so returned. ⌜*He throws
down the ring.*⌝ If it be worth stooping for, there it   15
lies in your eye; if not, be it his that finds it.

He exits.

VIOLA
I left no ring with her. What means this lady?
⌜*She picks up the ring.*⌝
Fortune forbid my outside have not charmed her!
She made good view of me, indeed so much
That methought her eyes had lost her tongue,   20
For she did speak in starts distractedly.
She loves me, sure! The cunning of her passion
Invites me in this churlish messenger.
None of my lord's ring? Why, he sent her none!
I am the man. If it be so, as 'tis,   25
Poor lady, she were better love a dream.
Disguise, I see thou art a wickedness
Wherein the pregnant enemy does much.
How easy is it for the proper false
In women's waxen hearts to set their forms!   30
Alas, ⌜our⌝ frailty is the cause, not we,
For such as we are made ⌜of,⌝ such we be.
How will this fadge? My master loves her dearly,
And I, poor monster, fond as much on him,
And she, mistaken, seems to dote on me.   35
What will become of this? As I am man,
My state is desperate for my master's love.
As I am woman (now, alas the day!),

39. **thriftless:** useless, fruitless

2.3   At Olivia's estate, Toby, Andrew, and the Fool hold a late night party. Maria comes in to quiet them, followed by Malvolio, who orders them to behave or be dismissed from the house. In retaliation, Maria plots to trap Malvolio with a forged letter that will persuade him that Olivia loves him.

———————

2. **betimes:** early in the morning

2–3. **diluculo surgere:** the first two words of a familiar Latin maxim that means "To rise early is good for the health"

6. **as:** i.e., as much as I do; **can:** drinking cup

9–10. **the . . . elements:** air, earth, water, and fire

14. **Marian:** i.e., Maria; **stoup:** tankard (a large drinking vessel)

17. **"We Three":** a familiar picture of two fools or asses, the title of which, "We Three," suggests that the viewer is the third fool or ass

18. **catch:** music written for three voices, sung as a round

19. **breast:** i.e., breath, singing voice

20. **leg:** i.e., for dancing

22. **fooling:** See longer note to 1.5.0 SD, page 191.

23–24. **Pigrogromitus . . . Queubus:**   examples of the Fool's wordplay (here, apparent mockery of astrological language)

25. **leman:** mistress, lover

What thriftless sighs shall poor Olivia breathe!
O Time, thou must untangle this, not I.   40
It is too hard a knot for me t' untie.

⌜*She exits.*⌝

Scene 3
Enter Sir Toby and Sir Andrew.

TOBY Approach, Sir Andrew. Not to be abed after
midnight is to be up betimes, and *"diluculo sur-*
gere," thou know'st—

ANDREW Nay, by my troth, I know not. But I know to
be up late is to be up late.   5

TOBY A false conclusion. I hate it as an unfilled can. To
be up after midnight and to go to bed then, is early,
so that to go to bed after midnight is to go to bed
betimes. Does not our lives consist of the four
elements?   10

ANDREW Faith, so they say, but I think it rather consists of eating and drinking.

TOBY Thou 'rt a scholar. Let us therefore eat and
drink. Marian, I say, a stoup of wine!

Enter ⌜Feste, the Fool.⌝

ANDREW Here comes the Fool, i' faith.   15

FOOL How now, my hearts? Did you never see the
picture of "We Three"?

TOBY Welcome, ass! Now let's have a catch.

ANDREW By my troth, the Fool has an excellent breast.
I had rather than forty shillings I had such a leg,   20
and so sweet a breath to sing, as the Fool has.—In
sooth, thou wast in very gracious fooling last night
when thou spok'st of Pigrogromitus of the Vapians
passing the equinoctial of Queubus. 'Twas very
good, i' faith. I sent thee sixpence for thy leman.   25
Hadst it?

27. **impeticos thy gratillity:** more of the Fool's wordplay (**Gratillity** sounds like "gratuity," i.e., tip.)

27–29. **for . . . houses:** apparent nonsense to please Sir Andrew **whipstock:** whip handle **white:** then synonymous with "beautiful" **Myrmidons:** the followers of Achilles, the Greek warrior in Homer's *Iliad* **bottle-ale houses:** inferior taverns

34. **testril:** tester, sixpence; **of:** from

35. **give a:** In the Folio, there is no punctuation after these words, which come at the end of the line. It is possible that the next line of Andrew's speech was simply dropped.

36–37. **a song . . . life:** a drinking song (Andrew, at line 39, appears to understand **good life** to mean a moral life.)

40. **"O mistress mine":** Tunes by this name were published in Shakespeare's time, and the words here may or may not be Shakespeare's.

43. **Trip:** go; **sweeting:** sweetheart

44. **in lovers meeting:** i.e., when lovers meet

48. **hereafter:** at some future time

50. **still:** always

51. **plenty:** abundance

55. **contagious:** foul (but understood by Andrew to be a compliment)

57. **To . . . nose:** i.e., if we heard with our noses; **dulcet:** sweet

58. **welkin:** heavens (See picture, page 152.)

59. **catch:** See note to line 18, above.

60. **weaver:** Weavers were said to be fond of singing.

FOOL   I did impeticos thy gratillity, for Malvolio's nose
   is no whipstock, my lady has a white hand, and the
   Myrmidons are no bottle-ale houses.

ANDREW   Excellent! Why, this is the best fooling when   30
   all is done. Now, a song.

TOBY, ⌜*giving money to the Fool*⌝ Come on, there is
   sixpence for you. Let's have a song.

ANDREW, ⌜*giving money to the Fool*⌝ There's a testril of
   me, too. If one knight give a—   35

FOOL   Would you have a love song or a song of good
   life?

TOBY   A love song, a love song.

ANDREW   Ay, ay, I care not for good life.

FOOL   *sings*

    O mistress mine, where are you roaming?   40
    O, stay and hear! Your truelove's coming,
      That can sing both high and low.
    Trip no further, pretty sweeting.
    Journeys end in lovers meeting,
      Every wise man's son doth know.   45

ANDREW   Excellent good, i' faith.

TOBY   Good, good.

FOOL ⌜*sings*⌝

    What is love? 'Tis not hereafter.
    Present mirth hath present laughter.
      What's to come is still unsure.   50
    In delay there lies no plenty,
    Then come kiss me, sweet and twenty.
      Youth's a stuff will not endure.

ANDREW   A mellifluous voice, as I am true knight.

TOBY   A contagious breath.   55

ANDREW   Very sweet and contagious, i' faith.

TOBY   To hear by the nose, it is dulcet in contagion.
   But shall we make the welkin dance indeed? Shall
   we rouse the night owl in a catch that will draw
   three souls out of one weaver? Shall we do that?   60

61. **An:** if; **dog:** i.e., expert

63. **By 'r Lady:** an oath, "By our Lady" (i.e., the Virgin Mary)

64–65. **"Thou Knave":** a catch or round also known as "Hold Thy Peace," in which the singers call each other, in turn, "thou knave" (**Knave** meant variously "servant, menial," "boy," and "villain.")

73. **caterwauling:** howling of cats

76. **Cataian:** i.e., untrustworthy boaster (See longer note, page 192.) **politicians:** shrewd fellows

77. **Peg-a-Ramsey:** the name of a popular song

77–78. **Three . . . we:** a line from another popular song

78–79. **of her blood:** related to her (i.e., **consanguineous**)

79. **Tillyvally:** an expression of impatience; **"Lady":** Toby mocks Maria's reference to Olivia.

79–80. **There . . . lady:** a line from a popular song

81. **Beshrew me:** i.e., curse me (a mild oath)

84. **natural:** i.e., naturally (with an unintended pun on "natural" meaning "like an idiot")

85. **O' . . . December:** a line from a popular song

87. **My masters:** i.e., gentlemen

88. **wit:** sense; **honesty:** decency, decorum

89. **tinkers:** wandering menders of utensils, known for their drinking

91. **coziers:** cobblers

91–92. **mitigation or remorse:** i.e., softening (See longer note, page 192.)

ANDREW An you love me, let's do 't. I am dog at a
catch.

FOOL By 'r Lady, sir, and some dogs will catch well.

ANDREW Most certain. Let our catch be "Thou
Knave."   65

FOOL "Hold thy peace, thou knave," knight? I shall be
constrained in 't to call thee "knave," knight.

ANDREW 'Tis not the first time I have constrained one
to call me "knave." Begin, Fool. It begins "Hold
thy peace."   70

FOOL I shall never begin if I hold my peace.

ANDREW Good, i' faith. Come, begin.   *Catch sung.*

Enter Maria.

MARIA What a caterwauling do you keep here! If my
lady have not called up her steward Malvolio and
bid him turn you out of doors, never trust me.   75

TOBY My lady's a Cataian, we are politicians, Malvolio's
a Peg-a-Ramsey, and ⌈*Sings.*⌉ *Three merry men be
we.* Am not I consanguineous? Am I not of her
blood? Tillyvally! "Lady"! ⌈*Sings.*⌉ *There dwelt a man
in Babylon, lady, lady.*   80

FOOL Beshrew me, the knight's in admirable fooling.

ANDREW Ay, he does well enough if he be disposed,
and so do I, too. He does it with a better grace, but
I do it more natural.

TOBY ⌈*sings*⌉ *O' the twelfth day of December—*   85

MARIA For the love o' God, peace!

Enter Malvolio.

MALVOLIO My masters, are you mad? Or what are you?
Have you no wit, manners, nor honesty but to
gabble like tinkers at this time of night? Do you
make an ale-house of my lady's house, that you   90
squeak out your coziers' catches without any mitigation or remorse of voice? Is there no respect of
place, persons, nor time in you?

94. **Sneck up:** hang yourself

95. **round:** straightforward

97. **disorders:** disturbances

99. **an:** if

102. **Farewell . . . gone:** the beginning of the song "Farewell Dear Love," which continues through line 112.

107. **lie:** i.e., do not tell the truth (In "Farewell," the words are "So long as I can spy.")

115. **cakes and ale:** associated with festivity

116. **Saint Anne:** mother of the Virgin Mary; **ginger:** used to spice ale

118–19. **rub . . . crumbs:** i.e., polish your steward's chain

A "viol-de-gamboys." (1.3.25–26)
From *Nieuwen ieucht spieghel . . .* (ca. 1620).

TOBY We did keep time, sir, in our catches. Sneck up!

MALVOLIO Sir Toby, I must be round with you. My lady 95
bade me tell you that, though she harbors you as her
kinsman, she's nothing allied to your disorders. If
you can separate yourself and your misdemeanors,
you are welcome to the house; if not, an it would
please you to take leave of her, she is very willing to 100
bid you farewell.

TOBY ⌜*sings*⌝
Farewell, dear heart, since I must needs be gone.

MARIA Nay, good Sir Toby.

FOOL ⌜*sings*⌝
His eyes do show his days are almost done.

MALVOLIO Is 't even so? 105

TOBY ⌜*sings*⌝
But I will never die.

FOOL ⌜*sings*⌝
Sir Toby, there you lie.

MALVOLIO This is much credit to you.

TOBY ⌜*sings*⌝
Shall I bid him go?

FOOL ⌜*sings*⌝
What an if you do? 110

TOBY ⌜*sings*⌝
Shall I bid him go, and spare not?

FOOL ⌜*sings*⌝
O no, no, no, no, you dare not.

TOBY Out o' tune, sir? You lie. Art any more than a
steward? Dost thou think, because thou art virtuous, there shall be no more cakes and ale? 115

FOOL Yes, by Saint Anne, and ginger shall be hot i' th'
mouth, too.

TOBY Thou 'rt i' th' right.—Go, sir, rub your chain
with crumbs.—A stoup of wine, Maria!

MALVOLIO Mistress Mary, if you prized my lady's favor 120
at anything more than contempt, you would not give

122. **uncivil rule:** uncivilized conduct

124. **shake . . . ears:** i.e., as if he were an ass

125–28. **'Twere . . . him:** In confused language (e.g., he means "thirsty" when he says **a-hungry**), Andrew threatens to challenge Malvolio to a duel and then not show up.

133. **out of quiet:** disquieted, troubled

133–34. **let . . . him:** i.e., leave him to me

134. **gull . . . nayword:** i.e., through trickery turn him into a byword (a figure of scorn)

135. **recreation:** i.e., figure of fun

138. **Possess:** inform

139. **puritan:** originally, a term of abuse used against members of the Church of England who were strict moralists, intent on stamping out sin and doing away with frivolity (The word comes from the Latin *purus*, "pure.")

145. **The devil . . . is:** i.e., he is not **a puritan** (contradicting line 139)

146. **constantly:** consistently; **time-pleaser:** opportunist, self-server; **affectioned:** affected

147. **cons . . . book:** i.e., memorizes high-sounding phrases

148. **the best . . . of:** i.e., holding the highest opinion of

156. **expressure:** expression

means for this uncivil rule. She shall know of it, by
this hand.   *He exits.*

MARIA   Go shake your ears!

ANDREW   'Twere as good a deed as to drink when a 125
man's a-hungry, to challenge him the field and
then to break promise with him and make a fool of
him.

TOBY   Do 't, knight. I'll write thee a challenge. Or I'll
deliver thy indignation to him by word of mouth. 130

MARIA   Sweet Sir Toby, be patient for tonight. Since the
youth of the Count's was today with my lady, she is
much out of quiet. For Monsieur Malvolio, let me
alone with him. If I do not gull him into ⌜a nayword⌝
and make him a common recreation, do not think I 135
have wit enough to lie straight in my bed. I know I
can do it.

TOBY   Possess us, possess us, tell us something of him.

MARIA   Marry, sir, sometimes he is a kind of puritan.

ANDREW   O, if I thought that, I'd beat him like a dog! 140

TOBY   What, for being a puritan? Thy exquisite reason,
dear knight?

ANDREW   I have no exquisite reason for 't, but I have
reason good enough.

MARIA   The devil a puritan that he is, or anything 145
constantly but a time-pleaser; an affectioned ass
that cons state without book and utters it by great
swaths; the best persuaded of himself, so crammed,
as he thinks, with excellencies, that it is his grounds
of faith that all that look on him love him. And on 150
that vice in him will my revenge find notable cause
to work.

TOBY   What wilt thou do?

MARIA   I will drop in his way some obscure epistles of
love, wherein by the color of his beard, the shape of 155
his leg, the manner of his gait, the expressure of his
eye, forehead, and complexion, he shall find himself

158. **feelingly personated:** accurately represented

159–60. **on . . . hands:** i.e., when we have forgotten who wrote something, we can barely distinguish her handwriting from mine

161. **device:** plan, scheme

170. **physic:** medicine

173. **construction:** interpretation

175. **Penthesilea:** queen of the Amazons (fierce warrior women) See picture, page 132.

176. **Before me:** a mild oath

182. **recover:** obtain

182–83. **a foul way out:** i.e., in financial trouble (literally, out in the dirt)

185. **Cut:** a horse (with a docked tail; or, gelded)

188. **burn some sack:** warm up some sherry

Taurus. (1.3.135)
From Johann Engel, *Astrolabium . . .* (1488).

most feelingly personated. I can write very like my
lady your niece; on a forgotten matter, we can
hardly make distinction of our hands.   160

TOBY   Excellent! I smell a device.

ANDREW   I have 't in my nose, too.

TOBY   He shall think, by the letters that thou wilt drop,
that they come from my niece, and that she's in
love with him.   165

MARIA   My purpose is indeed a horse of that color.

ANDREW   And your horse now would make him an ass.

MARIA   Ass, I doubt not.

ANDREW   O, 'twill be admirable!

MARIA   Sport royal, I warrant you. I know my physic   170
will work with him. I will plant you two, and let the
Fool make a third, where he shall find the letter.
Observe his construction of it. For this night, to bed,
and dream on the event. Farewell.

TOBY   Good night, Penthesilea.   *She exits.* 175

ANDREW   Before me, she's a good wench.

TOBY   She's a beagle true bred, and one that adores
me. What o' that?

ANDREW   I was adored once, too.

TOBY   Let's to bed, knight. Thou hadst need send for   180
more money.

ANDREW   If I cannot recover your niece, I am a foul way
out.

TOBY   Send for money, knight. If thou hast her not i'
th' end, call me "Cut."   185

ANDREW   If I do not, never trust me, take it how you
will.

TOBY   Come, come, I'll go burn some sack. 'Tis too
late to go to bed now. Come, knight; come, knight.
                                            They exit.

2.4 Orsino asks for a song to relieve his love-longing. In conversation about the capacities for love in men and in women, Viola expresses her love for Orsino through a story about "Cesario's sister." Orsino becomes curious about this sister's fate, but then turns back to his own longings and sends Cesario once again to visit Olivia.

1–2. **good morrow:** good morning

3. **but:** just

4. **antique:** old-fashioned (accent on first syllable)

5. **passion:** emotional suffering

6. **airs:** tunes, melodies; **recollected terms:** perhaps, unspontaneous or studied verse

7. **brisk and giddy-pacèd:** i.e., unpleasantly fast-moving

20. **Unstaid and skittish:** fickle, inconstant; **in . . . else: in all** other emotions or desires

21. **constant:** fixed, unchanging (referring to the **image**); faithful (referring to the lover)

23. **It . . . echo:** i.e., it echoes exactly

23–24. **the seat . . . throned:** i.e., the lover's heart

25. **masterly:** as an expert

27. **stayed . . . favor:** lingered over some face

29. **by your favor:** a courteous phrase, "if you please," with a punning reference to Orsino's "favor," or face

Scene 4
Enter ⌜Orsino,⌝ Viola, Curio, and others.

ORSINO
  Give me some music. ⌜*Music plays.*⌝ Now, good
    morrow, friends.—
  Now, good Cesario, but that piece of song,
  That old and antique song we heard last night.
  Methought it did relieve my passion much,   5
  More than light airs and recollected terms
  Of these most brisk and giddy-pacèd times.
  Come, but one verse.
CURIO   He is not here, so please your Lordship, that
    should sing it.   10
ORSINO   Who was it?
CURIO   Feste the jester, my lord, a Fool that the Lady
    Olivia's father took much delight in. He is about
    the house.
ORSINO
  Seek him out ⌜*Curio exits,*⌝ and play the tune the   15
    while.   *Music plays.*
  ⌜*To Viola.*⌝ Come hither, boy. If ever thou shalt love,
  In the sweet pangs of it remember me,
  For such as I am, all true lovers are,
  Unstaid and skittish in all motions else   20
  Save in the constant image of the creature
  That is beloved. How dost thou like this tune?
VIOLA
  It gives a very echo to the seat
  Where love is throned.
ORSINO   Thou dost speak masterly.   25
  My life upon 't, young though thou art, thine eye
  Hath stayed upon some favor that it loves.
  Hath it not, boy?
VIOLA   A little, by your favor.

31. **complexion:** temperament; appearance

34. **still:** always

35. **wears . . . him:** i.e., shapes herself to fit him

36. **sways she level:** The image may be of a ruler holding sway, or of a balance scale. (See picture, below.)

38. **fancies:** desires

41. **think:** believe

43. **hold the bent:** i.e., endure at its maximum tension, like a fully stretched bow (See picture, page 70.)

45. **Being . . . displayed:** i.e., having blossomed

49. **Mark:** pay attention to

50. **spinsters:** those who spin thread or yarn

51. **free:** carefree

51–52. **weave . . . bones:** use bone bobbins in making lace

53. **Do use to:** customarily; **silly sooth:** simple truth

54. **dallies:** plays

55. **the old age:** i.e., **the** good **old** days

A balance scale. (2.4.36)
From Silvestro Pietrasanta, . . . *Symbola heroica . . .* (1682).

ORSINO
  What kind of woman is 't?   30
VIOLA   Of your complexion.
ORSINO
  She is not worth thee, then. What years, i' faith?
VIOLA   About your years, my lord.
ORSINO
  Too old, by heaven. Let still the woman take
  An elder than herself. So wears she to him;   35
  So sways she level in her husband's heart.
  For, boy, however we do praise ourselves,
  Our fancies are more giddy and unfirm,
  More longing, wavering, sooner lost and worn,
  Than women's are.   40
VIOLA   I think it well, my lord.
ORSINO
  Then let thy love be younger than thyself,
  Or thy affection cannot hold the bent.
  For women are as roses, whose fair flower,
  Being once displayed, doth fall that very hour.   45
VIOLA
  And so they are. Alas, that they are so,
  To die even when they to perfection grow!

          Enter Curio and ⌈*Feste, the Fool.*⌉

ORSINO
  O, fellow, come, the song we had last night.—
  Mark it, Cesario. It is old and plain;
  The spinsters and the knitters in the sun   50
  And the free maids that weave their thread with
     bones
  Do use to chant it. It is silly sooth,
  And dallies with the innocence of love
  Like the old age.   55
FOOL   Are you ready, sir?
ORSINO   Ay, prithee, sing.   *Music.*

58. **away:** i.e., with me

59. **sad cypress:** i.e., a coffin of dark **cypress** wood

62. **yew:** i.e., sprigs of **yew** (The yew tree was often planted in churchyards and was a symbol of sadness.)

67. **strown:** strewn

68. **greet:** lament, bewail

74. **There's for:** i.e., **there's** payment **for**

77. **paid:** i.e., **paid** for

79. **Give . . . thee:** a polite dismissal of the Fool

80. **the . . . god:** i.e., Saturn, **god** of **melancholy**

81. **doublet:** jacket; **changeable taffeta:** a thin silky fabric woven so that the color appears to change when viewed from different perspectives

82. **opal:** a stone of variable colors

82–83. **such constancy:** i.e., so little **constancy**

84. **intent:** i.e., intended destination

A bow at the full bent. (2.4.43)
From Jacobus a. Bruck, *Emblemata moralia & bellica* (1615).

The Song.

⌜FOOL⌝

  Come away, come away, death,
    And in sad cypress let me be laid.
  ⌜*Fly*⌝ *away,* ⌜*fly*⌝ *away, breath,*   60
    I am slain by a fair cruel maid.
  My shroud of white, stuck all with yew,
    O, prepare it!
  My part of death, no one so true
    Did share it.   65

  Not a flower, not a flower sweet
    On my black coffin let there be strown;
  Not a friend, not a friend greet
    My poor corpse where my bones shall be thrown.
  A thousand thousand sighs to save,   70
    Lay me, O, where
  Sad true lover never find my grave
    To weep there.

ORSINO, ⌜*giving money*⌝   There's for thy pains.

FOOL   No pains, sir. I take pleasure in singing, sir.   75

ORSINO   I'll pay thy pleasure, then.

FOOL   Truly sir, and pleasure will be paid, one time or
another.

ORSINO   Give me now leave to leave thee.

FOOL   Now the melancholy god protect thee and the   80
tailor make thy doublet of changeable taffeta, for thy
mind is a very opal. I would have men of such
constancy put to sea, that their business might be
everything and their intent everywhere, for that's it
that always makes a good voyage of nothing. Fare-   85
well.   *He exits.*

ORSINO

  Let all the rest give place.
               ⌜*All but Orsino and Viola exit.*⌝
               Once more, Cesario,

89. sovereign cruelty: (1) the cruel woman who rules my life; (2) the queen of cruelty (Orsino speaks the exaggerated language of love poetry.)

91. quantity . . . lands: i.e., her property

92. parts . . . her: i.e., her wealth and status

93. hold as giddily as Fortune: Fortune is proverbially fickle. (See picture, page 142.)

94–95. that miracle . . . in: i.e., her own beauty, a gift of **nature   pranks:** dresses

98. Sooth: in truth

102. be answered: i.e., take that as final

104. bide: endure

108. No . . . palate: i.e., not a strong emotion whose seat is in **the liver, but** a casual appetite

109. suffer: experience; **surfeit, cloyment:** i.e., excessive consumption; **revolt:** revulsion

111–12. Make . . . Between: i.e., do not compare

113. that: i.e., that which; **owe:** have for

117. In faith: a mild oath

Mercury. (1.5.96)
From Innocenzio Ringhieri, *Cento giuochi liberali . . .* (1580).

Get thee to yond same sovereign cruelty.
Tell her my love, more noble than the world,   90
Prizes not quantity of dirty lands.
The parts that Fortune hath bestowed upon her,
Tell her, I hold as giddily as Fortune.
But 'tis that miracle and queen of gems
That nature pranks her in attracts my soul.   95

VIOLA   But if she cannot love you, sir—

ORSINO
⌜I⌝ cannot be so answered.

VIOLA   Sooth, but you must.
Say that some lady, as perhaps there is,
Hath for your love as great a pang of heart   100
As you have for Olivia. You cannot love her;
You tell her so. Must she not then be answered?

ORSINO   There is no woman's sides
Can bide the beating of so strong a passion
As love doth give my heart; no woman's heart   105
So big, to hold so much; they lack retention.
Alas, their love may be called appetite,
No motion of the liver but the palate,
That suffer surfeit, cloyment, and revolt;
But mine is all as hungry as the sea,   110
And can digest as much. Make no compare
Between that love a woman can bear me
And that I owe Olivia.

VIOLA   Ay, but I know—

ORSINO   What dost thou know?   115

VIOLA
Too well what love women to men may owe.
In faith, they are as true of heart as we.
My father had a daughter loved a man
As it might be, perhaps, were I a woman,
I should your Lordship.   120

ORSINO   And what's her history?

123. **worm i' th' bud:** i.e., a cankerworm inside a rosebud (See picture, below.)

124. **damask:** pink, rosy

129. **shows . . . will:** outer expressions are larger than actual desires; **still:** always

137. **give no place: give** way to no one; **bide no denay:** accept no denial

2.5 Maria lays her trap for Malvolio by placing her forged letter in his path. From their hiding place, Toby, Andrew, and Fabian observe Malvolio's delight in discovering the love letter. Malvolio promises to obey the letter: to smile, to put on yellow stockings cross-gartered, and to be haughty to Sir Toby. Delighted with their success, Maria and the others prepare to enjoy Malvolio's downfall.

---

1. **Come thy ways:** i.e., **come** along

2. **scruple:** i.e., tiny amount

5. **sheep-biter:** i.e., dog (Thomas Nashe, in his *Unfortunate Traveller*, 1594, uses the term to describe a hypocritical puritan.)

7. **bearbalting:** See note to 1.3.93 and picture, page 98.

A cankerworm. (2.4.123)
From John Johnstone, *Opera aliquot . . .* (1650–62).

VIOLA
  A blank, my lord. She never told her love,
  But let concealment, like a worm i' th' bud,
  Feed on her damask cheek. She pined in thought,
  And with a green and yellow melancholy   125
  She sat like Patience on a monument,
  Smiling at grief. Was not this love indeed?
  We men may say more, swear more, but indeed
  Our shows are more than will; for still we prove
  Much in our vows but little in our love.   130

ORSINO
  But died thy sister of her love, my boy?

VIOLA
  I am all the daughters of my father's house,
  And all the brothers, too—and yet I know not.
  Sir, shall I to this lady?

ORSINO   Ay, that's the theme.   135
  To her in haste. Give her this jewel. Say
  My love can give no place, bide no denay.
             ⌜*He hands her a jewel and*⌝ *they exit.*

Scene 5
Enter Sir Toby, Sir Andrew, and Fabian.

TOBY   Come thy ways, Signior Fabian.

FABIAN   Nay, I'll come. If I lose a scruple of this sport,
    let me be boiled to death with melancholy.

TOBY   Wouldst thou not be glad to have the niggardly
    rascally sheep-biter come by some notable shame?   5

FABIAN   I would exult, man. You know he brought me
    out o' favor with my lady about a bearbaiting here.

TOBY   To anger him, we'll have the bear again, and we
    will fool him black and blue, shall we not, Sir
    Andrew?   10

ANDREW   An we do not, it is pity of our lives.

12. **villain:** here, a term of affection

13. **metal of India:** i.e., golden one (an allusion to the Americas, source of gold in Shakespeare's day)

14. **boxtree:** boxwood shrubbery

16. **behavior:** elegant deportment

19. **Close:** i.e., stay hidden

21. **trout . . . tickling: Trout** can be lured from hiding places by stroking the gills. Here, Malvolio will be "stroked" with flattery.

23. **she did affect me:** i.e., Olivia loved me

24. **come . . . near:** i.e., say something close to this; **fancy:** fall in love

25. **complexion:** nature, appearance

26. **follows:** serves

29. **Contemplation:** thinking continuously (of himself)

30–31. **jets . . . plumes:** struts (like a **turkey-cock**) with his feathers spread

32. **'Slight:** By God's light (a strong oath)

36. **Pistol:** i.e., shoot

38. **example:** precedent

38–39. **The lady . . . wardrobe:** probably a topical allusion, now lost   **yeoman:** servant, officer

40. **Jezebel:** a proud queen in the Bible

41. **deeply in:** i.e., mired in his fantasy

42. **blows:** swells

Enter Maria.

TOBY Here comes the little villain.—How now, my
metal of India?

MARIA Get you all three into the boxtree. Malvolio's
coming down this walk. He has been yonder i' the   15
sun practicing behavior to his own shadow this half
hour. Observe him, for the love of mockery, for I
know this letter will make a contemplative idiot of
him. Close, in the name of jesting! ⌜*They hide.*⌝ Lie
thou there ⌜*putting down the letter,*⌝ for here comes   20
the trout that must be caught with tickling.

                                        She exits.

Enter Malvolio.

MALVOLIO 'Tis but fortune, all is fortune. Maria once
told me she did affect me, and I have heard herself
come thus near, that should she fancy, it should be
one of my complexion. Besides, she uses me with a   25
more exalted respect than anyone else that follows
her. What should I think on 't?

TOBY, ⌜*aside*⌝ Here's an overweening rogue.

FABIAN, ⌜*aside*⌝ O, peace! Contemplation makes a rare
turkeycock of him. How he jets under his advanced   30
plumes!

ANDREW, ⌜*aside*⌝ 'Slight, I could so beat the rogue!

TOBY, ⌜*aside*⌝ Peace, I say.

MALVOLIO To be Count Malvolio.

TOBY, ⌜*aside*⌝ Ah, rogue!   35

ANDREW, ⌜*aside*⌝ Pistol him, pistol him!

TOBY, ⌜*aside*⌝ Peace, peace!

MALVOLIO There is example for 't. The lady of the
Strachy married the yeoman of the wardrobe.

ANDREW, ⌜*aside*⌝ Fie on him, Jezebel!   40

FABIAN, ⌜*aside*⌝ O, peace, now he's deeply in. Look how
imagination blows him.

44. **state:** i.e., chair of **state** (as Count Malvolio)

45. **stone-bow:** a crossbow that propels stones (See picture below.)

47. **branched:** perhaps, embroidered with figures

51. **have . . . state:** assume a haughty manner fitting my position

52. **a demure . . . regard:** perhaps, soberly surveying my officers

54. **Toby:** Malvolio drops Sir Toby's title.

57. **start:** sudden movement

62–63. **drawn . . . cars:** i.e., forced from us through torture   **cars:** chariots

65–66. **regard of control:** look of mastery

67. **take . . . o':** i.e., give **you** a **blow** on

75–76. **break . . . plot:** i.e., cripple, destroy, our scheme

A stone-bow. (2.5.45)
From Jan van der Straet, *Venationes ferarum, auium . . .* (ca. 1630?).

MALVOLIO Having been three months married to her, sitting in my state—

TOBY, ⌜*aside*⌝ O, for a stone-bow, to hit him in the eye!   45

MALVOLIO Calling my officers about me, in my branched velvet gown, having come from a daybed where I have left Olivia sleeping—

TOBY, ⌜*aside*⌝ Fire and brimstone!

FABIAN, ⌜*aside*⌝ O, peace, peace!   50

MALVOLIO And then to have the humor of state; and after a demure travel of regard, telling them I know my place, as I would they should do theirs, to ask for my kinsman Toby—

TOBY, ⌜*aside*⌝ Bolts and shackles!   55

FABIAN, ⌜*aside*⌝ O, peace, peace, peace! Now, now.

MALVOLIO Seven of my people, with an obedient start, make out for him. I frown the while, and perchance wind up my watch, or play with my—some rich jewel. Toby approaches; curtsies there to me—   60

TOBY, ⌜*aside*⌝ Shall this fellow live?

FABIAN, ⌜*aside*⌝ Though our silence be drawn from us with cars, yet peace.

MALVOLIO I extend my hand to him thus, quenching my familiar smile with an austere regard of control—   65

TOBY, ⌜*aside*⌝ And does not Toby take you a blow o' the lips then?

MALVOLIO Saying "Cousin Toby, my fortunes, having cast me on your niece, give me this prerogative of speech—"   70

TOBY, ⌜*aside*⌝ What, what?

MALVOLIO "You must amend your drunkenness."

TOBY, ⌜*aside*⌝ Out, scab!

FABIAN, ⌜*aside*⌝ Nay, patience, or we break the sinews of our plot.   75

MALVOLIO "Besides, you waste the treasure of your time with a foolish knight—"

83. **employment:** i.e., business

85. **woodcock:** a proverbially stupid bird; **gin:** trap (See picture, page 150.)

86. **spirit of humors:** i.e., that which controls moods

86–87. **intimate . . . him:** i.e., suggest to him that he read aloud

89. **hand:** handwriting

89–90. **her very *c*'s, her *u*'s, and her *t*'s . . . great *P*'s:** See longer note, page 192.

90. **great:** capital

90–91. **in contempt of question:** i.e., without a doubt

94. **By your leave:** i.e., with your permission (Malvolio's apology to the wax seal before he breaks it)

95. **impressure:** image stamped on the wax; **Lucrece:** i.e., a picture of the chaste Lucretia, whose story Shakespeare had told in his poem *Lucrece* (See picture, page 170.)

96. **uses to seal:** is accustomed to sealing

98. **liver:** seat of the passions

103. **numbers:** meter

106. **brock:** a term of contempt (literally, badger)

108. **Lucrece knife:** Lucretia stabbed herself after being raped by Tarquin. (See note on line 95, above.)

110. **sway:** rule

111. **fustian:** pretentious, pompous

112. **Excellent wench:** i.e., Maria

ANDREW, ⌜*aside*⌝ That's me, I warrant you.

MALVOLIO "One Sir Andrew."   80

ANDREW, ⌜*aside*⌝ I knew 'twas I, for many do call me fool.

MALVOLIO, ⌜*seeing the letter*⌝ What employment have we here?

FABIAN, ⌜*aside*⌝ Now is the woodcock near the gin.   85

TOBY, ⌜*aside*⌝ O, peace, and the spirit of humors intimate reading aloud to him.

MALVOLIO, ⌜*taking up the letter*⌝ By my life, this is my lady's hand! These be her very *c*'s, her *u*'s, and her *t*'s, and thus makes she her great *P*'s. It is in   90 contempt of question her hand.

ANDREW, ⌜*aside*⌝ Her *c*'s, her *u*'s, and her *t*'s. Why that?

MALVOLIO ⌜*reads*⌝ *To the unknown beloved, this, and my good wishes*—Her very phrases! By your leave, wax. Soft. And the impressure her Lucrece, with which   95 she uses to seal—'tis my lady! ⌜*He opens the letter.*⌝ To whom should this be?

FABIAN, ⌜*aside*⌝ This wins him, liver and all.

MALVOLIO ⌜*reads*⌝

> *Jove knows I love,*
>   *But who?*   100
> *Lips, do not move;*
>   *No man must know.*

"No man must know." What follows? The numbers altered. "No man must know." If this should be thee, Malvolio!   105

TOBY, ⌜*aside*⌝ Marry, hang thee, brock!

MALVOLIO ⌜*reads*⌝

> *I may command where I adore,*
>   *But silence, like a Lucrece knife,*
> *With bloodless stroke my heart doth gore;*
>   *M.O.A.I. doth sway my life.*   110

FABIAN, ⌜*aside*⌝ A fustian riddle!

TOBY, ⌜*aside*⌝ Excellent wench, say I.

115. **What dish:** i.e., **what** a **dish; dressed:** prepared for

117. **staniel:** an inferior kind of hawk

117–18. **checks at it:** turns to fly after it

121. **formal capacity:** i.e., sane mind

122. **obstruction:** difficulty

125. **make up:** i.e., **make** sense out of

125–26. **He . . . scent:** i.e., he's like a hound who has lost the trail of his quarry (Language describing Malvolio as a dog following a scent continues in lines 127–28, where **Sowter** seems to be the dog's name and **cry upon 't** means "bark loudly," and in line 132, where **faults** is a technical term for lost scents. See picture, page 114.)

128. **rank:** strong smelling

133–34. **no consonancy . . . sequel:** i.e., no harmony in the letters that follow (See longer note to 2.3.91–92, page 192.)

134. **suffers under probation:** i.e., stands up to testing

136. **O:** perhaps a reference to the hangman's noose

141. **detraction:** loss of reputation

143–44. **This simulation . . . former:** i.e., this part of the letter does not resemble me as clearly as does the first part ("I may command where I adore.")

147. **revolve:** consider

148. **stars:** i.e., destiny

MALVOLIO   "M.O.A.I. doth sway my life." Nay, but first
let me see, let me see, let me see.

FABIAN, ⌈*aside*⌉   What dish o' poison has she dressed   115
him!

TOBY, ⌈*aside*⌉   And with what wing the ⌈staniel⌉ checks
at it!

MALVOLIO   "I may command where I adore." Why, she
may command me; I serve her; she is my lady. Why,   120
this is evident to any formal capacity. There is
no obstruction in this. And the end—what should that
alphabetical position portend? If I could make that
resemble something in me! Softly! "M.O.A.I."—

TOBY, ⌈*aside*⌉   O, ay, make up that.—He is now at a cold   125
scent.

FABIAN, ⌈*aside*⌉   Sowter will cry upon 't for all this,
though it be as rank as a fox.

MALVOLIO   "M"—Malvolio. "M"—why, that begins
my name!   130

FABIAN, ⌈*aside*⌉   Did not I say he would work it out? The
cur is excellent at faults.

MALVOLIO   "M." But then there is no consonancy in
the sequel that suffers under probation. "A" should
follow, but "O" does.   135

FABIAN, ⌈*aside*⌉   And "O" shall end, I hope.

TOBY, ⌈*aside*⌉   Ay, or I'll cudgel him and make him cry
"O."

MALVOLIO   And then "I" comes behind.

FABIAN, ⌈*aside*⌉   Ay, an you had any eye behind you, you   140
might see more detraction at your heels than fortunes before you.

MALVOLIO   "M.O.A.I." This simulation is not as the
former, and yet to crush this a little, it would bow
to me, for every one of these letters are in my name.   145
Soft, here follows prose.
⌈*He reads.*⌉ *If this fall into thy hand, revolve. In my
stars I am above thee, but be not afraid of greatness.*

150–51. **open their hands:** i.e., have become generous

152. **inure:** accustom; **like:** likely

152–53. **cast . . . slough:** discard your humble attitude (as a snake discards its old skin)

153. **opposite:** confrontational

154–55. **tang . . . state:** ring out with political opinions

155–56. **Put . . . singularity:** i.e., adopt conspicuous idiosyncrasies

158. **cross-gartered:** wearing garters around the knees (See pictures, pages 86 and 112.)

159. **Go to:** an expression of protest (like "Come, come"); **thou art:** i.e., your fortunes are

160. **still:** always

162. **alter services:** i.e., change positions

164. **champian:** open country; **discovers:** reveals

165. **open:** perfectly clear; **politic:** (1) political; (2) wise

166. **baffle:** publicly humiliate; **gross:** base

167. **point-devise . . . man:** i.e., precisely **the man** described in the letter

168. **jade:** dupe, delude

173. **these . . . liking:** i.e., wear the kind of clothes and/or show the behavior that she likes

174. **strange:** extraordinary, exceptional; or distant, aloof; **stout:** proud, arrogant

179. **thou entertain'st:** you accept

Some are ⌜born⌝ great, some ⌜achieve⌝ greatness, and
some have greatness thrust upon 'em. Thy fates open 150
their hands. Let thy blood and spirit embrace them.
And, to inure thyself to what thou art like to be, cast
thy humble slough and appear fresh. Be opposite with
a kinsman, surly with servants. Let thy tongue tang
arguments of state. Put thyself into the trick of singu- 155
larity. She thus advises thee that sighs for thee.
Remember who commended thy yellow stockings and
wished to see thee ever cross-gartered. I say, remem-
ber. Go to, thou art made, if thou desir'st to be so. If
not, let me see thee a steward still, the fellow of 160
servants, and not worthy to touch Fortune's fingers.
Farewell. She that would alter services with thee.
　　　　　　　　　　　　　　The Fortunate-Unhappy.
Daylight and champian discovers not more! This is
open. I will be proud, I will read politic authors, I 165
will baffle Sir Toby, I will wash off gross acquaintance, I will be point-devise the very man. I do not
now fool myself, to let imagination jade me; for
every reason excites to this, that my lady loves me.
She did commend my yellow stockings of late, she 170
did praise my leg being cross-gartered, and in this
she manifests herself to my love and, with a kind of
injunction, drives me to these habits of her liking. I
thank my stars, I am happy. I will be strange, stout,
in yellow stockings, and cross-gartered, even with 175
the swiftness of putting on. Jove and my stars be
praised! Here is yet a postscript.
⌜*He reads.*⌝ *Thou canst not choose but know who I*
am. If thou entertain'st my love, let it appear in thy
smiling; thy smiles become thee well. Therefore in my 180
presence still smile, dear my sweet, I prithee.
Jove, I thank thee! I will smile. I will do everything
that thou wilt have me. 　　　　　　　　*He exits.*

185. **Sophy:** Shah of Persia

191. **gull-catcher:** A gull is a person easily cheated.

194. **play:** bet; **tray-trip:** a gambling game

200. **aqua vitae:** strong drink, usually brandy

208. **notable contempt:** i.e., well-known object of **contempt**

210. **Tartar:** i.e., Tartarus, hell

212. **make one, too:** i.e., join you

Legs cross-gartered. (2.5.158, 204; 3.2.72, 3.4.22–23)
From Abraham de Bruyn, *Omnium pene Europae,
Asiae . . . gentium habitus . . .* (1581).

FABIAN   I will not give my part of this sport for a
pension of thousands to be paid from the Sophy.   185
TOBY   I could marry this wench for this device.
ANDREW   So could I, too.
TOBY   And ask no other dowry with her but such
another jest.
ANDREW   Nor I neither.   190

Enter Maria.

FABIAN   Here comes my noble gull-catcher.
TOBY   Wilt thou set thy foot o' my neck?
ANDREW   Or o' mine either?
TOBY   Shall I play my freedom at tray-trip and become
thy bondslave?   195
ANDREW   I' faith, or I either?
TOBY   Why, thou hast put him in such a dream that
when the image of it leaves him he must run mad.
MARIA   Nay, but say true, does it work upon him?
TOBY   Like aqua vitae with a midwife.   200
MARIA   If you will then see the fruits of the sport,
mark his first approach before my lady. He will
come to her in yellow stockings, and 'tis a color
she abhors, and cross-gartered, a fashion she de-
tests; and he will smile upon her, which will now   205
be so unsuitable to her disposition, being ad-
dicted to a melancholy as she is, that it cannot
but turn him into a notable contempt. If you will
see it, follow me.
TOBY   To the gates of Tartar, thou most excellent dev- 210
il of wit!
ANDREW   I'll make one, too.

They exit.

TWELFTH NIGHT,
OR,
WHAT
YOU WILL

ACT 3

3.1 Viola (as Cesario), on her way to see Olivia, encounters first the Fool and then Sir Toby and Sir Andrew. Olivia, meeting Cesario, sends the others away and declares her love.

———————

0 SD. **tabor:** small drum (See picture, page 96.)

1. **Save thee:** i.e., God **save thee** (a friendly greeting)

1–2. **Dost thou live by:** i.e., do you make your living by playing

4. **churchman:** clergyman

5. **No such matter:** i.e., not at all

11. **You have said:** i.e., you're right; **this age:** i.e., the **age** in which we live

12. **chev'ril:** kid leather, which stretches easily

14. **dally nicely:** play with precise meanings (**Dally** also means "flirt, play with amorously.")

15. **wanton:** changeable, ambiguous (also "immoral, unchaste")

21. **bonds:** i.e., the legal requirement that one's pledge (**word**) be backed by a written contract, or bond

ACT 3

Scene 1
Enter Viola and ⌜Feste, the Fool, playing a tabor.⌝

VIOLA   Save thee, friend, and thy music. Dost thou live
   by thy tabor?

FOOL   No, sir, I live by the church.

VIOLA   Art thou a churchman?

FOOL   No such matter, sir. I do live by the church, for I   5
   do live at my house, and my house doth stand by the
   church.

VIOLA   So thou mayst say the ⌜king⌝ lies by a beggar if a
   beggar dwell near him, or the church stands by thy
   tabor if thy tabor stand by the church.   10

FOOL   You have said, sir. To see this age! A sentence is
   but a chev'ril glove to a good wit. How quickly the
   wrong side may be turned outward!

VIOLA   Nay, that's certain. They that dally nicely with
   words may quickly make them wanton.   15

FOOL   I would therefore my sister had had no name,
   sir.

VIOLA   Why, man?

FOOL   Why, sir, her name's a word, and to dally with
   that word might make my sister wanton. But,   20
   indeed, words are very rascals since bonds disgraced them.

VIOLA   Thy reason, man?

91

27. **I warrant:** i.e., I'm sure.

36. **pilchers:** pilchards, small fish related to the herring

39. **late:** lately, recently

40. **walk . . . orb:** move around the earth

41–42. **but . . . be:** i.e., unless **the Fool** were

43. **your Wisdom:** an ironic title (analogous to "your Honor")

44. **an thou . . . me:** i.e., if you attack me; **I'll no more:** i.e., **I'll** have **no more** to do

46. **in . . . commodity:** i.e., out of his next supply

51. **Would . . . bred:** The Fool, begging for money, suggests that money can breed, i.e., reproduce. Viola continues the wordplay in her response, where **put to use** means "invested to earn interest," but also has a sexual meaning.

53–54. **Lord . . . Troilus:** The allusion is to the story of **Troilus** and **Cressida,** lovers who were brought together by **Pandarus.** The story was told by Chaucer, and by Shakespeare in his *Troilus and Cressida.* **Phrygia:** the country where Troy was said to be located, Troilus being a prince of Troy

57. **Cressida . . . beggar:** In some versions of the story, **Cressida** becomes **a beggar** before her death.

FOOL   Troth, sir, I can yield you none without words,
and words are grown so false I am loath to prove   25
reason with them.

VIOLA   I warrant thou art a merry fellow and car'st for
nothing.

FOOL   Not so, sir. I do care for something. But in my
conscience, sir, I do not care for you. If that be to   30
care for nothing, sir, I would it would make you
invisible.

VIOLA   Art not thou the Lady Olivia's Fool?

FOOL   No, indeed, sir. The Lady Olivia has no folly. She
will keep no Fool, sir, till she be married, and Fools   35
are as like husbands as pilchers are to herrings: the
husband's the bigger. I am indeed not her Fool but
her corrupter of words.

VIOLA   I saw thee late at the Count Orsino's.

FOOL   Foolery, sir, does walk about the orb like the   40
sun; it shines everywhere. I would be sorry, sir, but
the Fool should be as oft with your master as with
my mistress. I think I saw your Wisdom there.

VIOLA   Nay, an thou pass upon me, I'll no more with
thee. Hold, there's expenses for thee. ⌜*Giving a*   45
coin.⌝

FOOL   Now Jove, in his next commodity of hair, send
thee a beard!

VIOLA   By my troth I'll tell thee, I am almost sick for
one, ⌜*aside*⌝ though I would not have it grow on my
chin.—Is thy lady within?   50

FOOL   Would not a pair of these have bred, sir?

VIOLA   Yes, being kept together and put to use.

FOOL   I would play Lord Pandarus of Phrygia, sir, to
bring a Cressida to this Troilus.

VIOLA   I understand you, sir. 'Tis well begged. ⌜*Giving*   55
another coin.⌝

FOOL   The matter I hope is not great, sir, begging but a
beggar: Cressida was a beggar. My lady is within, sir.

58. **conster to them:** i.e., construe (explain) to those in the house

59. **out . . . welkin:** i.e., beyond my comprehension, **out of my** element (The wordplay here is on **welkin** as "sky," which, as "air," is an **element.**)

64. **quality:** rank; nature

65. **haggard:** wild hawk; **check at:** turn to follow; **feather:** i.e., bird

66. **practice:** profession

67. **art:** learning, skill

68. **fit:** i.e., fitting, appropriate

69. **wit:** intelligence (or reputation for it)

72. **Dieu . . . monsieur:** God save you, sir.

73. **Et . . . serviteur!:** And you as well. Your servant!

75. **encounter:** i.e., approach (Toby uses affected language, and Viola answers him in kind.)

78. **list:** limit, boundary

80. **understand:** i.e., stand under, hold me up

84. **with . . . entrance:** i.e., by going and entering

85. **we are prevented:** i.e., Olivia's appearance anticipates our entrance

I will conster to them whence you come. Who you
are and what you would are out of my welkin—I
might say "element," but the word is overworn.   60

He exits.

VIOLA
This fellow is wise enough to play the Fool,
And to do that well craves a kind of wit.
He must observe their mood on whom he jests,
The quality of persons, and the time,
And, like the haggard, check at every feather   65
That comes before his eye. This is a practice
As full of labor as a wise man's art:
For folly that he wisely shows is fit;
But ⌜wise men,⌝ folly-fall'n, quite taint their wit.

Enter Sir Toby and Andrew.

TOBY   Save you, gentleman.   70
VIOLA   And you, sir.
ANDREW   *Dieu vous garde, monsieur.*
VIOLA   *Et vous aussi. Votre serviteur!*
ANDREW   I hope, sir, you are, and I am yours.
TOBY   Will you encounter the house? My niece is   75
desirous you should enter, if your trade be to her.
VIOLA   I am bound to your niece, sir; I mean, she is the
list of my voyage.
TOBY   Taste your legs, sir; put them to motion.
VIOLA   My legs do better understand me, sir, than I   80
understand what you mean by bidding me taste my
legs.
TOBY   I mean, to go, sir, to enter.
VIOLA   I will answer you with gait and entrance—but
we are prevented.   85

Enter Olivia, and ⌜Maria, her⌝ Gentlewoman.

Most excellent accomplished lady, the heavens rain
odors on you!

90. **My . . . but:** i.e., my message cannot be spoken except

91. **pregnant:** receptive; **vouchsafed:** willing, graciously attentive

97. **service:** respect

101. **lowly feigning:** i.e., pretending to be humble; **was called:** i.e., began to be considered

105. **For:** as for; **on him:** i.e., about him

113. **music . . . spheres:** In Ptolemaic astronomy, the stars move about the earth in crystalline spheres, giving out incredibly beautiful music that humans cannot hear. (See picture, page xxxii.)

115. **Give . . . you:** i.e., permit me to speak, I beg you

Tabor. (3.1.2)
From William Kemp, *Kemps nine daies wonder . . .* (1600; 1884 facs.).

ANDREW, ⌜*aside*⌝ That youth's a rare courtier. "Rain
  odors," well.

VIOLA My matter hath no voice, lady, but to your own   90
  most pregnant and vouchsafed ear.

ANDREW, ⌜*aside*⌝ "Odors," "pregnant," and "vouchsafed." I'll get 'em all three all ready.

OLIVIA Let the garden door be shut, and leave me to
  my hearing. ⌜*Sir Toby, Sir Andrew, and Maria exit.*⌝   95
  Give me your hand, sir.

VIOLA
  My duty, madam, and most humble service.

OLIVIA What is your name?

VIOLA
  Cesario is your servant's name, fair princess.

OLIVIA
  My servant, sir? 'Twas never merry world   100
  Since lowly feigning was called compliment.
  You're servant to the Count Orsino, youth.

VIOLA
  And he is yours, and his must needs be yours.
  Your servant's servant is your servant, madam.

OLIVIA
  For him, I think not on him. For his thoughts,   105
  Would they were blanks rather than filled with me.

VIOLA
  Madam, I come to whet your gentle thoughts
  On his behalf.

OLIVIA   O, by your leave, I pray you.
  I bade you never speak again of him.   110
  But would you undertake another suit,
  I had rather hear you to solicit that
  Than music from the spheres.

VIOLA   Dear lady—

OLIVIA
  Give me leave, beseech you. I did send,   115
  After the last enchantment you did here,

117. **abuse:** deceive; wrong

119–21. **Under . . . yours:** i.e., I must be judged harshly by you, since I used **shameful cunning to force on you** something **you knew** was not **yours**

123–25. **Have . . . think:** The image here is of a bearbaiting. Olivia imagines her honor as a bear tied to the stake, attacked (**baited**) by the **unmuzzled** dogs that are Cesario's **thoughts.** (See picture, below.)

126. **receiving:** perceptiveness

127. **cypress:** thin (almost transparent) cloth veil

130, 131. **degree, grize:** step

131. **a . . . proof:** an ordinary experience

140. **proper:** handsome

142. **westward ho!:** the cry of Thames watermen headed from London to Westminster

144. **You'll nothing . . . ?:** i.e., you have no message . . . ?

A bearbaiting. (1.3.93; 3.1.123–25)
From [William Lily,] *Antibossicon* (1521).

A ring in chase of you. So did I abuse
Myself, my servant, and, I fear me, you.
Under your hard construction must I sit,
To force that on you in a shameful cunning   120
Which you knew none of yours. What might you
   think?
Have you not set mine honor at the stake
And baited it with all th' unmuzzled thoughts
That tyrannous heart can think? To one of your   125
   receiving
Enough is shown. A cypress, not a bosom,
Hides my heart. So, let me hear you speak.

VIOLA
I pity you.

OLIVIA   That's a degree to love.   130

VIOLA
No, not a grize, for 'tis a vulgar proof
That very oft we pity enemies.

OLIVIA
Why then methinks 'tis time to smile again.
O world, how apt the poor are to be proud!
If one should be a prey, how much the better   135
To fall before the lion than the wolf.   *Clock strikes.*
The clock upbraids me with the waste of time.
Be not afraid, good youth, I will not have you.
And yet when wit and youth is come to harvest,
Your wife is like to reap a proper man.   140
There lies your way, due west.

VIOLA   Then westward ho!
Grace and good disposition attend your Ladyship.
You'll nothing, madam, to my lord by me?

OLIVIA
Stay. I prithee, tell me what thou think'st of me.   145

VIOLA
That you do think you are not what you are.

148. **think you right:** i.e., **you think** correctly

152. **deal:** quantity

155–56. **Love's . . . noon:** i.e., love cannot be hidden

159. **maugre . . . pride:** i.e., despite your scorn

160. **Nor . . . nor:** neither . . . nor

161. **extort thy reasons:** i.e., force out excuses; **clause:** premise

162. **For . . . cause:** i.e., because I am the wooer, you have **no cause** (to woo me)

163. **reason . . . fetter:** i.e., restrain such rationalizing by considering the following sentence

166. **bosom:** desire

167. **nor never none:** nor anyone ever

168. **save:** except

Cupid with his bow. (1.1.37)
From Johannes ab Indagine, *The booke of palmestry* (1666).

OLIVIA
  If I think so, I think the same of you.

VIOLA
  Then think you right. I am not what I am.

OLIVIA
  I would you were as I would have you be.

VIOLA
  Would it be better, madam, than I am?   150
  I wish it might, for now I am your fool.

OLIVIA, ⌐aside¬
  O, what a deal of scorn looks beautiful
  In the contempt and anger of his lip!
  A murd'rous guilt shows not itself more soon
  Than love that would seem hid. Love's night is   155
      noon.—
  Cesario, by the roses of the spring,
  By maidhood, honor, truth, and everything,
  I love thee so, that, maugre all thy pride,
  Nor wit nor reason can my passion hide.   160
  Do not extort thy reasons from this clause,
  For that I woo, thou therefore hast no cause;
  But rather reason thus with reason fetter:
  Love sought is good, but given unsought is better.

VIOLA
  By innocence I swear, and by my youth,   165
  I have one heart, one bosom, and one truth,
  And that no woman has, nor never none
  Shall mistress be of it, save I alone.
  And so adieu, good madam. Nevermore
  Will I my master's tears to you deplore.   170

OLIVIA
  Yet come again, for thou perhaps mayst move
  That heart, which now abhors, to like his love.
          They exit ⌐*in different directions.*¬

3.2 Sir Andrew, convinced that Olivia will never love him, threatens to leave. Sir Toby persuades him that he can win her love if he challenges Cesario to a duel. Sir Andrew goes off to prepare a letter for Cesario. Maria enters to say that Malvolio has followed every point in the letter and is about to incur disaster when he appears before Olivia.

———

3. **must needs yield:** i.e., must give

4. **do more favors:** show **more** good will

6. **orchard:** garden

10. **argument:** token, evidence

13. **prove it legitimate:** i.e., make good my case; **oaths of:** i.e., testimony sworn under oath by

15. **they:** i.e., **judgment and reason; grand-jurymen:** those who decide whether there is sufficient evidence to bring a case to trial

16. **Noah:** survivor in his ark of the flood in Genesis (See picture, page 146.)

18. **dormouse:** i.e., sleeping (The **dormouse** becomes torpid in cold weather. See picture, page 172.)

23. **at your hand:** i.e., from you

24. **balked:** passed up, neglected; **gilt:** gold plating (Fabian plays with the idea of a missed "golden **opportunity**.")

25–26. **sailed . . . opinion:** i.e., earned **my lady's** cold regard

29. **policy:** statesmanlike wisdom (Andrew, in his response, gives the word its meaning of "political cunning.")

(continued)

Scene 2
Enter Sir Toby, Sir Andrew, and Fabian.

ANDREW No, faith, I'll not stay a jot longer.

TOBY Thy reason, dear venom, give thy reason.

FABIAN You must needs yield your reason, Sir Andrew.

ANDREW Marry, I saw your niece do more favors to the
Count's servingman than ever she bestowed upon 5
me. I saw 't i' th' orchard.

TOBY Did she see ⌐thee⌐ the while, old boy? Tell me
that.

ANDREW As plain as I see you now.

FABIAN This was a great argument of love in her toward 10
you.

ANDREW 'Slight, will you make an ass o' me?

FABIAN I will prove it legitimate, sir, upon the oaths of
judgment and reason.

TOBY And they have been grand-jurymen since before 15
Noah was a sailor.

FABIAN She did show favor to the youth in your sight
only to exasperate you, to awake your dormouse
valor, to put fire in your heart and brimstone in
your liver. You should then have accosted her, and 20
with some excellent jests, fire-new from the mint,
you should have banged the youth into dumbness.
This was looked for at your hand, and this was
balked. The double gilt of this opportunity you let
time wash off, and you are now sailed into the north 25
of my lady's opinion, where you will hang like an
icicle on a Dutchman's beard, unless you do redeem it by some laudable attempt either of valor or
policy.

ANDREW An 't be any way, it must be with valor, for 30
policy I hate. I had as lief be a Brownist as a
politician.

TOBY Why, then, build me thy fortunes upon the basis

31. **as lief:** i.e., just as soon; **Brownist:** a believer in the then-revolutionary ideas about religion preached by Robert Browne (c. 1550–1633)

33. **build me:** i.e., **build** (ethical dative)

34. **Challenge me:** i.e., **challenge** (another ethical dative)

37. **love-broker:** go-between

41. **curst:** fierce, savage

42. **so it be:** i.e., as long as it is

43. **invention:** arguments; inventiveness

43–44. **with . . . ink:** i.e., with the freedom given to one who puts his challenge in writing

44. **"thou"-est . . . thrice:** i.e., address him three times as "thou" instead of "you" (The use of the familiar "thou" to a stranger would be an insult.)

45. **lies:** perhaps accusations of lying, so as to provoke a fight

47. **bed of Ware:** a famous eleven-foot-wide bed (now in a museum in London)

48. **gall:** (1) oak galls, used in making ink; (2) bitterness

49. **goose-pen:** (1) a pen made with a goose quill; (2) a pen used by a goose (i.e., a fool)

51. **call:** call on; **cubiculo:** bedchamber

52. **dear manikin:** i.e., affectionate little man (**Manikin** is a term of contempt.)

53. **dear:** expensive, costly

58. **wainropes:** i.e., wagon ropes

59. **hale:** haul, pull, drag

60. **blood . . . liver:** Cowards were supposed to have white or bloodless livers.

62. **anatomy:** i.e., the body being dissected

(continued)

of valor. Challenge me the Count's youth to fight
with him. Hurt him in eleven places. My niece shall   35
take note of it, and assure thyself there is no
love-broker in the world can more prevail in man's
commendation with woman than report of valor.

FABIAN   There is no way but this, Sir Andrew.

ANDREW   Will either of you bear me a challenge to him?   40

TOBY   Go, write it in a martial hand. Be curst and
brief. It is no matter how witty, so it be eloquent
and full of invention. Taunt him with the license of
ink. If thou "thou"-est him some thrice, it shall not
be amiss, and as many lies as will lie in thy sheet of   45
paper, although the sheet were big enough for the
bed of Ware in England, set 'em down. Go, about it.
Let there be gall enough in thy ink, though thou
write with a goose-pen, no matter. About it.

ANDREW   Where shall I find you?   50

TOBY   We'll call thee at the cubiculo. Go.

Sir Andrew exits.

FABIAN   This is a dear manikin to you, Sir Toby.

TOBY   I have been dear to him, lad, some two thousand
strong or so.

FABIAN   We shall have a rare letter from him. But you'll   55
not deliver 't?

TOBY   Never trust me, then. And by all means stir on
the youth to an answer. I think oxen and wainropes
cannot hale them together. For Andrew, if he were
opened and you find so much blood in his liver as   60
will clog the foot of a flea, I'll eat the rest of th'
anatomy.

FABIAN   And his opposite, the youth, bears in his visage
no great presage of cruelty.

Enter Maria.

TOBY   Look where the youngest wren of mine comes.   65

MARIA   If you desire the spleen, and will laugh your-

63. **opposite:** opponent

65. **wren:** another reference to Maria's short stature

66. **desire the spleen:** i.e., want to laugh

67. **gull:** dupe

68. **a very renegado:** i.e., no longer a Christian

69. **means:** intends

70. **passages:** acts

73. **villainously:** atrociously; **pedant:** i.e., teacher

77. **new map:** an allusion to a map published in 1599, filled with prominent lines (See page xxxiv.)

78. **augmentation . . . Indies:** i.e., more complete mappings of the East **Indies**

3.3 Antonio, having followed Sebastian, explains the incident in his past that keeps him from safely venturing into the streets of Orsino's city. Giving his money to Sebastian, Antonio sets off to their inn while Sebastian goes off to see the sights.

———————

1. **by my will:** i.e., willingly

3. **chide:** blame

5. **filèd:** ground to a sharp edge with a file

6. **not all love:** i.e., not only a desire

8. **jealousy:** fear of

9. **skill-less in:** i.e., without knowledge of

12. **The . . . fear:** i.e., spurred by these anxieties

13. **your pursuit: pursuit** of you

selves into stitches, follow me. Yond gull Malvolio is
turned heathen, a very renegado; for there is no
Christian that means to be saved by believing rightly
can ever believe such impossible passages of gross-   70
ness. He's in yellow stockings.

TOBY   And cross-gartered?

MARIA   Most villainously, like a pedant that keeps a
school i' th' church. I have dogged him like his
murderer. He does obey every point of the letter   75
that I dropped to betray him. He does smile his face
into more lines than is in the new map with the
augmentation of the Indies. You have not seen such
a thing as 'tis. I can hardly forbear hurling things at
him. I know my lady will strike him. If she do, he'll   80
smile and take 't for a great favor.

TOBY   Come, bring us, bring us where he is.

They all exit.

Scene 3
Enter Sebastian and Antonio.

SEBASTIAN
I would not by my will have troubled you,
But, since you make your pleasure of your pains,
I will no further chide you.

ANTONIO
I could not stay behind you. My desire,
More sharp than filèd steel, did spur me forth;   5
And not all love to see you, though so much
As might have drawn one to a longer voyage,
But jealousy what might befall your travel,
Being skill-less in these parts, which to a stranger,
Unguided and unfriended, often prove   10
Rough and unhospitable. My willing love,
The rather by these arguments of fear,
Set forth in your pursuit.

16–17. oft . . . pay: i.e., **good** acts are often rewarded with mere words   **uncurrent:** not negotiable, worthless

18. worth: possessions, wealth; **conscience:** i.e., recognition of obligation (to you)

20. relics: i.e., antiquities, old buildings, etc.

22. to: until

25. renown this city: i.e., make **this city** famous

26. Would . . . me: i.e., please excuse me

28. Count his: Count's

29. of such note: i.e., so memorable

30. ta'en: captured; **it . . . answered:** i.e., I would hardly be able (1) to defend myself before the law, or (2) to endure the penalty exacted from me

31. Belike: perhaps

34. bloody argument: a reason worth shedding blood for

35. answered: recompensed

36. for traffic's sake: i.e., for the sake of trade

37. stood out: i.e., refused

38. be lapsèd: i.e., am caught

39. dear: dearly, at great cost

40. open: i.e., much in public view

41. It . . . me: it is not fitting for me

43. bespeak: arrange for; **diet:** meals

SEBASTIAN　　　　　　　　My kind Antonio,
　I can no other answer make but thanks,　　　　　　15
　And thanks, and ever ⌈thanks; and⌉ oft good turns
　Are shuffled off with such uncurrent pay.
　But were my worth, as is my conscience, firm,
　You should find better dealing. What's to do?
　Shall we go see the relics of this town?　　　　　　20
ANTONIO
　Tomorrow, sir. Best first go see your lodging.
SEBASTIAN
　I am not weary, and 'tis long to night.
　I pray you, let us satisfy our eyes
　With the memorials and the things of fame
　That do renown this city.　　　　　　　　　　25
ANTONIO　Would you'd pardon me.
　I do not without danger walk these streets.
　Once in a sea fight 'gainst the Count his galleys
　I did some service, of such note indeed
　That were I ta'en here it would scarce be answered.　30
SEBASTIAN
　Belike you slew great number of his people?
ANTONIO
　Th' offense is not of such a bloody nature,
　Albeit the quality of the time and quarrel
　Might well have given us bloody argument.
　It might have since been answered in repaying　　35
　What we took from them, which, for traffic's sake,
　Most of our city did. Only myself stood out,
　For which, if I be lapsèd in this place,
　I shall pay dear.
SEBASTIAN　　　　　Do not then walk too open.　　40
ANTONIO
　It doth not fit me. Hold, sir, here's my purse.
　　　　　　　　　　⌈*Giving him money.*⌉
　In the south suburbs, at the Elephant,
　Is best to lodge. I will bespeak our diet

44. **beguile:** while away

46. **There . . . me:** i.e., **you** will find **me there** (at the Elephant)

48. **Haply:** perhaps; **toy:** trifle

49. **store:** supply of money

50. **is . . . markets:** i.e., will not cover whimsical purchases

3.4 Malvolio, dressed ridiculously and smiling grotesquely, appears before an astonished Olivia. Thinking him insane, she puts him in the care of Sir Toby, who decides to treat him as a madman by having him bound and put in a dark room. Toby also decides to deliver Sir Andrew's challenge to Cesario in person in order to force the two of them into a duel. Terrified, they prepare to fight. At that moment, Antonio enters, thinks that Cesario is Sebastian, and comes to his defense. Antonio is immediately arrested by Orsino's officers. Since he is sure that Viola is Sebastian, Antonio is bitter about the apparent denial of their friendship. Viola is herself delighted by Antonio's angry words because, since he called her Sebastian, there is hope that her brother may in fact be alive.

———————

2. **bestow of: bestow** on, give

6. **sad and civil:** serious-minded and polite

10. **possessed:** i.e., by the devil (This was one popular explanation of insanity.)

11. **rave:** speak incoherently

14. **in 's:** in his

16. **equal be:** i.e., are **equal**

Whiles you beguile the time and feed your
  knowledge   45
With viewing of the town. There shall you have me.

SEBASTIAN   Why I your purse?

ANTONIO
Haply your eye shall light upon some toy
You have desire to purchase, and your store,
I think, is not for idle markets, sir.   50

SEBASTIAN
I'll be your purse-bearer and leave you
For an hour.

ANTONIO   To th' Elephant.

SEBASTIAN   I do remember.
They exit ⌜in different directions.⌝

Scene 4
Enter Olivia and Maria.

OLIVIA, ⌜*aside*⌝
I have sent after him. He says he'll come.
How shall I feast him? What bestow of him?
For youth is bought more oft than begged or
  borrowed.
I speak too loud.—   5
Where's Malvolio? He is sad and civil
And suits well for a servant with my fortunes.
Where is Malvolio?

MARIA   He's coming, madam, but in very strange manner. He is sure possessed, madam.   10

OLIVIA   Why, what's the matter? Does he rave?

MARIA   No, madam, he does nothing but smile. Your
Ladyship were best to have some guard about you if
he come, for sure the man is tainted in 's wits.

OLIVIA
Go call him hither. ⌜*Maria exits.*⌝ I am as mad as he,   15
If sad and merry madness equal be.

19. **sad:** serious (Malvolio takes the word to mean "sorrowful.")

23. **one:** i.e., Olivia

24. **sonnet:** song ("Please one, and please all" is the refrain of a ballad about the wishes of women.)

28. **black in my mind:** i.e., melancholy

29. **It:** i.e., the letter of 2.5

30–31. **Roman hand:** Italian-style handwriting

33–34. **Ay . . . thee:** a line from a popular song

38–39. **nightingales answer daws:** i.e., fine birds don't respond to the call of crows

Legs cross-gartered. (2.5.158, 204; 3.2.72, 3.4.22–23)
From Abraham de Bruyn, *Omnium pene Europae, Asiae . . . gentium habitus . . .* (1581).

Enter ⌜Maria with⌝ Malvolio.

How now, Malvolio?

MALVOLIO   Sweet lady, ho, ho!

OLIVIA   Smil'st thou? I sent for thee upon a sad
    occasion.   20

MALVOLIO   Sad, lady? I could be sad. This does make
    some obstruction in the blood, this cross-garter-
    ing, but what of that? If it please the eye of one, it is
    with me as the very true sonnet is: "Please one, and
    please all."   25

⌜OLIVIA⌝   Why, how dost thou, man? What is the matter
    with thee?

MALVOLIO   Not black in my mind, though yellow in my
    legs. It did come to his hands, and commands shall
    be executed. I think we do know the sweet Roman   30
    hand.

OLIVIA   Wilt thou go to bed, Malvolio?

MALVOLIO   To bed? "Ay, sweetheart, and I'll come to
    thee."

OLIVIA   God comfort thee! Why dost thou smile so, and   35
    kiss thy hand so oft?

MARIA   How do you, Malvolio?

MALVOLIO   At your request? Yes, nightingales answer
    daws!

MARIA   Why appear you with this ridiculous boldness   40
    before my lady?

MALVOLIO   "Be not afraid of greatness." 'Twas well
    writ.

OLIVIA   What mean'st thou by that, Malvolio?

MALVOLIO   "Some are born great—"   45

OLIVIA   Ha?

MALVOLIO   "Some achieve greatness—"

OLIVIA   What sayst thou?

MALVOLIO   "And some have greatness thrust upon
    them."   50

61. **very:** genuine, true; **midsummer madness:** insanity (The midsummer moon was thought to cause madness.)

63. **hardly:** i.e., only with great difficulty

68. **miscarry:** come to harm

78. **consequently:** i.e., subsequently, later

79. **a reverend carriage:** distinguished manners

79–80. **in . . . note:** i.e., dressed like some note-worthy gentleman

80. **limed:** trapped, as with birdlime

81. **it is Jove's doing:** a possible allusion to Psalm 118.23, "This was the Lord's doing." (The names "God" and "Jove" are used almost interchangeably in this play.)

82. **fellow:** used dismissively by Olivia but heard by Malvolio as meaning "companion"

A hound on the scent. (2.5.125–32)
From George Turberville, *The noble arte of venerie . . .* (1611).

OLIVIA   Heaven restore thee!

MALVOLIO   "Remember who commended thy yellow stockings—"

OLIVIA   Thy yellow stockings?

MALVOLIO   "And wished to see thee cross-gartered."   55

OLIVIA   Cross-gartered?

MALVOLIO   "Go to, thou art made, if thou desir'st to be so—"

OLIVIA   Am I made?

MALVOLIO   "If not, let me see thee a servant still."   60

OLIVIA   Why, this is very midsummer madness!

Enter Servant.

SERVANT   Madam, the young gentleman of the Count Orsino's is returned. I could hardly entreat him back. He attends your Ladyship's pleasure.

OLIVIA   I'll come to him. ⌜*Servant exits.*⌝ Good Maria, let   65
this fellow be looked to. Where's my Cousin Toby?
Let some of my people have a special care of him. I
would not have him miscarry for the half of my
dowry.
      ⌜*Olivia and Maria*⌝ *exit* ⌜*in different directions.*⌝

MALVOLIO   O ho, do you come near me now? No worse   70
man than Sir Toby to look to me. This concurs
directly with the letter. She sends him on purpose
that I may appear stubborn to him, for she incites
me to that in the letter: "Cast thy humble slough,"
says she. "Be opposite with a kinsman, surly with   75
servants; let thy tongue ⌜tang⌝ with arguments of
state; put thyself into the trick of singularity," and
consequently sets down the manner how: as, a sad
face, a reverend carriage, a slow tongue, in the habit
of some Sir of note, and so forth. I have limed her,   80
but it is Jove's doing, and Jove make me thankful!
And when she went away now, "Let this fellow be
looked to." "Fellow!" Not "Malvolio," nor after my

84. **degree:** i.e., my rank as her steward

84–85. **adheres together:** i.e., coheres, fits

85. **dram:** tiniest bit (literally, an apothecaries' weight of 60 grains); **scruple:** doubt (also, an apothecaries' weight of 20 grains)

86. **incredulous:** incredible; **unsafe:** unreliable, untrustworthy

92. **drawn in little:** (1) made into a miniature painting; (2) brought together into the small space (of Malvolio's body); **Legion:** In Mark 5.8–9, Jesus asks the name of the "unclean spirit" possessing the demoniac, whose response to Jesus is "My name is Legion: for we are many."

97. **private:** i.e., privacy

98. **hollow:** i.e., tonelessly

107. **an:** if

108. **at heart:** i.e., to **heart**

110. **water:** urine (for medical diagnosis); **wise-woman:** a woman who used charms or herbs to treat diseases

111. **Marry:** a mild oath, meaning "truly" or "indeed"

117. **move:** excite

117–18. **Let . . . him:** i.e., don't interfere

degree, but "fellow." Why, everything adheres together, that no dram of a scruple, no scruple of a   85
scruple, no obstacle, no incredulous or unsafe
circumstance—what can be said? Nothing that can
be can come between me and the full prospect of
my hopes. Well, Jove, not I, is the doer of this, and
he is to be thanked.   90

Enter Toby, Fabian, and Maria.

TOBY Which way is he, in the name of sanctity? If all
the devils of hell be drawn in little, and Legion
himself possessed him, yet I'll speak to him.

FABIAN Here he is, here he is.—How is 't with you, sir?
How is 't with you, man?   95

MALVOLIO Go off, I discard you. Let me enjoy my
private. Go off.

MARIA, ⌈*to Toby*⌉ Lo, how hollow the fiend speaks
within him! Did not I tell you? Sir Toby, my lady
prays you to have a care of him.   100

MALVOLIO Aha, does she so?

TOBY, ⌈*to Fabian and Maria*⌉ Go to, go to! Peace, peace.
We must deal gently with him. Let me alone.—How
do you, Malvolio? How is 't with you? What, man,
defy the devil! Consider, he's an enemy to mankind. 105

MALVOLIO Do you know what you say?

MARIA, ⌈*to Toby*⌉ La you, an you speak ill of the devil,
how he takes it at heart! Pray God he be not
bewitched!

FABIAN Carry his water to th' wisewoman.   110

MARIA Marry, and it shall be done tomorrow morning
if I live. My lady would not lose him for more than
I'll say.

MALVOLIO How now, mistress?

MARIA O Lord!   115

TOBY Prithee, hold thy peace. This is not the way. Do
you not see you move him? Let me alone with
him.

120. **rough:** violent; **used:** treated

121. **bawcock:** fine bird (French: *beau coq*) This word, along with **chuck** and **biddy** (both of which mean "chicken"), seems to be addressed to "the fiend" supposedly possessing Malvolio.

125. **for gravity:** i.e., appropriate for a dignified person; **cherry-pit:** a children's game

126. **foul collier:** dirty coal-dealer (applicable to Satan, who is pictured as black)

129. **minx:** hussy, insolent girl

132. **idle:** frivolous

138. **genius:** i.e., soul

139. **device:** plot

140–41. **take . . . taint:** be exposed to the **air** (i.e., become known) and thus be ruined

144–45. **in . . . bound:** a standard treatment for insanity at the time

146. **carry it thus:** proceed in this way

149. **bar:** perhaps, **the bar** of justice, the open court

151. **matter . . . morning:** perhaps, sport fit for a holiday

FABIAN   No way but gentleness, gently, gently. The
    fiend is rough and will not be roughly used.   120
TOBY, ⌜*to Malvolio*⌝ Why, how now, my bawcock? How
    dost thou, chuck?
MALVOLIO   Sir!
TOBY   Ay, biddy, come with me.—What, man, 'tis not
    for gravity to play at cherry-pit with Satan. Hang 125
    him, foul collier!
MARIA   Get him to say his prayers, good Sir Toby; get
    him to pray.
MALVOLIO   My prayers, minx?
MARIA, ⌜*to Toby*⌝ No, I warrant you, he will not hear of 130
    godliness.
MALVOLIO   Go hang yourselves all! You are idle, shal-
    low things. I am not of your element. You shall
    know more hereafter.   *He exits.*
TOBY   Is 't possible?   135
FABIAN   If this were played upon a stage now, I could
    condemn it as an improbable fiction.
TOBY   His very genius hath taken the infection of the
    device, man.
MARIA   Nay, pursue him now, lest the device take air 140
    and taint.
FABIAN   Why, we shall make him mad indeed.
MARIA   The house will be the quieter.
TOBY   Come, we'll have him in a dark room and
    bound. My niece is already in the belief that he's 145
    mad. We may carry it thus, for our pleasure and his
    penance, till our very pastime, tired out of breath,
    prompt us to have mercy on him, at which time we
    will bring the device to the bar and crown thee for a
    finder of madmen. But see, but see!   150

Enter Sir Andrew.

FABIAN   More matter for a May morning.
ANDREW, ⌜*presenting a paper*⌝ Here's the challenge.
    Read it. I warrant there's vinegar and pepper in 't.

154. **saucy:** (1) flavored with seasoning; (2) insolent, rude

155. **warrant him:** perhaps, I can assure him (Cesario)

157. **scurvy:** contemptible

159. **admire:** marvel

162–63. **keeps . . . law:** i.e., protects **you from** arrest (for disturbing the peace, or for libel)

165. **thou liest in thy throat:** i.e., you are a complete liar

172. **o' th' windy side:** on the windward side, and therefore safe from attack

176. **look to:** i.e., **look** out for, take care of

177. **thou usest:** you treat

179. **move him:** prompt him to action; or, arouse his feelings

182. **commerce:** dealings

182–83. **by and by:** soon

184. **Scout me:** i.e., keep a lookout

185. **bum-baily:** a bailiff (sheriff's officer)

186. **draw:** i.e., **draw** your sword

189. **approbation:** reputation (for courage); **proof:** testing, trial

FABIAN   Is 't so saucy?

ANDREW   Ay, is 't. I warrant him. Do but read.   155

TOBY   Give me. ⌜*He reads.*⌝ *Youth, whatsoever thou art,*
thou art but a scurvy fellow.

FABIAN   Good, and valiant.

TOBY ⌜*reads*⌝ *Wonder not nor admire not in thy mind*
why I do call thee so, for I will show thee no reason   160
for 't.

FABIAN   A good note, that keeps you from the blow of
the law.

TOBY ⌜*reads*⌝ *Thou com'st to the Lady Olivia, and in my*
sight she uses thee kindly. But thou liest in thy throat;   165
that is not the matter I challenge thee for.

FABIAN   Very brief, and to exceeding good sense—less.

TOBY ⌜*reads*⌝ *I will waylay thee going home, where if it be*
thy chance to kill me—

FABIAN   Good.   170

TOBY ⌜*reads*⌝ *Thou kill'st me like a rogue and a villain.*

FABIAN   Still you keep o' th' windy side of the law.
Good.

TOBY ⌜*reads*⌝ *Fare thee well, and God have mercy upon*
one of our souls. He may have mercy upon mine, but   175
my hope is better, and so look to thyself. Thy friend, as
thou usest him, and thy sworn enemy,

                        Andrew Aguecheek.

If this letter move him not, his legs cannot. I'll
give 't him.   180

MARIA   You may have very fit occasion for 't. He is now
in some commerce with my lady and will by and
by depart.

TOBY   Go, Sir Andrew. Scout me for him at the corner
of the orchard like a bum-baily. So soon as ever   185
thou seest him, draw, and as thou draw'st, swear
horrible, for it comes to pass oft that a terrible oath,
with a swaggering accent sharply twanged off, gives
manhood more approbation than ever proof itself
would have earned him. Away!   190

191. **let . . . swearing:** i.e., don't worry about my ability to swear

193. **gives him out:** shows him

194. **capacity:** intelligence; **breeding:** education; or, parentage; **his employment:** i.e., the service he performs

198. **clodpoll:** blockhead

199–200. **set . . . valor:** i.e., describe **Aguecheek** as notably courageous

204. **cockatrices:** mythical serpents (with the head, wings, and feet of a cock) whose looks could kill (See picture, page 128.)

205–6. **Give . . . leave:** i.e., let them alone till he leaves

206. **presently after him:** immediately go after him

207. **horrid:** terrifying

210. **laid:** wagered; **unchary:** impetuously; **on 't:** perhaps, on that stony heart (Many editors change "on 't" to "out," and interpret the phrase as meaning "expended my honor too lavishly.")

214. **With . . . havior:** i.e., in the same way

215. **Goes on:** i.e., go on, persist

216. **jewel:** i.e., jeweled miniature portrait

220. **saved:** i.e., uncompromised

ANDREW   Nay, let me alone for swearing.   *He exits.*

TOBY   Now will not I deliver his letter, for the behavior
of the young gentleman gives him out to be of good
capacity and breeding; his employment between
his lord and my niece confirms no less. Therefore,   195
this letter, being so excellently ignorant, will breed
no terror in the youth. He will find it comes from a
clodpoll. But, sir, I will deliver his challenge by
word of mouth, set upon Aguecheek a notable
report of valor, and drive the gentleman (as I know   200
his youth will aptly receive it) into a most hideous
opinion of his rage, skill, fury, and impetuosity. This
will so fright them both that they will kill one
another by the look, like cockatrices.

Enter Olivia and Viola.

FABIAN   Here he comes with your niece. Give them   205
way till he take leave, and presently after him.

TOBY   I will meditate the while upon some horrid
message for a challenge.
                    ⌜*Toby, Fabian, and Maria exit.*⌝

OLIVIA
I have said too much unto a heart of stone
And laid mine honor too unchary on 't.   210
There's something in me that reproves my fault,
But such a headstrong potent fault it is
That it but mocks reproof.

VIOLA
With the same havior that your passion bears
Goes on my master's griefs.   215

OLIVIA
Here, wear this jewel for me. 'Tis my picture.
Refuse it not. It hath no tongue to vex you.
And I beseech you come again tomorrow.
What shall you ask of me that I'll deny,
That honor, saved, may upon asking give?   220

229. **defense:** ability as a fencer; **betake thee:** commit yourself (Sir Toby speaks to Cesario in very contorted language throughout this scene.)

231. **thy intercepter:** i.e., the one who wants to cut you off; **despite:** anger, defiance

232. **hunter:** perhaps, huntsman; or, perhaps, hunting dog; **attends thee:** waits for you

232–33. **Dismount thy tuck:** draw your sword

233. **yare:** quick

236. **to:** i.e., with; **remembrance:** memory; **free:** innocent

239. **price:** value

239–40. **betake . . . guard:** put yourself in a defensive position (See picture, page 130.)

240. **opposite:** adversary

241. **withal:** i.e., with

243. **dubbed:** made a knight; **unhatched:** unhacked, not used (This charge, and the admission that Sir Andrew's knighthood was for **carpet consideration** [line 244]—i.e., that he was knighted at court rather than on the battlefield—acknowledge that he is no soldier.)

246. **incensement:** anger

247. **satisfaction . . . by:** i.e., he can be satisfied only by

248–49. **"Hob, nob," "give 't or take 't":** Both phrases mean that the challenger wants to fight to the death. **word:** motto

VIOLA
  Nothing but this: your true love for my master.

OLIVIA
  How with mine honor may I give him that
  Which I have given to you?

VIOLA   I will acquit you.

OLIVIA
  Well, come again tomorrow. Fare thee well.   225
  A fiend like thee might bear my soul to hell.

                        ⌜*She exits.*⌝

Enter Toby and Fabian.

TOBY   Gentleman, God save thee.

VIOLA   And you, sir.

TOBY   That defense thou hast, betake thee to 't. Of what
    nature the wrongs are thou hast done him, I know   230
    not, but thy intercepter, full of despite, bloody as
    the hunter, attends thee at the orchard end. Dis-
    mount thy tuck, be yare in thy preparation, for thy
    assailant is quick, skillful, and deadly.

VIOLA   You mistake, sir. I am sure no man hath any   235
    quarrel to me. My remembrance is very free and
    clear from any image of offense done to any man.

TOBY   You'll find it otherwise, I assure you. Therefore,
    if you hold your life at any price, betake you to your
    guard, for your opposite hath in him what youth,   240
    strength, skill, and wrath can furnish man withal.

VIOLA   I pray you, sir, what is he?

TOBY   He is knight dubbed with unhatched rapier and
    on carpet consideration, but he is a devil in private
    brawl. Souls and bodies hath he divorced three, and   245
    his incensement at this moment is so implacable
    that satisfaction can be none but by pangs of death
    and sepulcher. "Hob, nob" is his word; "give 't or
    take 't."

VIOLA   I will return again into the house and desire   250

251. **conduct:** escort; **of:** from
252–53. **put quarrels . . . on:** i.e., provoke **quarrels** with
253. **taste:** test; **Belike:** perhaps
255. **derives itself:** i.e., grows
256. **competent injury:** i.e., an insult sufficient to demand satisfaction
258. **that:** i.e., a duel
259. **answer:** fight with
260. **meddle:** fight
261–62. **forswear . . . you:** i.e., give up your right to wear a sword (admit your cowardice)
263. **uncivil:** rude
264. **office:** kindness, service; **as . . . of:** i.e., find out from
266. **negligence:** oversight; **purpose:** intention
271. **a . . . arbitrament:** i.e., a fight to the death
274. **read:** judge
275. **form:** appearance; **like:** likely
277. **fatal:** deadly
283. **mettle:** character

some conduct of the lady. I am no fighter. I have
heard of some kind of men that put quarrels pur-
posely on others to taste their valor. Belike this is a
man of that quirk.

TOBY   Sir, no. His indignation derives itself out of a very   255
competent injury. Therefore get you on and give
him his desire. Back you shall not to the house,
unless you undertake that with me which with as
much safety you might answer him. Therefore on,
or strip your sword stark naked, for meddle you   260
must, that's certain, or forswear to wear iron about
you.

VIOLA   This is as uncivil as strange. I beseech you, do
me this courteous office, as to know of the knight
what my offense to him is. It is something of my   265
negligence, nothing of my purpose.

TOBY   I will do so.—Signior Fabian, stay you by this
gentleman till my return.   *Toby exits.*

VIOLA   Pray you, sir, do you know of this matter?

FABIAN   I know the knight is incensed against you even   270
to a mortal arbitrament, but nothing of the circumstance more.

VIOLA   I beseech you, what manner of man is he?

FABIAN   Nothing of that wonderful promise, to read
him by his form, as you are like to find him in the   275
proof of his valor. He is indeed, sir, the most skillful,
bloody, and fatal opposite that you could possibly
have found in any part of Illyria. Will you walk
towards him? I will make your peace with him if I
can.   280

VIOLA   I shall be much bound to you for 't. I am one
that had rather go with Sir Priest than Sir Knight; I
care not who knows so much of my mettle.

                              They exit.

Enter Toby and Andrew.

285. **firago:** virago; **pass:** bout
286. **stuck-in:** stoccata (a fencing thrust)
288. **answer:** return thrust
290. **Sophy:** Shah of Persia
291. **Pox on 't:** a mild oath
295. **fence:** i.e., fencing
299. **motion:** offer
300. **on 't:** of it
303. **take up:** settle
305. **He:** Cesario; **is . . . conceited:** has as horrible an image
310. **his quarrel:** i.e., the insult to him
311–12. **for . . . vow:** so that he can keep his oath

A cockatrice. (3.4.204)
From Joachim Camerarius, *Symbolorum et emblematum . . .* (1605).

TOBY   Why, man, he's a very devil. I have not seen such
a firago. I had a pass with him, rapier, scabbard,   285
and all, and he gives me the stuck-in with such
a mortal motion that it is inevitable; and on the
answer, he pays you as surely as your feet hits the
ground they step on. They say he has been fencer
to the Sophy.   290

ANDREW   Pox on 't! I'll not meddle with him.

TOBY   Ay, but he will not now be pacified. Fabian can
scarce hold him yonder.

ANDREW   Plague on 't! An I thought he had been
valiant and so cunning in fence, I'd have seen him   295
damned ere I'd have challenged him. Let him let
the matter slip, and I'll give him my horse, gray
Capilet.

TOBY   I'll make the motion. Stand here, make a good
show on 't. This shall end without the perdition of   300
souls. ⌈*Aside.*⌉ Marry, I'll ride your horse as well as I
ride you.

Enter Fabian and Viola.

⌈*Toby crosses to meet them.*⌉
⌈*Aside to Fabian.*⌉ I have his horse to take up the
quarrel. I have persuaded him the youth's a devil.

FABIAN, ⌈*Aside to Toby*⌉   He is as horribly conceited of   305
him, and pants and looks pale as if a bear were at his
heels.

TOBY, ⌈*to Viola*⌉   There's no remedy, sir; he will fight
with you for 's oath sake. Marry, he hath better
bethought him of his quarrel, and he finds that now   310
scarce to be worth talking of. Therefore, draw for
the supportance of his vow. He protests he will not
hurt you.

VIOLA   Pray God defend me! ⌈*Aside.*⌉ A little thing
would make me tell them how much I lack of a   315
man.

320. **duello:** dueling code

332. **undertaker:** i.e., one who takes up a challenge to fight

334. **anon:** soon

337. **for that:** as **for that** which (i.e., my horse)

339. **reins:** tolerates reins

"Betake you to your guard." (3.4.239–40)
From George Silver, *Paradoxes of defence* (1599).

FABIAN　Give ground if you see him furious.

⌜*Toby crosses to Andrew.*⌝

TOBY　Come, Sir Andrew, there's no remedy. The
gentleman will, for his honor's sake, have one bout
with you. He cannot by the *duello* avoid it. But he　320
has promised me, as he is a gentleman and a soldier,
he will not hurt you. Come on, to 't.

ANDREW, ⌜*drawing his sword*⌝　Pray God he keep his
oath!

VIOLA, ⌜*drawing her sword*⌝
I do assure you, 'tis against my will.　　　　　　325

Enter Antonio.

ANTONIO, ⌜*to Andrew*⌝
Put up your sword. If this young gentleman
Have done offense, I take the fault on me.
If you offend him, I for him defy you.

TOBY　You, sir? Why, what are you?

ANTONIO, ⌜*drawing his sword*⌝
One, sir, that for his love dares yet do more　　330
Than you have heard him brag to you he will.

TOBY, ⌜*drawing his sword*⌝
Nay, if you be an undertaker, I am for you.

Enter Officers.

FABIAN　O, good Sir Toby, hold! Here come the officers.

TOBY, ⌜*to Antonio*⌝　I'll be with you anon.

VIOLA, ⌜*to Andrew*⌝　Pray, sir, put your sword up, if　335
you please.

ANDREW　Marry, will I, sir. And for that I promised
you, I'll be as good as my word. He will bear you
easily, and reins well.

FIRST OFFICER　This is the man. Do thy office.　　340

SECOND OFFICER　Antonio, I arrest thee at the suit of
Count Orsino.

ANTONIO　You do mistake me, sir.

344. **favor:** face
347. **with:** as a consequence of
349. **answer:** pay the penalty for
353. **amazed:** bewildered, perplexed
359. **part:** i.e., partly
360. **ability:** financial resources
361. **My having:** i.e., the money that I have
362. **present:** i.e., present funds
363. **coffer:** literally, money box
365. **deserts:** good deeds, services
366. **lack persuasion:** i.e., fail to persuade (you to help me)
367. **unsound:** wicked
373. **vainness:** (1) vanity; (2) foolishness
375. **blood:** nature

An Amazon. (2.3.175)
From Giovanni Battista Cavalleriis;
Antiquarum statuarum . . . (1585–94).

FIRST OFFICER
No, sir, no jot. I know your favor well,
Though now you have no sea-cap on your head.— 345
Take him away. He knows I know him well.

ANTONIO
I must obey. ⌈*To Viola.*⌉ This comes with seeking
   you.
But there's no remedy. I shall answer it.
What will you do, now my necessity 350
Makes me to ask you for my purse? It grieves me
Much more for what I cannot do for you
Than what befalls myself. You stand amazed,
But be of comfort.

SECOND OFFICER   Come, sir, away. 355

ANTONIO, ⌈*to Viola*⌉
I must entreat of you some of that money.

VIOLA   What money, sir?
For the fair kindness you have showed me here,
And part being prompted by your present trouble,
Out of my lean and low ability 360
I'll lend you something. My having is not much.
I'll make division of my present with you.
Hold, there's half my coffer.   ⌈*Offering him money.*⌉

ANTONIO   Will you deny me now?
Is 't possible that my deserts to you 365
Can lack persuasion? Do not tempt my misery,
Lest that it make me so unsound a man
As to upbraid you with those kindnesses
That I have done for you.

VIOLA   I know of none, 370
Nor know I you by voice or any feature.
I hate ingratitude more in a man
Than lying, vainness, babbling drunkenness,
Or any taint of vice whose strong corruption
Inhabits our frail blood— 375

ANTONIO   O heavens themselves!

379. **one half . . . death:** i.e., half-dead

385. **done . . . shame:** i.e., disgraced your **good** looks

386. **the mind:** i.e., what happens in one's **mind** or heart

389. **empty . . . devil:** i.e., elaborately decorated chests, made beautiful by **the devil** but with nothing inside

393. **passion:** intense feelings

398. **saws:** sayings

399–400. **I . . . glass:** i.e., I am the mirror image of **my brother**

401. **favor:** looks, features

402. **Still:** always

Luna. (1.5.198)
From Johann Engel, *Astrolabium . . .* (1488).

SECOND OFFICER   Come, sir, I pray you go.

ANTONIO
Let me speak a little. This youth that you see here
I snatched one half out of the jaws of death,
Relieved him with such sanctity of love,   380
And to his image, which methought did promise
Most venerable worth, did I devotion.

FIRST OFFICER
What's that to us? The time goes by. Away!

ANTONIO
But O, how vile an idol proves this god!
Thou hast, Sebastian, done good feature shame.   385
In nature there's no blemish but the mind;
None can be called deformed but the unkind.
Virtue is beauty, but the beauteous evil
Are empty trunks o'erflourished by the devil.

FIRST OFFICER
The man grows mad. Away with him.—Come,   390
    come, sir.

ANTONIO   Lead me on.
                            ⌜*Antonio and Officers*⌝ *exit.*

VIOLA, ⌜*aside*⌝
Methinks his words do from such passion fly
That he believes himself; so do not I.
Prove true, imagination, O, prove true,   395
That I, dear brother, be now ta'en for you!

TOBY   Come hither, knight; come hither, Fabian. We'll
    whisper o'er a couplet or two of most sage saws.
                        ⌜*Toby, Fabian, and Andrew move aside.*⌝

VIOLA, ⌜*aside*⌝
He named Sebastian. I my brother know
Yet living in my glass. Even such and so   400
In favor was my brother, and he went
Still in this fashion, color, ornament,
For him I imitate. O, if it prove,
Tempests are kind, and salt waves fresh in love!
                                            ⌜*She exits.*⌝

405. **dishonest:** dishonorable, shameful
409–10. **religious in:** i.e., devoted to
411. **'Slid:** an oath "by God's eyelid"
415. **event:** outcome
416. **yet:** after all

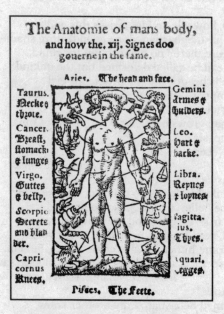

The signs governing the body. (1.3.135)
From Walter Gray, *An almanacke . . .* (1591).

TOBY   A very dishonest, paltry boy, and more a coward   405
     than a hare. His dishonesty appears in leaving his
     friend here in necessity and denying him; and for
     his cowardship, ask Fabian.

FABIAN   A coward, a most devout coward, religious
     in it.   410

ANDREW   'Slid, I'll after him again and beat him.

TOBY   Do, cuff him soundly, but never draw thy
     sword.

ANDREW   An I do not—

FABIAN   Come, let's see the event.   415

TOBY   I dare lay any money 'twill be nothing yet.

                                     ⌜*They*⌝ *exit.*

TWELFTH NIGHT,

OR,

WHAT
YOU WILL

ACT 4

4.1 The Fool encounters Sebastian, whom he mistakes for Cesario. When Sir Andrew and Sir Toby attack Sebastian, the Fool fetches Olivia, who again declares her love—this time to a delighted Sebastian.

---

3. **Go to:** an expression of impatience

5. **held out:** kept up, maintained

5–9. **I . . . so:** These lines are said sarcastically.

10. **vent:** give expression to

14. **lubber:** oaf

15. **cockney:** sissy; **ungird:** remove

15–16. **strangeness:** distance (i.e., pretense that you and I are strangers)

18. **foolish Greek:** A "merry Greek" was a buffoon or jester.

23. **report:** name, reputation; **purchase:** i.e., making payments

A Fool.
From August Casimir Redel, *Apophtegmata symbolica . . .* (n.d.).

ACT 4

Scene 1
Enter Sebastian and ⌈Feste, the Fool.⌉

FOOL   Will you make me believe that I am not sent for
  you?

SEBASTIAN   Go to, go to, thou art a foolish fellow. Let
  me be clear of thee.

FOOL   Well held out, i' faith. No, I do not know you, nor   5
  I am not sent to you by my lady to bid you come
  speak with her, nor your name is not Master
  Cesario, nor this is not my nose neither. Nothing
  that is so is so.

SEBASTIAN   I prithee, vent thy folly somewhere else.   10
  Thou know'st not me.

FOOL   Vent my folly? He has heard that word of some
  great man and now applies it to a Fool. Vent my
  folly? I am afraid this great lubber the world will
  prove a cockney. I prithee now, ungird thy strange-   15
  ness and tell me what I shall vent to my lady. Shall I
  vent to her that thou art coming?

SEBASTIAN   I prithee, foolish Greek, depart from me.
  There's money for thee. ⌈*Giving money.*⌉ If you
  tarry longer, I shall give worse payment.   20

FOOL   By my troth, thou hast an open hand. These wise
  men that give Fools money get themselves a good
  report—after fourteen years' purchase.

28. **your dagger:** These words have suggested to some editors that Sebastian beats Andrew with the hilt of his dagger. If such is the case, however unlikely, Toby's command to Sebastian at line 39, "put up your iron," would mean "sheathe your dagger."

30. **straight:** straightway, immediately

34. **action of battery:** i.e., lawsuit accusing him of unlawfully beating me

39. **well fleshed:** eager for battle; or, hardened to battle

45. **malapert:** impudent

Fortune. (2.4.92)
From George Wither, *A collection of emblemes* . . . (1635).

Enter Andrew, Toby, and Fabian.

ANDREW, ⌜*to Sebastian*⌝   Now, sir, have I met you again?
  There's for you.   ⌜*He strikes Sebastian.*⌝   25
SEBASTIAN, ⌜*returning the blow*⌝   Why, there's for thee,
  and there, and there.—Are all the people mad?
TOBY   Hold, sir, or I'll throw your dagger o'er the
  house.
FOOL, ⌜*aside*⌝   This will I tell my lady straight. I would   30
  not be in some of your coats for twopence.
                                   ⌜*He exits.*⌝
TOBY, ⌜*seizing Sebastian*⌝   Come on, sir, hold!
ANDREW   Nay, let him alone. I'll go another way to
  work with him. I'll have an action of battery against
  him, if there be any law in Illyria. Though I struck   35
  him first, yet it's no matter for that.
SEBASTIAN, ⌜*to Toby*⌝   Let go thy hand!
TOBY   Come, sir, I will not let you go. Come, my young
  soldier, put up your iron. You are well fleshed.
  Come on.   40
SEBASTIAN
  I will be free from thee.
                 ⌜*He pulls free and draws his sword.*⌝
                      What wouldst thou now?
  If thou dar'st tempt me further, draw thy sword.
TOBY   What, what? Nay, then, I must have an ounce or
  two of this malapert blood from you.   45
                                   ⌜*He draws his sword.*⌝

Enter Olivia.

OLIVIA
  Hold, Toby! On thy life I charge thee, hold!
TOBY   Madam.
OLIVIA
  Will it be ever thus? Ungracious wretch,
  Fit for the mountains and the barbarous caves,

53. **Rudesby:** rude, ill-mannered person

56. **extent:** assault

59. **botched up:** clumsily put together

61. **deny:** refuse; **Beshrew:** literally, curse (but the harshness of the word was lost through repeated use)

62. **started . . . thee:** i.e., made my **heart** (residing in you) leap with fear (There is a play on **heart** and "hart" and on *start* as "startle" and "rouse an animal from its hiding place.")

63. **What . . . this:** i.e., what does this mean? (literally, how does this taste?)

64. **Or . . . or:** either . . . or

65. **Let . . . steep:** i.e., let me continue in this dreamlike state **fancy:** imagination **sense:** senses, awareness of the waking world **Lethe:** the mythological river in the underworld that washes away one's memory of one's former life **steep:** immerse

67. **Would:** i.e., I wish

4.2 Under directions from Sir Toby, the Fool disguises himself as a parish priest and visits the imprisoned Malvolio. In his own person, the Fool agrees to fetch pen, paper, and a candle for the supposed madman.

---

2. **Sir:** English term for Latin *dominus*, the title given a clergyman; **curate:** parish priest

3. **the whilst:** i.e., in the meantime

4. **dissemble:** disguise

5. **dissembled:** played the hypocrite

Where manners ne'er were preached! Out of my   50
    sight!—
Be not offended, dear Cesario.—
Rudesby, begone!   ⌜*Toby, Andrew, and Fabian exit.*⌝
             I prithee, gentle friend,
Let thy fair wisdom, not thy passion, sway   55
In this uncivil and unjust extent
Against thy peace. Go with me to my house,
And hear thou there how many fruitless pranks
This ruffian hath botched up, that thou thereby
Mayst smile at this. Thou shalt not choose but go.   60
Do not deny. Beshrew his soul for me!
He started one poor heart of mine, in thee.

SEBASTIAN, ⌜*aside*⌝
What relish is in this? How runs the stream?
Or I am mad, or else this is a dream.
Let fancy still my sense in Lethe steep;   65
If it be thus to dream, still let me sleep!

OLIVIA
Nay, come, I prithee. Would thou 'dst be ruled by
    me!

SEBASTIAN
Madam, I will.

OLIVIA   O, say so, and so be!   70
                          They exit.

Scene 2
Enter Maria and ⌜*Feste, the Fool.*⌝

MARIA   Nay, I prithee, put on this gown and this beard;
make him believe thou art Sir Topas the curate. Do
it quickly. I'll call Sir Toby the whilst.   ⌜*She exits.*⌝

FOOL   Well, I'll put it on and I will dissemble myself in
't, and I would I were the first that ever dissembled   5
in such a gown. ⌜*He puts on gown and beard.*⌝ I am

7. **become:** befit; **the function:** i.e., of a priest

9. **housekeeper:** hospitable person

11. **The competitors:** i.e., my colleagues

13. **Bonos dies:** good day (in bad Latin)

13–14. **the . . . Prague:** The Fool once again invents an authority to quote in his foolery.

15. **Gorboduc:** a legendary king of Britain

18. **To him:** i.e., begin your attack on Malvolio

21. **knave:** a playful term of endearment

21 SD. **Malvolio within:** This Folio direction indicates that Malvolio speaks from offstage or from behind a door or curtain.

27. **Out . . . fiend:** addressed to the devil that supposedly possesses Malvolio **hyperbolical:** i.e., ranting (literally, using hyperbole or exaggeration)

33. **dishonest:** dishonorable; lying

34. **modest:** moderate

Noah's ark. (3.2.16)
From Vincentius, *The myrrour: dyscrypcyon
of the worlde . . .* [1527?].

not tall enough to become the function well, nor
lean enough to be thought a good student, but to be
said an honest man and a good housekeeper goes as
fairly as to say a careful man and a great scholar. 10
The competitors enter.

Enter Toby ⌐and Maria.⌐

TOBY   Jove bless thee, Master Parson.

FOOL   *Bonos dies*, Sir Toby; for, as the old hermit of
Prague, that never saw pen and ink, very wittily said
to a niece of King Gorboduc "That that is, is," so I, 15
being Master Parson, am Master Parson; for what is
"that" but "that" and "is" but "is"?

TOBY   To him, Sir Topas.

FOOL, ⌐*disguising his voice*⌐   What ho, I say! Peace in this
prison! 20

TOBY   The knave counterfeits well. A good knave.

Malvolio within.

MALVOLIO   Who calls there?

FOOL   Sir Topas the curate, who comes to visit Malvolio the lunatic.

MALVOLIO   Sir Topas, Sir Topas, good Sir Topas, go to 25
my lady—

FOOL   Out, hyperbolical fiend! How vexest thou this
man! Talkest thou nothing but of ladies?

TOBY, ⌐*aside*⌐   Well said, Master Parson.

MALVOLIO   Sir Topas, never was man thus wronged. 30
Good Sir Topas, do not think I am mad. They have
laid me here in hideous darkness—

FOOL   Fie, thou dishonest Satan! I call thee by the most
modest terms, for I am one of those gentle ones
that will use the devil himself with courtesy. Sayst 35
thou that house is dark?

MALVOLIO   As hell, Sir Topas.

38–39. **barricadoes:** barricades, barriers

39. **clerestories:** high windows

45. **puzzled:** confused

46. **the . . . fog:** In stories about Moses, one of the plagues visited by God on the Egyptians was "a black darkness in all the land of Egypt three days" (Exodus 10.22).

50–51. **any constant question:** perhaps, any consistent line of questioning

52. **Pythagoras:** This ancient Greek philosopher taught the transmigration of souls. Ovid's *Metamorphoses* (a book used frequently by Shakespeare) has a speech by Pythagoras urging humans not to kill animals because "Our souls survive . . . death; as they depart / Their local habitations in the flesh, / They enter new-found bodies that preserve them. / . . . the spirit takes its way / To different kinds of being as it chooses, / From beast to man, from man to beast." (Book 15, trans. Horace Gregory)

54. **haply:** perhaps

61. **allow . . . wits:** agree that you're sane; **and fear:** and (until) you shall **fear**

66. **I . . . waters:** perhaps, I can do anything

71–72. **delivered:** freed

FOOL   Why, it hath bay windows transparent as barricadoes, and the ⌜clerestories⌝ toward the south-
north are as lustrous as ebony; and yet complainest   40
thou of obstruction?

MALVOLIO   I am not mad, Sir Topas. I say to you this
house is dark.

FOOL   Madman, thou errest. I say there is no darkness
but ignorance, in which thou art more puzzled than   45
the Egyptians in their fog.

MALVOLIO   I say this house is as dark as ignorance,
though ignorance were as dark as hell. And I say
there was never man thus abused. I am no more
mad than you are. Make the trial of it in any   50
constant question.

FOOL   What is the opinion of Pythagoras concerning
wildfowl?

MALVOLIO   That the soul of our grandam might haply
inhabit a bird.   55

FOOL   What thinkst thou of his opinion?

MALVOLIO   I think nobly of the soul, and no way
approve his opinion.

FOOL   Fare thee well. Remain thou still in darkness.
Thou shalt hold th' opinion of Pythagoras ere I will   60
allow of thy wits, and fear to kill a woodcock lest
thou dispossess the soul of thy grandam. Fare thee
well.

MALVOLIO   Sir Topas, Sir Topas!

TOBY   My most exquisite Sir Topas!   65

FOOL   Nay, I am for all waters.

MARIA   Thou mightst have done this without thy beard
and gown. He sees thee not.

TOBY   To him in thine own voice, and bring me word
how thou find'st him. I would we were well rid   70
of this knavery. If he may be conveniently delivered, I would he were, for I am now so far in
offense with my niece that I cannot pursue with

74. **the upshot:** i.e., to its final conclusion

76. **Hey, Robin . . . :** a song the words for which may be Thomas Wyatt's

79. **perdy:** for sure (*par Dieu*, by God)

91. **fell you besides:** i.e., did you lose; **five wits:** five senses; or, common wit, imagination, fantasy, estimation, and memory (the five wits, according to Stephen Hawes in *The Pastime of Pleasure*)

94. **But:** i.e., only, no more than

96. **propertied me:** treated me like a lifeless object

98. **face:** bully

99. **Advise you:** i.e., be careful

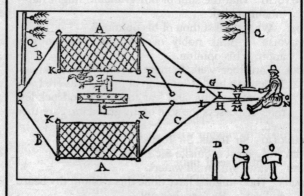

A woodcock in a "gin." (2.5.85)
From Gervase Markham, *Hungers prevention, or, The whole art of fowling . . .* (1655).

any safety this sport the upshot. Come by and by   75
to my chamber.

⌜*Toby and Maria* ⌝ *exit.*

FOOL ⌜*sings, in his own voice* ⌝
    Hey, Robin, jolly Robin,
    Tell me how thy lady does.

MALVOLIO   Fool!

FOOL ⌜*sings* ⌝
        My lady is unkind, perdy.

MALVOLIO   Fool!   80

FOOL ⌜*sings* ⌝
        Alas, why is she so?

MALVOLIO   Fool, I say!

FOOL ⌜*sings* ⌝
        She loves another—
    Who calls, ha?

MALVOLIO   Good Fool, as ever thou wilt deserve well at   85
    my hand, help me to a candle, and pen, ink, and
    paper. As I am a gentleman, I will live to be thankful
    to thee for 't.

FOOL   Master Malvolio?

MALVOLIO   Ay, good Fool.   90

FOOL   Alas, sir, how fell you besides your five wits?

MALVOLIO   Fool, there was never man so notoriously
    abused. I am as well in my wits, Fool, as thou art.

FOOL   But as well? Then you are mad indeed, if you be
    no better in your wits than a Fool.   95

MALVOLIO   They have here propertied me, keep me in
    darkness, send ministers to me—asses!—and do
    all they can to face me out of my wits.

FOOL   Advise you what you say. The minister is here.
    ⌜*In the voice of Sir Topas.* ⌝ Malvolio, Malvolio, thy   100
    wits the heavens restore. Endeavor thyself to sleep
    and leave thy vain bibble-babble.

MALVOLIO   Sir Topas!

105–6. God buy you: i.e., **God** be with **you,** good-bye

110. shent: rebuked

114. Welladay that: i.e., alas, if only

117. advantage: benefit, profit

118. letter: i.e., a **letter**

128. the old Vice: a comic character in earlier drama, whose props (**dagger of lath,** or wood) and antics are described in the lines of the song

133. goodman: a title indicating a low social rank

"Shall we make the welkin dance?" (2.3.58)
From Vincentius, *The myrrour: dyscrypcyon of the worlde . . .* (1527).

FOOL, ⌜*as Sir Topas*⌝ Maintain no words with him, good
fellow. ⌜*As Fool.*⌝ Who, I, sir? Not I, sir! God buy 105
you, good Sir Topas. ⌜*As Sir Topas.*⌝ Marry, amen.
⌜*As Fool.*⌝ I will, sir, I will.

MALVOLIO Fool! Fool! Fool, I say!

FOOL Alas, sir, be patient. What say you, sir? I am
shent for speaking to you. 110

MALVOLIO Good Fool, help me to some light and some
paper. I tell thee, I am as well in my wits as any
man in Illyria.

FOOL Welladay that you were, sir!

MALVOLIO By this hand, I am. Good Fool, some ink, 115
paper, and light; and convey what I will set down to
my lady. It shall advantage thee more than ever the
bearing of letter did.

FOOL I will help you to 't. But tell me true, are you not
mad indeed, or do you but counterfeit? 120

MALVOLIO Believe me, I am not. I tell thee true.

FOOL Nay, I'll ne'er believe a madman till I see his
brains. I will fetch you light and paper and ink.

MALVOLIO Fool, I'll requite it in the highest degree. I
prithee, begone. 125

FOOL ⌜*sings*⌝
I am gone, sir, and anon, sir,
    I'll be with you again,
In a trice, like to the old Vice,
    Your need to sustain.
Who with dagger of lath, in his rage and his wrath, 130
    Cries "aha!" to the devil;
Like a mad lad, "Pare thy nails, dad!
    Adieu, goodman devil."

                                                    He exits.

4.3 While Sebastian is sure that neither he nor Olivia is insane, he is amazed by the wonder of his new situation. When Olivia asks him to enter into a formal betrothal with her, he readily agrees.

---

3. **wonder:** astonishment, amazement

6. **there he was:** i.e., he had been there; **credit:** report

7. **range:** roam, wander around

9. **my soul . . . sense:** i.e., my reason and my senses agree in arguing

12. **instance:** example; **discourse:** reasoning

15. **trust:** belief

17. **sway:** rule

19. **Take . . . dispatch:** i.e., "**take affairs**" (undertake business matters) and "**give back their dispatch**" (complete them promptly)

22. **deceivable:** deceptive

25. **chantry:** chapel; **by:** nearby

27. **Plight . . . faith:** i.e., assure me of your fidelity (through a promise to marry me)

28. **jealous:** anxious; **doubtful:** filled with doubts, insecure

29. **He:** i.e., the priest

Scene 3
Enter Sebastian.

⌜SEBASTIAN⌝
 This is the air; that is the glorious sun.
 This pearl she gave me, I do feel 't and see 't.
 And though 'tis wonder that enwraps me thus,
 Yet 'tis not madness. Where's Antonio, then?
 I could not find him at the Elephant.   5
 Yet there he was; and there I found this credit,
 That he did range the town to seek me out.
 His counsel now might do me golden service.
 For though my soul disputes well with my sense
 That this may be some error, but no madness, 10
 Yet doth this accident and flood of fortune
 So far exceed all instance, all discourse,
 That I am ready to distrust mine eyes
 And wrangle with my reason that persuades me
 To any other trust but that I am mad—   15
 Or else the lady's mad. Yet if 'twere so,
 She could not sway her house, command her
   followers,
 Take and give back affairs and their dispatch
 With such a smooth, discreet, and stable bearing 20
 As I perceive she does. There's something in 't
 That is deceivable. But here the lady comes.

Enter Olivia and ⌜*a*⌝ *Priest.*

OLIVIA, ⌜*to Sebastian*⌝
 Blame not this haste of mine. If you mean well,
 Now go with me and with this holy man
 Into the chantry by. There, before him   25
 And underneath that consecrated roof,
 Plight me the full assurance of your faith,
 That my most jealous and too doubtful soul
 May live at peace. He shall conceal it

30. **Whiles:** until; **come to note:** become known
31. **What time:** at which time; **our . . . keep:** i.e., celebrate our marriage
32. **birth:** social rank
37. **fairly note:** look favorably on; or, show that they approve

Dancing the galliard. (1.3.117)
From Fabritio Caroso, *Il ballarino . . .* (1581).

Whiles you are willing it shall come to note,   30
What time we will our celebration keep
According to my birth. What do you say?

SEBASTIAN
I'll follow this good man and go with you,
And, having sworn truth, ever will be true.

OLIVIA
Then lead the way, good father, and heavens so   35
    shine
That they may fairly note this act of mine.

They exit.

TWELFTH NIGHT,
OR,
WHAT
YOU WILL

ACT 5

5.1   Orsino, at Olivia's estate, sends the Fool to bring Olivia to him. Antonio is brought in by officers, and he tells the incredulous Orsino about Cesario's treacherous behavior. At Olivia's entrance, Orsino expresses his anger that Cesario has become Olivia's darling. Cesario's expressions of love for Orsino lead Olivia to send for the "holy father," who confirms Olivia's claim that she is formally betrothed to Cesario. Sir Andrew and Sir Toby enter with bloody heads, which they blame on Cesario. Sebastian's entry at this moment untangles a series of knots: Sebastian addresses Olivia with love, greets Antonio warmly, and recognizes Cesario as the image of himself. When Cesario admits to being Sebastian's sister Viola, Orsino asks Viola to become his wife. On the day that Sebastian marries Olivia, Viola will marry Orsino.

---

1. **his:** i.e., Malvolio's

11. **friends:** likely alluding to Orsino's **friends** (line 7)

18. **abused:** deceived

18–20. **conclusions ... affirmatives:** possibly an allusion to a sonnet by Sir Philip Sidney, in which the lady's twice saying "no" to the offer of a kiss is taken as a "yes" because, in grammar, two **negatives** make an affirmative

ACT 5

Scene 1
Enter ⌜Feste, the Fool⌝ and Fabian.

FABIAN   Now, as thou lov'st me, let me see his letter.

FOOL   Good Master Fabian, grant me another request.

FABIAN   Anything.

FOOL   Do not desire to see this letter.

FABIAN   This is to give a dog and in recompense desire   5
my dog again.

Enter ⌜Orsino,⌝ Viola, Curio, and Lords.

ORSINO
Belong you to the Lady Olivia, friends?

FOOL   Ay, sir, we are some of her trappings.

ORSINO
I know thee well. How dost thou, my good fellow?

FOOL   Truly, sir, the better for my foes and the worse   10
for my friends.

ORSINO
Just the contrary: the better for thy friends.

FOOL   No, sir, the worse.

ORSINO   How can that be?

FOOL   Marry, sir, they praise me and make an ass of me.   15
Now my foes tell me plainly I am an ass; so that by
my foes, sir, I profit in the knowledge of myself, and
by my friends I am abused. So that, conclusions to
be as kisses, if your four negatives make your two

161

26. **double-dealing:** (1) giving twice; (2) duplicity

29. **grace:** virtue (with a pun on the phrase—"your Grace"—with which the duke is normally addressed)

30. **obey it:** i.e., obey the Fool's **ill counsel**

33. **Primo, secundo, tertio:** first, second, third (perhaps an allusion to a game, or **play**)

34. **triplex:** triple time in music (i.e., a three-beat rhythm)

35. **tripping:** quick and light, or dancing

35. **Saint Bennet:** i.e., the church of St. Benedict

37. **fool:** beg through clever wordplay

38. **throw:** i.e., time (literally, throw of the dice)

43. **desire of having:** i.e., wish to possess

45. **anon:** very soon

49. **Vulcan:** Roman god of fire and blacksmith to the gods

50. **baubling:** tiny, insignificant

Vulcan. (5.1.49)
From Johann Basilius Herold, *Heydenweldt* . . . (1554).

affirmatives, why then the worse for my friends and 20
the better for my foes.

ORSINO Why, this is excellent.

FOOL By my troth, sir, no—though it please you to be
one of my friends.

ORSINO, ⌐*giving a coin*⌐
Thou shalt not be the worse for me; there's gold. 25

FOOL But that it would be double-dealing, sir, I would
you could make it another.

ORSINO O, you give me ill counsel.

FOOL Put your grace in your pocket, sir, for this once,
and let your flesh and blood obey it. 30

ORSINO Well, I will be so much a sinner to be a
double-dealer: there's another. ⌐*He gives a coin.*⌐

FOOL *Primo, secundo, tertio* is a good play, and the old
saying is, the third pays for all. The triplex, sir, is a
good tripping measure, or the bells of Saint Bennet, 35
sir, may put you in mind—one, two, three.

ORSINO You can fool no more money out of me at this
throw. If you will let your lady know I am here to
speak with her, and bring her along with you, it
may awake my bounty further. 40

FOOL Marry, sir, lullaby to your bounty till I come
again. I go, sir, but I would not have you to think
that my desire of having is the sin of covetousness.
But, as you say, sir, let your bounty take a nap. I
will awake it anon. *He exits.* 45

Enter Antonio and Officers.

VIOLA
Here comes the man, sir, that did rescue me.

ORSINO
That face of his I do remember well.
Yet when I saw it last, it was besmeared
As black as Vulcan in the smoke of war.
A baubling vessel was he captain of, 50

51. **For . . . unprizable:** i.e., worthless because of its **shallow draught** and its small **bulk**

52. **With which:** i.e., **with which** worthless vessel; **scatheful:** harmful

53. **bottom:** ship

54. **very:** even; **tongue of loss:** i.e., voices of those whom he defeated

55. **Cried:** called out

57, 58. *Phoenix, Tiger:* names of Orsino's ships

57. **fraught:** freight, that which the ship carries; **Candy:** Candia (capital of Crete)

60. **desperate of:** i.e., as if unconcerned with; **state:** i.e., his situation

61. **brabble:** brawl

62. **drew . . . side:** i.e., **drew** his sword to defend me

63. **put . . . me:** talked to me strangely

64. **distraction:** madness

65. **Notable:** excellent; conspicuous

67. **dear:** dire

73. **base and ground:** evidence

74. **witchcraft:** bewitching attraction

76. **rude:** violent, rough

77. **wrack:** piece of wreckage

79. **retention:** holding back

80. **All . . . dedication:** i.e., dedicating all (my love) to him

81. **pure:** purely, simply

82. **adverse:** hostile

For shallow draught and bulk unprizable,
With which such scatheful grapple did he make
With the most noble bottom of our fleet
That very envy and the tongue of loss
Cried fame and honor on him.—What's the matter?   55

FIRST OFFICER
Orsino, this is that Antonio
That took the *Phoenix* and her fraught from Candy,
And this is he that did the *Tiger* board
When your young nephew Titus lost his leg.
Here in the streets, desperate of shame and state,   60
In private brabble did we apprehend him.

VIOLA
He did me kindness, sir, drew on my side,
But in conclusion put strange speech upon me.
I know not what 'twas but distraction.

ORSINO
Notable pirate, thou saltwater thief,   65
What foolish boldness brought thee to their mercies
Whom thou, in terms so bloody and so dear,
Hast made thine enemies?

ANTONIO   Orsino, noble sir,
Be pleased that I shake off these names you give   70
  me.
Antonio never yet was thief or pirate,
Though, I confess, on base and ground enough,
Orsino's enemy. A witchcraft drew me hither.
That most ingrateful boy there by your side   75
From the rude sea's enraged and foamy mouth
Did I redeem; a wrack past hope he was.
His life I gave him and did thereto add
My love, without retention or restraint,
All his in dedication. For his sake   80
Did I expose myself, pure for his love,
Into the danger of this adverse town;
Drew to defend him when he was beset;

85. **Not meaning to:** i.e., choosing not to
86. **face . . . out of:** shamelessly exclude . . . from
88. **While . . . wink:** i.e., in the time it takes to blink one's eyes
89. **recommended:** consigned, given
94. **No int'rim:** without interruption
99. **tended . . . me:** attended me as a servant
102. **What . . . that:** i.e., what does my lord wish, except for that
103. **serviceable:** willing to be of service
104. **keep promise with:** i.e., **keep** your **promise** to
110. **fat, fulsome:** disgusting

Woman with a distaff. (1.3.100)
From Johann Engel, *Astrolabium* . . . (1488).

Where, being apprehended, his false cunning
(Not meaning to partake with me in danger)   85
Taught him to face me out of his acquaintance
And grew a twenty years' removèd thing
While one would wink; denied me mine own purse,
Which I had recommended to his use
Not half an hour before.   90

VIOLA   How can this be?

ORSINO, ⌜*to Antonio*⌝   When came he to this town?

ANTONIO
Today, my lord; and for three months before,
No int'rim, not a minute's vacancy,
Both day and night did we keep company.   95

Enter Olivia and Attendants.

ORSINO
Here comes the Countess. Now heaven walks on
    Earth!—
But for thee, fellow: fellow, thy words are madness.
Three months this youth hath tended upon me—
But more of that anon. ⌜*To an Officer.*⌝ Take him   100
    aside.

OLIVIA
What would my lord, but that he may not have,
Wherein Olivia may seem serviceable?—
Cesario, you do not keep promise with me.

VIOLA   Madam?   105

ORSINO   Gracious Olivia—

OLIVIA
What do you say, Cesario?—Good my lord—

VIOLA
My lord would speak; my duty hushes me.

OLIVIA
If it be aught to the old tune, my lord,
It is as fat and fulsome to mine ear   110
As howling after music.

113. **constant:** steadfast, immovable
114. **uncivil:** barbarous, rude
115. **ingrate:** ungrateful; **unauspicious:** inauspicious, unfavorable
117. **tendered:** offered
118. **become him:** accord with his rank or wishes
120. **th' Egyptian thief:** an allusion to a novel by Heliodorus, in which the robber chief, threatened with death, tries to kill the woman he loves to prevent her being taken by another
122. **savors nobly:** i.e., smacks of nobility
123. **to nonregardance cast:** i.e., fail to take notice of
124. **that:** i.e., since
125. **screws:** twists
126. **Live you:** i.e., continue to live as
127. **minion:** darling
128. **tender:** regard, esteem
135. **jocund, apt:** jocundly, aptly (i.e., happily, readily)
136. **do you rest:** i.e., give you peace
141. **you witnesses above:** i.e., you heavenly powers
142. **tainting of:** corrupting, injuring

ORSINO
Still so cruel?

OLIVIA   Still so constant, lord.

ORSINO
What, to perverseness? You, uncivil lady,
To whose ingrate and unauspicious altars   115
My soul the faithful'st off'rings have breathed out
That e'er devotion tendered—what shall I do?

OLIVIA
Even what it please my lord that shall become him.

ORSINO
Why should I not, had I the heart to do it,
Like to th' Egyptian thief at point of death,   120
Kill what I love?—a savage jealousy
That sometimes savors nobly. But hear me this:
Since you to nonregardance cast my faith,
And that I partly know the instrument
That screws me from my true place in your favor,   125
Live you the marble-breasted tyrant still.
But this your minion, whom I know you love,
And whom, by heaven I swear, I tender dearly,
Him will I tear out of that cruel eye
Where he sits crownèd in his master's spite.—   130
Come, boy, with me. My thoughts are ripe in
    mischief.
I'll sacrifice the lamb that I do love
To spite a raven's heart within a dove.

VIOLA
And I, most jocund, apt, and willingly,   135
To do you rest a thousand deaths would die.

OLIVIA
Where goes Cesario?

VIOLA   After him I love
More than I love these eyes, more than my life,
More by all mores than e'er I shall love wife.
If I do feign, you witnesses above,   140
Punish my life for tainting of my love.

143. **beguiled:** cheated, deceived

151. **sirrah:** a term of address that, here, emphasizes the speaker's authority

153. **baseness:** contemptibleness, ignobleness

154. **strangle thy propriety:** i.e., conceal what you are; or, perhaps, hide the fact that I belong to you

156. **that:** that which (i.e., my husband)

157. **that thou fear'st:** i.e., Orsino **that:** that which

159. **charge:** order

160. **unfold:** disclose

163. **newly:** recently

165. **joinder:** joining

166. **close:** union

Lucrece. (2.5.95)
From Silvestro Pietrasanta, . . . *Symbola heroica* . . . (1682).

OLIVIA
  Ay me, detested! How am I beguiled!
VIOLA
  Who does beguile you? Who does do you wrong?
OLIVIA
  Hast thou forgot thyself? Is it so long?—   145
  Call forth the holy father.   ⌜*An Attendant exits.*⌝
ORSINO, ⌜*to Viola*⌝   Come, away!
OLIVIA
  Whither, my lord?—Cesario, husband, stay.
ORSINO
  Husband?
OLIVIA   Ay, husband. Can he that deny?   150
ORSINO
  Her husband, sirrah?
VIOLA   No, my lord, not I.
OLIVIA
  Alas, it is the baseness of thy fear
  That makes thee strangle thy propriety.
  Fear not, Cesario. Take thy fortunes up.   155
  Be that thou know'st thou art, and then thou art
  As great as that thou fear'st.

               Enter Priest.

                    O, welcome, father.
  Father, I charge thee by thy reverence
  Here to unfold (though lately we intended   160
  To keep in darkness what occasion now
  Reveals before 'tis ripe) what thou dost know
  Hath newly passed between this youth and me.
PRIEST
  A contract of eternal bond of love,
  Confirmed by mutual joinder of your hands,   165
  Attested by the holy close of lips,
  Strengthened by interchangement of your rings,
  And all the ceremony of this compact

169. **Sealed . . . function:** ratified by me in my role as priest

173. **dissembling:** hypocritical

174. **a grizzle:** gray hair; **case:** skin

175. **craft:** craftiness

176. **trip:** wrestling move in which one trips one's opponent

181. **Hold little:** i.e., keep a bit of

183. **presently:** immediately

185. **Has . . . across:** i.e., he has cut my head

186. **coxcomb:** i.e., head

191–92. **incardinate:** a mistake for "incarnate"

194. **'Od's lifelings:** by God's little lives

199. **bespake . . . fair:** addressed . . . courteously

The dormouse. (3.2.18)
From Edward Topsell, *The historie of foure-footed beastes . . .* (1607).

Sealed in my function, by my testimony;
Since when, my watch hath told me, toward my   170
  grave
I have traveled but two hours.

ORSINO ⌜*to Viola*⌝
O thou dissembling cub! What wilt thou be
When time hath sowed a grizzle on thy case?
Or will not else thy craft so quickly grow   175
That thine own trip shall be thine overthrow?
Farewell, and take her, but direct thy feet
Where thou and I henceforth may never meet.

VIOLA
My lord, I do protest—

OLIVIA   O, do not swear.   180
Hold little faith, though thou hast too much fear.

Enter Sir Andrew.

ANDREW   For the love of God, a surgeon! Send one
  presently to Sir Toby.

OLIVIA   What's the matter?

ANDREW   Has broke my head across, and has given Sir   185
  Toby a bloody coxcomb too. For the love of God,
  your help! I had rather than forty pound I were at
  home.

OLIVIA   Who has done this, Sir Andrew?

ANDREW   The Count's gentleman, one Cesario. We took   190
  him for a coward, but he's the very devil incardinate.

ORSINO   My gentleman Cesario?

ANDREW   'Od's lifelings, here he is!—You broke my
  head for nothing, and that that I did, I was set on to   195
  do 't by Sir Toby.

VIOLA
Why do you speak to me? I never hurt you.
You drew your sword upon me without cause,
But I bespake you fair and hurt you not.

201. **set nothing by:** think nothing of
202. **halting:** limping
203. **in drink:** drunk
204. **tickled:** beaten; **othergates:** otherwise
206. **That's all one:** i.e., it doesn't matter
209. **set . . . morning:** perhaps, fixed in place, like the hands of a stopped clock
210. **passy-measures pavin:** perhaps a comment on the surgeon's slowness (A **pavin** is a stately dance, and the Italian word *passemezzo* means a slow tune.)
215. **dressed:** i.e., have our wounds **dressed**
216. **coxcomb:** fool; literally, the cap worn by a Fool (See picture, page 176.)
217. **gull:** dupe
220. **the . . . blood:** i.e., **my** own **brother**
221. **with wit and safety:** i.e., with reasonable regard for my safety
222. **throw . . . me:** look at me strangely (or, perhaps, coldly)
224. **even for:** precisely because of
225. **so late ago:** so recently
226. **habit:** outfit; costume, clothes
227. **A . . . perspective:** i.e., an optical illusion created naturally, without mirrors or other optical devices (*perspectives*)

ANDREW If a bloody coxcomb be a hurt, you have hurt 200
me. I think you set nothing by a bloody coxcomb.

Enter Toby and ⌜Feste, the Fool.⌝

Here comes Sir Toby halting. You shall hear
more. But if he had not been in drink, he would
have tickled you othergates than he did.

ORSINO How now, gentleman? How is 't with you? 205

TOBY That's all one. Has hurt me, and there's th' end
on 't. ⌜*To Fool.*⌝ Sot, didst see Dick Surgeon, sot?

FOOL O, he's drunk, Sir Toby, an hour agone; his eyes
were set at eight i' th' morning.

TOBY Then he's a rogue and a passy-measures pavin. I 210
hate a drunken rogue.

OLIVIA Away with him! Who hath made this havoc
with them?

ANDREW I'll help you, Sir Toby, because we'll be
dressed together. 215

TOBY Will you help?—an ass-head, and a coxcomb,
and a knave, a thin-faced knave, a gull?

OLIVIA
Get him to bed, and let his hurt be looked to.
⌜*Toby, Andrew, Fool, and Fabian exit.*⌝

Enter Sebastian.

SEBASTIAN
I am sorry, madam, I have hurt your kinsman,
But, had it been the brother of my blood, 220
I must have done no less with wit and safety.
You throw a strange regard upon me, and by that
I do perceive it hath offended you.
Pardon me, sweet one, even for the vows
We made each other but so late ago. 225

ORSINO
One face, one voice, one habit, and two persons!
A natural perspective, that is and is not!

229. **racked:** The *rack* was an instrument of torture that tore the body apart. (See picture, page 180.)

232. **Fear'st thou:** i.e., are you in doubt about

238–39. **Nor . . . everywhere:** i.e., nor do I have the power to be omnipresent, like a god

241. **Of charity:** i.e., out of kindness (i.e., please tell me)

245. **suited:** dressed

246. **suit:** clothing

249–50. **am . . . participate:** i.e., am the same flesh-and-blood creature that I've been from my birth **dimension:** bodily form **grossly:** materially **clad:** dressed **participate:** "have in common with others" (Elam)

251. **as . . . even:** i.e., since everything else fits together

A fool wearing a coxcomb. (5.1.216)
From George Wither, *A collection of emblemes . . .* (1635).

SEBASTIAN
  Antonio, O, my dear Antonio!
  How have the hours racked and tortured me
  Since I have lost thee!   230
ANTONIO
  Sebastian are you?
SEBASTIAN   Fear'st thou that, Antonio?
ANTONIO
  How have you made division of yourself?
  An apple cleft in two is not more twin
  Than these two creatures. Which is Sebastian?   235
OLIVIA Most wonderful!
SEBASTIAN, ⌜*looking at Viola*⌝
  Do I stand there? I never had a brother,
  Nor can there be that deity in my nature
  Of here and everywhere. I had a sister
  Whom the blind waves and surges have devoured.   240
  Of charity, what kin are you to me?
  What countryman? What name? What parentage?
VIOLA
  Of Messaline. Sebastian was my father.
  Such a Sebastian was my brother, too.
  So went he suited to his watery tomb.   245
  If spirits can assume both form and suit,
  You come to fright us.
SEBASTIAN   A spirit I am indeed,
  But am in that dimension grossly clad
  Which from the womb I did participate.   250
  Were you a woman, as the rest goes even,
  I should my tears let fall upon your cheek
  And say "Thrice welcome, drownèd Viola."
VIOLA
  My father had a mole upon his brow.
SEBASTIAN And so had mine.   255
VIOLA
  And died that day when Viola from her birth
  Had numbered thirteen years.

258. **record:** memory (accent on second syllable)

261. **lets:** hinders

262. **But . . . attire:** except for the male clothing I have appropriated

264. **cohere, jump:** agree

265. **That:** i.e., to demonstrate that

267. **Where:** i.e., at whose house; **maiden weeds:** woman's clothing; **gentle:** kind, courteous

269. **All . . . fortune:** i.e., **all** that has happened

271. **mistook:** mistaken

272. **nature . . . that:** i.e., nature caused your desire, mistakenly directed to Viola, to swerve to me (The **bias** is the curve that brings the ball to the desired point in the game of bowls. See picture, page 182.)

275. **maid and man:** i.e., a **man** who is a virgin

276. **right:** assuredly

277. **the glass seems true:** i.e., the **perspective** (line 227) **glass** seems to be representing the truth rather than a distortion

278. **wrack:** wreck, shipwreck; or, that which has washed up from the shipwreck

280. **like to me:** i.e., as much as you love me

281. **overswear:** i.e., swear over again

283. **that orbèd continent:** i.e., the sun (A **continent** is a container; the sun is pictured as containing **fire**.)

SEBASTIAN
  O, that record is lively in my soul!
  He finishèd indeed his mortal act
  That day that made my sister thirteen years.   260

VIOLA
  If nothing lets to make us happy both
  But this my masculine usurped attire,
  Do not embrace me till each circumstance
  Of place, time, fortune, do cohere and jump
  That I am Viola; which to confirm,   265
  I'll bring you to a captain in this town,
  Where lie my maiden weeds; by whose gentle help
  I was preserved to serve this noble count.
  All the occurrence of my fortune since
  Hath been between this lady and this lord.   270

SEBASTIAN, ⌜*to Olivia*⌝
  So comes it, lady, you have been mistook.
  But nature to her bias drew in that.
  You would have been contracted to a maid.
  Nor are you therein, by my life, deceived:
  You are betrothed both to a maid and man.   275

ORSINO, ⌜*to Olivia*⌝
  Be not amazed; right noble is his blood.
  If this be so, as yet the glass seems true,
  I shall have share in this most happy wrack.—
  Boy, thou hast said to me a thousand times
  Thou never shouldst love woman like to me.   280

VIOLA
  And all those sayings will I overswear,
  And all those swearings keep as true in soul
  As doth that orbèd continent the fire
  That severs day from night.

ORSINO   Give me thy hand,   285
  And let me see thee in thy woman's weeds.

VIOLA
  The Captain that did bring me first on shore

288. **upon some action:** as a result of legal **action**

289. **in durance:** imprisoned

291. **He . . . him:** i.e., Malvolio shall free the captain

293. **remember me:** i.e., **remember**

294. **much distract:** quite mad

295. **extracting:** distracting; **frenzy:** temporary insanity

296. **his:** i.e., Malvolio's "frenzy"

298–99. **he . . . end:** i.e., he keeps the devil at a distance **Beelzebub:** the devil

299. **Has:** i.e., he has

300–301. **today morning:** i.e., this **morning**

302. **skills not much:** makes little difference

305. **delivers:** reads the words of

310. **allow vox:** permit me to use the appropriate "voice"

313. **thus:** i.e., like a madman; **perpend:** ponder, consider

Men being "racked." (5.1.229)
From Girolamo Maggi, *De tintinnabulis liber . . . Accedit . . . De equuleo liber . . .* (1689).

Hath my maid's garments. He, upon some action,
Is now in durance at Malvolio's suit,
A gentleman and follower of my lady's.   290

OLIVIA
He shall enlarge him.

Enter ⌜Feste, the Fool⌝ with a letter, and Fabian.

               Fetch Malvolio hither.
And yet, alas, now I remember me,
They say, poor gentleman, he's much distract.
A most extracting frenzy of mine own   295
From my remembrance clearly banished his.
⌜*To the Fool.*⌝ How does he, sirrah?

FOOL   Truly, madam, he holds Beelzebub at the stave's
    end as well as a man in his case may do. Has here
    writ a letter to you. I should have given 't you today 300
    morning. But as a madman's epistles are no gos-
    pels, so it skills not much when they are delivered.

OLIVIA   Open 't and read it.

FOOL   Look then to be well edified, when the Fool
    delivers the madman. ⌜*He reads.*⌝ *By the Lord,* 305
    madam—

OLIVIA   How now, art thou mad?

FOOL   No, madam, I do but read madness. An your
    Ladyship will have it as it ought to be, you must
    allow *vox.*   310

OLIVIA   Prithee, read i' thy right wits.

FOOL   So I do, madonna. But to read his right wits is to
    read thus. Therefore, perpend, my princess, and
    give ear.

OLIVIA, ⌜*giving letter to Fabian*⌝   Read it you, sirrah. 315

FABIAN (*reads*) *By the Lord, madam, you wrong me, and*
    the world shall know it. Though you have put me into
    darkness and given your drunken cousin rule over
    me, yet have I the benefit of my senses as well as your
    Ladyship. I have your own letter that induced me to 320

321. **semblance:** appearance (i.e., smiling, with yellow stockings); **the which:** i.e., your own letter

329. **delivered:** released

330–32. **so . . . wife:** i.e., if you are willing, once we've thought more about these things, to think as well of me as a sister-in-law as you were thinking of me **as a wife**

333. **crown . . . on 't:** i.e., celebrate the **alliance** that will make us kin (i.e., you can marry Viola at the same time I marry Sebastian)

335. **at my proper cost:** i.e., **at my** expense

337. **quits:** releases

339. **mettle:** nature

340. **breeding:** upbringing

The game of bowls. (5.1.272)
From *Le centre de l'amour . . .* [1650?].

the semblance I put on, with the which I doubt not but
to do myself much right or you much shame. Think of
me as you please. I leave my duty a little unthought of
and speak out of my injury.

        The madly used Malvolio.   325

OLIVIA Did he write this?

FOOL Ay, madam.

ORSINO
 This savors not much of distraction.

OLIVIA
 See him delivered, Fabian. Bring him hither.

          ⌜*Fabian exits.*⌝

 ⌜*To Orsino.*⌝ My lord, so please you, these things   330
    further thought on,
 To think me as well a sister as a wife,
 One day shall crown th' alliance on 't, so please
    you,
 Here at my house, and at my proper cost.   335

ORSINO
 Madam, I am most apt t' embrace your offer.
 ⌜*To Viola.*⌝ Your master quits you; and for your
    service done him,
 So much against the mettle of your sex,
 So far beneath your soft and tender breeding,   340
 And since you called me "master" for so long,
 Here is my hand. You shall from this time be
 Your master's mistress.

OLIVIA, ⌜*to Viola*⌝   A sister! You are she.

     Enter Malvolio ⌜*and Fabian.*⌝

ORSINO
 Is this the madman?   345

OLIVIA   Ay, my lord, this same.—
 How now, Malvolio?

MALVOLIO   Madam, you have done me
    wrong,
 Notorious wrong.   350

353. **hand:** handwriting

354. **from it:** differently (from the way you wrote in the letter)

355. **invention:** composition

357. **in . . . honor:** i.e., with the moderation that should go with **honor**

358. **lights:** perhaps, signs

361. **lighter:** lesser

362. **acting this:** i.e., doing what you said

363. **suffered:** allowed

365. **geck, gull:** dupe

366. **invention:** i.e., plotting, scheming; **played on:** victimized

368. **the character:** my handwriting

371. **cam'st:** i.e., you came

372–73. **forms . . . were presupposed / Upon:** i.e., style . . . was prescribed for

374. **This . . . thee:** i.e., this plot has maliciously tricked you

375. **authors:** inventors

381. **wondered:** been astonished

383. **device:** scheme

384–85. **Upon . . . him:** i.e., because of some rude and ill-mannered characteristics of his that made us dislike him

OLIVIA   Have I, Malvolio? No.
MALVOLIO, ⌈*handing her a paper*⌉
  Lady, you have. Pray you peruse that letter.
  You must not now deny it is your hand.
  Write from it if you can, in hand or phrase,
  Or say 'tis not your seal, not your invention.   355
  You can say none of this. Well, grant it then,
  And tell me, in the modesty of honor,
  Why you have given me such clear lights of favor?
  Bade me come smiling and cross-gartered to you,
  To put on yellow stockings, and to frown   360
  Upon Sir Toby and the lighter people?
  And, acting this in an obedient hope,
  Why have you suffered me to be imprisoned,
  Kept in a dark house, visited by the priest,
  And made the most notorious geck and gull   365
  That e'er invention played on? Tell me why.
OLIVIA
  Alas, Malvolio, this is not my writing,
  Though I confess much like the character.
  But out of question, 'tis Maria's hand.
  And now I do bethink me, it was she   370
  First told me thou wast mad; then cam'st in smiling,
  And in such forms which here were presupposed
  Upon thee in the letter. Prithee, be content.
  This practice hath most shrewdly passed upon thee.
  But when we know the grounds and authors of it,   375
  Thou shalt be both the plaintiff and the judge
  Of thine own cause.
FABIAN   Good madam, hear me speak,
  And let no quarrel nor no brawl to come
  Taint the condition of this present hour,   380
  Which I have wondered at. In hope it shall not,
  Most freely I confess, myself and Toby
  Set this device against Malvolio here,
  Upon some stubborn and uncourteous parts
  We had conceived against him. Maria writ   385

386. **importance:** importuning, urgent request

388. **sportful:** playful; **it was followed:** i.e., the plot was carried out

389. **pluck on:** induce

392. **baffled thee:** put you to shame

395. **interlude:** comedy

399. **whirligig:** continual whirling

405. **convents:** perhaps, is convenient for all

409. **so you shall be:** i.e., that's what I'll call you

410. **habits:** clothes

411. **mistress:** (1) the woman he loves; (2) the person he obeys; **fancy's:** love's

414. **toy:** trifle

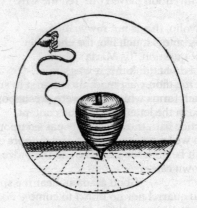

A top. (1.3.42)
From Giovanni Ferro, *Teatro d'imprese* . . . (1623).

The letter at Sir Toby's great importance,
In recompense whereof he hath married her.
How with a sportful malice it was followed
May rather pluck on laughter than revenge,
If that the injuries be justly weighed   390
That have on both sides passed.

OLIVIA, ⌜*to Malvolio*⌝
Alas, poor fool, how have they baffled thee!

FOOL Why, "some are born great, some achieve greatness, and some have greatness thrown upon them."
I was one, sir, in this interlude, one Sir Topas, sir,   395
but that's all one. "By the Lord, Fool, I am not
mad"—but, do you remember "Madam, why laugh
you at such a barren rascal; an you smile not, he's
gagged"? And thus the whirligig of time brings in
his revenges.   400

MALVOLIO
I'll be revenged on the whole pack of you! ⌜*He exits.*⌝

OLIVIA
He hath been most notoriously abused.

ORSINO
Pursue him and entreat him to a peace. ⌜*Some exit.*⌝
He hath not told us of the Captain yet.
When that is known, and golden time convents,   405
A solemn combination shall be made
Of our dear souls.—Meantime, sweet sister,
We will not part from hence.—Cesario, come,
For so you shall be while you are a man.
But when in other habits you are seen,   410
Orsino's mistress, and his fancy's queen.
⌜*All but the Fool*⌝ *exit.*

FOOL *sings*
    When that I was and a little tiny boy,
        With hey, ho, the wind and the rain,
    A foolish thing was but a toy,
        For the rain it raineth every day.   415

416. **came . . . estate:** i.e., grew up to be a man

426. **tosspots:** drunkards (The meaning of this stanza continues to be debated.)

430. **that's all one:** i.e., none of that matters

"Arion on the dolphin's back." (1.2.16)
From Sigmund, freiherr von Herberstein, *Rerum Moscouiticarum commentarij . . . Russiae . . . descriptio . . .* (1557).

But when I came to man's estate,
　　With hey, ho, the wind and the rain,
'Gainst knaves and thieves men shut their gate,
　　For the rain it raineth every day.

But when I came, alas, to wive,   420
　　With hey, ho, the wind and the rain,
By swaggering could I never thrive,
　　For the rain it raineth every day.

But when I came unto my beds,
　　With hey, ho, the wind and the rain,   425
With tosspots still had drunken heads,
　　For the rain it raineth every day.

A great while ago the world begun,
　　⌜With⌝ hey, ho, the wind and the rain,
But that's all one, our play is done,   430
　　And we'll strive to please you every day.
　　　　　　　　　　　　　　⌜*He exits.*⌝

Longer Notes

1.1.3 die: As the *Oxford English Dictionary* (*OED*) notes, the use of the verb *die* to mean "experience sexual orgasm" is "most common as a poetical metaphor in the late 16th and 17th cent[uries]." *OED* lists as its first example a passage from Shakespeare's *Much Ado About Nothing*: "CLAUDIO Nay, but I know who loves him . . . and, in despite of all, dies for him. PRINCE She shall be buried with her face upwards" (3.2.59–64). In his *Dictionary of Sexual Language* (see Further Reading, page 249), Gordon Williams provides a host of other examples from Shakespeare's period. In Thomas Kyd's play *The Spanish Tragedy* (written by 1590), responding to Bel-imperia's "life in passion dies," her would-be lover Horatio says "O stay awhile and I will die with thee, / So shalt thou yield and yet have conquered me" (2.4.47–49). In John Fletcher's play *Valentinian* (1610–14), a court pander answers a lady's declaration that "The gods shall kill me" before she will yield to seduction by the Emperor: "there's better dying, / I' th' Emperours arms" (2.5.90–91).

1.5.0 SD Feste, the Fool: In the Folio, this character, in stage directions and speech prefixes, is simply called "Clown" (an indication that the role was played by the troupe's comic actor). In dialogue, he is always called "Fool." He is at one point (in 2.4) referred to as "Feste, the jester," which leads some editors to name him "Feste" in speech prefixes and stage directions. (See Susan Snyder, "Naming Names in *All's Well That Ends Well*," *Shakespeare Quarterly* 43 [1992]: 265–79.)

Feste is a professional fool; i.e., he makes his living by entertaining his aristocratic patron and by amusing others in the household, who reward him for his **foolery** (line 13). Feste's **foolery** depends primarily on the way he uses words.

2.3.76. Cataian: As Timothy Billings demonstrates in "Caterwauling Cataians: The Genealogy of a Gloss," *Shakespeare Quarterly* 54 (2003): 1–28, Shakespeare editors long misunderstood the term **Cataian.** Beginning with George Steevens in his edition of 1773, **Cataian** was understood to be Shakespeare's racial slur against the Chinese, who are all, according to Steevens, thieves and cheats. However, as Billings reveals, the term refers not to anything Chinese but to a kind of European adventurer "who reported truly incredible marvels or promised ever-elusive riches from that ever-elusive realm of semi-fantasy," Cataia (p. 7). Hence the use of the term **Cataian** to refer to any kind of untrustworthy boaster.

2.3.91–92. mitigation or remorse: These words suggest "softening," but neither seems appropriate as used here to refer to the **voice. Mitigation** is usually applied to a lessening of violence or disease; **remorse** is a theological term that applies to the conscience of a sinner. Malvolio's language often has odd quirks that contemporary audiences might have associated with his supposed puritanism. (See line 2.3.139.)

2.5.89–90. her very *c*'s, her *u*'s, and her *t*'s . . . great *P*'s: Editors have sought significance in Shakespeare's choice of these particular letters with a view to how the choice may cast additional ridicule on the speaker, Malvolio. In **great *P*'s** they find plausible unintended reference by Malvolio to urination. In *c u t*, or *cut*, they find reference to genitalia, particularly to the pudendum. Gordon Williams (see Further Reading, p. 249) finds a passage in Nathan Field, John Fletcher, and Philip Massinger's *The Honest Man's Fortune* (1613) where through wordplay *cut* may mean both a straw and a penis, and another passage in Thomas Middleton's *A Chaste Maid in Cheapside* (1611–13) where *cut* may, again through wordplay, mean both a misfortune and a pudendum. However, these uses of *cut* depend on an elaborate context of wordplay for their reference to genitalia. *Twelfth Night* here supplies no such context, and therefore it is difficult to establish a sexual reference for *cut* in Malvolio's speech. At the same time, it is equally difficult to rule it out altogether, especially when **her very c's, her u's, and her t's** are immediately followed in the speech by her **great P's,** with the unmistakable suggestion of urination. Must we not suspect some purpose in the selection of the particular letters when Shakespeare has Malvolio refer to the letters *c, u,* and *t* even though so far Malvolio has seen only the address on the outside of the letter—**To the unknown beloved, this, and my good wishes** (lines 93–94)—in which there is no **c** to be seen? Nonetheless, it is rather embarrassing to join so many past editors by asking exactly the same question that Shakespeare gives the fool Sir Andrew: **"Her c's, her u's, and her t's. Why that?"** (line 92).

Textual Notes

The reading of the present text appears to the left of the square bracket. The earliest sources of readings not in **F,** the First Folio text (upon which this edition is based), are indicated as follows: **F2** is the Second Folio of 1632; **F3** is the Third Folio of 1663–64; **F4** is the Fourth Folio of 1685. **Ed.** is an earlier editor of Shakespeare, beginning with Rowe in 1709. No sources are given for emendations of punctuation or for corrections of obvious typographical errors, like turned letters that produce no known word. **SD** means stage direction; **SP** means speech prefix; **uncorr.** means the first or uncorrected state of the First Folio; **corr.** means the second or corrected state of the First Folio; ~ stands in place of a word already quoted before the square bracket; ʌ indicates the omission of a punctuation mark.

1.1	1.	SP *and hereafter throughout.* ORSINO] Ed.; *Duke* F (*"Duke."* or *"Du."* *throughout* F)
	10–11.	capacityʌ . . . sea, naught] ~, . . . ~. ~ F
	24.	SD *One-half line later in* F
	40.	supplied, and] ~ʌ ~ F
1.2	15.	strong] sttong F
	16.	Arion] Ed.; *Orion* F
1.3	1.	SP TOBY] F (*Sir To.*)
	7	*and throughout.* SP TOBY] F (*To.*)
	36.	moreover] moreour F
	51.	SP ANDREW] F2; *Ma.* F
	54.	Maryʌ Accost] Ed.; *Mary,* accost F
	97.	will] wlll F
	97.	curl by] Ed.; coole my F
	99.	me] F2; we F

	99.	does 't] F (dost)
	105.	Count] Connt F
	109.	swear 't] swear∧ F
	113.	kickshawses] F (kicke-chawses)
	132.	dun-colored] Ed.; dam'd colour'd F
	132.	set] Ed.; sit F
	136.	That's] F3; That F
1.4	9.	SD *one-half line earlier in* F; *Orsino*] Ed.; *Duke* F
	15.	the] rhe F
1.5	0.	SD *Feste, the Fool*] This ed.; *Clowne* F
	5	*and throughout.* SP FOOL] This ed.; *Clo.* F
	86.	gagged] F (gag'd)
	90–91.	guiltless] guiltesse F
	113.	for—here he comes—one] ∼∧ ∼∼∼. ∼ F
	114.	SD *1 line earlier in* F
	157.	peascod] F (pescod)
	165.	SD *Viola*] F2; *Violenta* F
	179.	I] F *catch-word; omit* F *dialogue*
	182.	swear∧ I] ∼) ∼ F
	204, 205.	SP OLIVIA, VIOLA] Ed.; *speech continues as Viola's in* F
	308.	County's] F (Countes)
	318.	SD *She exits.*] *Finis, Actus primus.* F
2.1	19.	heavens] Heanens F
2.2	3.	sir. On] ∼, ∼ F
	31.	our] F2; O F
	32.	made of,] Ed.; made, if F
2.3	2.	*diluculo*] Ed.; *Deliculo* F
	14.	drink. Marian] ∼∧ ∼ F
	14.	SD *Feste, the Fool*] This ed.; *Clowne* F
	24.	Queubus] *Quenbus* F
	79.	Tillyvally! "Lady"!] tilly vally. Ladie, F
	133.	Malvolio] Malnolio F
	134.	a nayword] Ed.; an ayword F
	175.	SD *1 line earlier in* F

2.4   0. SD *Orsino*] Ed.; *Duke* F
             17. boy. If] ~, ~ F
             25. masterly.] ~, F
             47. SD *Feste, the Fool*] This ed.; *Clowne* F
             60. *Fly . . . fly*] Ed.; *Fye . . . fie* F
             62. *yew*] F (*Ew*)
             97. I] Ed.; It F
2.5   59. my—some] ~∧ ~ F
             90. her] het F
            101. *Lips, do*] ~∧ ~ F
            104. altered] alter d F
            117. staniel] Ed.; stallion F
            123. portend? If] ~, ~ F
            149. *born*] Ed.; become F
            149. *achieve*] F2; atcheeues F
            158. *thee*] thce F
        161–62. *fingers. Farewell*] ~∧ ~ F
            163. *The*] tht F
        163–64. *Fortunate-Unhappy. Daylight*] ~∧ ~∧ ~ F
            165. politic] pollticke F
            181. *dear*] deero F
            190. SD *1 line earlier in* F
            200. vitae] vite F
            212. SD *They exit.*] *Exeunt. Finis Actus*
                 secnndus [*sic*] F
3.1   0. SD *Feste, the Fool*] This ed.; *Clowne* F
              8. king] F2; Kings F
              9. church] Chureh F
             58. come.] ~, F
             69. wise men, folly-fall'n] Ed.; wisemens
                 folly falne F
             72. *vous*] vou F
             93. all ready] F (already)
            152. beautiful∧] ~? F
            153. lip!] ~, F
3.2   7. thee the] F3; the F

	35. him.] ~∧ F
3.3	8. travel] rrauell F
	16. thanks; and ever thanks; and oft] Ed.;
	thankes: and euer oft F
	21. sir.] ~, F
	22. night.] ~∧ F
	32. Th' offense] Th∧ offence F
3.4	16. merry] metry F
	16. SD *2 lines earlier in* F
	21. Sad, lady?] ~∧ ~, F
	26. SP OLIVIA] F2; *Mal.* F
	60. let] ler F
	66. looked] look d F
	76. tang] langer F
	179. If] *To.* If F
	181. You . . . fit . . . for 't] Yon . . . sit . . . fot't F
	229. thee] F (the)
	274. promise, to] ~∧ ~ F
	325. SD *1 line earlier in* F
	395. O, prove true] oh proue ttue F
4.1	0. SD *Feste, the Fool*] This ed.; *Clowne* F
4.2	0. SD *Feste, the Fool*] This ed.; *Clowne* F
	6. in] in in F
12, 16, 29, 89.	Master] M. F
	15. Gorboduc] F (*Gorbodacke*)
	39. clerestories] Ed.; cleere stores F
	54. haply] F (happily)
	125. begone] be goue F
4.3	1. SP *omit* F
	37. SD *They exit.*] *Exeunt. Finis Actus Quartus.* F
5.1	0. SD *Feste, the Fool*] This ed.; *Clowne* F
	2. Master] M. F
	6. SD *Orsino*] Ed.; *Duke* F
	35. Saint] F (S.)
	188. home] homc F

191–92. incardinate] incardinatc F
   201. SD *Feste, the Fool*] This ed.; *Clowne* F,
       where SD is 2 lines earlier
   210. pavin] F (*panyn*)
   216. help?—] ~∧ F
   284. from] ftom F
   291. SD *Feste, the Fool*] This ed.; *Clowne* F,
       where SD is 2 1/2 lines later
   396. Lord] Lotd F
   412. *tiny*] F (*tine*)
417, 421, 425. *With hey, ho, the wind and the rain*] Ed.;
       with hey ho, &c. F
419, 423, 427. *For the rain it raineth every day*] Ed.; *for
       the raine, &c.* F
   428. *begun*] Ed.; *begon* F
   429. *With hey, ho, the wind and the rain*] F2
       (*which adds "With"*); *hey ho, &c.* F
   431. SD *He exits.*] FINIS. F

Twelfth Night:
A Modern Perspective

Catherine Belsey

Who is it that Olivia falls in love with?[1]

In 1.5 of *Twelfth Night*, the self-imposed seclusion of the Lady Olivia, in mourning for her brother, whose death has left her in control of an aristocratic household, is disrupted by the latest in a succession of messengers pressing the suit of Duke Orsino. This messenger, more insistent than all the others, brooks no denial and demands access to her. Olivia, curious, is equally insistent that Malvolio should describe the messenger: "What kind o' man is he? . . . What manner of man? . . . Of what personage and years is he?" (1.5.149–54). Malvolio's reply points to a certain elusiveness in the messenger's identity, defining Cesario primarily in terms of what he is not:

> Not yet old enough for a man, nor young enough for a boy—as a squash is before 'tis a peascod, or a codling when 'tis almost an apple. 'Tis with him in standing water, between boy and man. He is very well-favored, and he speaks very shrewishly. One would think his mother's milk were scarce out of him.   (1.5.155–61)

Orsino's messenger is identifiable by the traces he bears of other identities that are not his own: not quite a man, not exactly a boy; at the same time he evokes something of the feminine by his high-pitched voice, and perhaps a vestige of his mother's milk. There is a certain indeterminacy here. The veiled Olivia, traditional Petrarchan lady, aloof and mysterious, herself until now the object of Orsino's and the audience's curiosity, is caught and held by another mystery, the undecidable identity of her suitor's representative.

It is important, of course, for the audience to be reminded that Cesario is a woman in disguise, especially in an all-male theater, where the part was played by a male actor. And it is important too that we should know the disguise is effective. But this is not the first time that the play has dwelt on the elusiveness of Cesario's sexual identity. Orsino tells him:

> . . . they shall yet belie thy happy years
> That say thou art a man. Diana's lip
> Is not more smooth and rubious, thy small pipe
> Is as the maiden's organ, shrill and sound,
> And all is semblative a woman's part.

> (1.4.33–37)

Ironically, Orsino too, though he does not yet know it, is in the process of falling in love. Here again Cesario is not, we are to understand, a man. He resembles a woman, but he is not quite that either. His voice is *as* a maiden's. He is *like* Diana, goddess of chastity, perpetual virgin, who passed her time hunting in the forest and was the least stereotypically feminine of the female immortals.

Each time, some quality evades the speakers in these definitions, and the romantic comedy depends on the elusiveness of Viola-Cesario's sexual identity. Olivia falls in love with Cesario, but Viola cannot love Olivia. Orsino apparently fails to fall in love with Cesario, and Viola loves Orsino. From the point of view of the audience, this double dramatic irony, and the uncertainty about how the play will untangle the love knots it has tied, constitutes much of the pleasure of the romantic story.

The shipwrecked Viola, frustrated in her initial desire to seek employment with Olivia, resolves to present herself to Orsino as a eunuch, since she is skilled in music. (Ladies could properly become companions to other ladies, but the household of an unmarried man offered no scope for ladies-in-waiting.) In Terence's Roman comedy *The Eunuch* (almost certainly familiar to Shakespeare from the grammar-school curriculum[2]), Chaerea, defined in the English translation of 1598 as a "stripling," disguises himself in the clothes of a eunuch in order to gain entry to a household which includes the woman he loves. His value to the lady of the house is his skill in literature, athletics, and music. Once alone with the object of his desire, however, Chaerea promptly rapes her, and his cover is blown.

Terence's play thus gives very little idea of what eunuchs might usefully do once they took up residence as members of a household. Cesario's role as a eunuch is not referred to again. In practice he is treated as a page, and it is the Fool who does the singing. But something of the indeterminacy of the eunuch invests Viola to the end of the play, where Orsino continues to call her Cesario, and defers beyond the edges of the fiction the moment when she will change back into a woman's dress and become "Orsino's mistress, and his fancy's queen" (5.1.411).

While the male-female body of Cesario-Viola is repeatedly set before us by the words of the text, its undecidability would have been materially underlined for Shakespeare's audience by the body of the male actor. It is very difficult to reconstruct the experience of an audience accustomed to an all-male theater, where women's parts were always played by men or boys. Probably for much of the time the sex of the actor was irrelevant. No doubt in general the audience simply entered into the illusion created by the fiction, without forgetting, any more than we do, that it *was* an illusion. The body of Olivia, for instance, is not in question (though that role, too, was played by a boy), and her body is described as perfectly feminine in the most conventional sense: ". . . beauty truly blent, whose red and white / Nature's own sweet and cunning hand laid on" (1.5.238–39).

Orsino, meanwhile, is equally conventionally handsome. Even Olivia concedes that he is "in dimension and the shape of nature / A gracious person" (1.5.263–64). These ideal romance protagonists are in direct contrast to the grotesque bodies that surround them: Sir Toby Belch, whose name and perpetual revelry probably indicate a resemblance to the gross allegorical figure of Gluttony; Sir Andrew Aguecheek, Toby's antithesis, a puny "manikin" (3.2.52) whose thin, stringy hair "hangs like flax on a distaff" (1.3.100); and above all, of course, Malvolio, dressed up for Olivia's benefit, absurd in outmoded yellow stockings, crossgartered, and smiling relentlessly.

Each of these bodies proclaims an identity. Only Viola-Cesario's physical form specifies an enigma. Is it this which constitutes her-him as an object of desire for Olivia? Certainly Cesario's body is not a matter of indifference to Olivia:

"I am a gentleman." I'll be sworn thou art.
Thy tongue, thy face, thy limbs, actions, and spirit
Do give thee fivefold blazon. . . .
. . . How now?
. . .
Methinks I feel this youth's perfections
With an invisible and subtle stealth
To creep in at mine eyes.   (1.5.296–304)

In the event, since marriage is the issue, Viola's body will not do. Sebastian's apparently identical but this time unequivocally masculine body will prove more adequate, and equally desirable.

And yet Cesario's body is not, for Olivia, the whole story. "Thy tongue, thy face, thy limbs, actions, and spirit . . .": these are the features that both show Cesario to be a gentleman and constitute his seductive perfections. They include his behavior, his "spirit" (something much less material: a disposition, a temperament, an animating principle), and perhaps above all his "tongue," his way of speaking, probably, rather than the organ itself, Cesario's eloquence and his wit. And here too Olivia repeatedly identifies a certain elusiveness, an enigma which she tries—and fails—to resolve. Cesario begins his address to her in the grand style: "Most radiant, exquisite, and unmatchable beauty. . . ." But no sooner has he begun than he draws attention to the absurdity of such rhetoric aimed anonymously:

> I pray you, tell me if this be the lady of the house,
> for I never saw her. I would be loath to cast away
> my speech, for, besides that it is excellently well
> penned, I have taken great pains to con it.
>
> (1.5.169–72)

Cesario here speaks initially as if from the place of Orsino, whose representative he is, and then shifts, within the sentence, to the position of the messenger, comically going on to betray that the "message" is of his own making. Who, then, is the "author" of Cesario's words?

Olivia's response can be seen as an indirect attempt to elicit an answer to that question, to locate the *origin* of what Cesario says: "Whence came you, sir?"; and then, since the answer is an evasion, she asks, "Are you a comedian [an actor]?" (175, 180). Cesario denies it, naturally, but then goes on, "And yet . . . I swear I am not that I play" (181–82). Who is speaking now? Not Cesario, but Viola, of course. But is this simply the Viola who is a woman pretending to be a man? Or is it more specifically the Viola who is a substitute for Orsino, pretending on his behalf to represent him, *re-presenting* his love for Olivia, when she is herself in love with Orsino?

Cesario presses Olivia to declare herself the lady of the house, and Olivia is able to reply with a quibble that only establishes more firmly her identity in the fiction: "If I do not usurp myself, I am" (184). She speaks from a single place. But Viola occupies a whole range of subject positions in rapid succession, and perhaps it is this above all that constitutes her as an enigma, and correspondingly as an object of desire, not only for the characters in the play but also, in a sense, for the audience.

"If I did love you in my master's flame," Viola-Cesario tells Olivia, I would not acknowledge or accept your rejection. "Why," Olivia asks, "what would you?" (1.5.266–70). What does Olivia want to hear? Not about Orsino, of course, but what Cesario would do if *he* loved her. And what does the audience hear as Viola replies non-ironically, lyrically, but conditionally, about love's insistent, repetitive *naming* of the beloved?

> Make me a willow cabin at your gate
> And call upon my soul within the house,
> Write loyal cantons of contemnèd love
> And sing them loud even in the dead of night,
> Hallow your name to the reverberate hills
> And make the babbling gossip of the air
> Cry out "Olivia!"   (1.5.271–77)

Who is speaking here? Cesario, loyally affirming Orsino's love? Yes, in a sense. Or Viola declaring her own love for Orsino? Yes and no: the name that Echo repeats is "Olivia," but then Echo can only repeat the speech of another; its origin is a matter of indifference to her. Or is it a voice beyond either, which is the condition of the possibility of Orsino's love and Viola's, and of our uncertainty about which is in question here, the strangely impersonal, shared because culturally specified, and thus always in one sense *echoed* voice of love "itself"?

A similar indeterminacy informs Viola-Cesario's history of her-his father's daughter, who pined for love like Patience on a monument (2.4.122–30). It is too easy to ascribe this account to Viola herself. As a story of any unrequited love, recounted by a woman who is shown within the fiction to be exceptionally active, busy, and witty, this both is and is not Viola's own story: "I am all the daughters of my father's house, / And all the brothers, too—and yet I know not" (2.4.132–33).

Viola, who is named only once, very late in the text (5.1.253), has no fixed location in the play. Even when she speaks "in her own person"—and it is not easy to be sure when that is—the play does not always make clear where we are to find "her" identity. In this sense she acts as a figure for the desire that circulates in the play. Though Viola's own desire is constant, the desire of the others keeps moving: from Olivia to Cesario, and on to Sebastian; from Orsino to Olivia, and then on to Viola. If it finds a fixed place in Act 5, perhaps arbitrarily, that may be simply because the play must end, and romantic comedies traditionally end in marriage. The objects of desire, the play implies, are in some senses interchangeable, so that Sebastian can easily take the place of Cesario, Viola of Olivia. Love itself invests the object with value. As a love story *Twelfth Night* is remarkably unsentimental about the romances it depicts with such sympathy.

Viola's counterpart outside the love story is the Fool, who is named Feste only once (2.4.12), and who equally has no fixed place to be. He was Olivia's father's jester, but he is also to be found at Orsino's court, moving easily between the two, just as Viola does. And he too is emblematic, a figure for the folly that also circulates in the play, since "Foolery . . . does walk about the orb like the sun; it shines everywhere" (3.1.40–41). Folly motivates the world of the comic subplot. It is to be found in the late-night carousing of Sir Toby Belch and his cronies. It is especially evident in the deportment of Sir Andrew Aguecheek, the "foolish knight" who solemnly declares, "Methinks sometimes I have no more wit than a Christian or an ordinary man has. But I am a great eater of beef, and I believe that does harm to my wit" (1.3.15–16, 83–86). (It would be worth counting the number of absurdities in that utterance alone.) And folly is displayed supremely in the narcissistic posturings of Malvolio, who loves for advancement, and who knows how to do so only according to the letter.

But folly also inhabits the world of romance, or so the Fool assures us. Olivia, he argues, "will keep no Fool, sir, till she be married, and Fools are as like husbands as pilchers are to herrings: the husband's the bigger" (3.1.35–37). And yet, he slyly indicates to Cesario, the foolery of love already inhabits Olivia's house as commonly as it accompanies Orsino—and it is Cesario (ironically addressed as "your Wisdom") who provokes it: "I would be sorry, sir, but the Fool should be as oft with your master as with my mistress. I think I saw your Wisdom there" (3.1.41–43).

The Fool works with words. They are his living. He invests their carnivalesque duplicity with materiality and makes money out of them. Folly throws into relief the ways in which language is opaque rather than transparent, an end and not a means. The Fool exploits the anarchic instability of meaning, introducing by a pun, a double entendre, or an equivocation an unexpected sense which obscures what is predictable and produces unforeseen significances. To Olivia's "Take the Fool away," he replies, "Take away the Lady," and justifies his case (1.5.36–70). Words, his foolery demonstrates, live a life of their own, independent of the intentions of his interlocutors.

But in this respect, too, folly is only the degree zero of courtship, where Malvolio, at the mercy of the letter, closely resembles Sir Andrew, who actively scoops up Cesario's fine phrases in order to put them to work on his own behalf. Love's script is always already written in advance, and the lover can do no more than put together a text and a mode of behavior from the existing repertoire. Both Malvolio and Sir Andrew may be seen as parodies of Orsino in love, aimlessly punning and poeticizing in the absence of the object of his desire. "Love," Julia Kristeva proposes, "is something spoken, and it is only that: poets have always known it."[3] The play does not go quite that far, but it points to the way the world of love inhabits the world of words— and shares in the process their anarchic, unstable, arbitrary nature.

Paradoxically, it follows that the work of the Fool (like the work of the dramatist?) is highly skilled, since it takes advantage of this anarchic character without submitting to it. Moreover, foolery (like drama?) is a discipline involving a strong awareness of what is appropriate. Folly (like the stage?) is licensed to say what might not be acceptable in another mode (1.5.92– 93), but it also confronts quite stringent constraints:

> This fellow is wise enough to play the Fool,
> And to do that well craves a kind of wit.
> He must observe their mood on whom he jests,
> The quality of persons, and the time,
> And, like the haggard, check at every feather
> That comes before his eye. This is a practice
> As full of labor as a wise man's art. . . .
> (3.1.61–67)

The Fool, who is independent of the love story, draws the attention of the audience to the absurdity of love, even while the romantic narrative enlists our sympathy. By turns lyrical, sad, and ridiculous, love in *Twelfth Night* shares something of the elusiveness which characterizes the play's cross-dressed protagonist. It never settles in a single place long enough for us to feel that we have resolved its enigmas or eliminated its indeterminacies. And this is perhaps one of the effects of romantic comedy, which constantly shifts the perspective it offers its audience. The spectators of *Twelfth Night* are at one moment detached observers of love's extravagance and its self-indulgence, while at another they are invited to participate in its pains and pleasures, sharing the point of view of the fictional lovers themselves.

The truth about love, beyond its enigmas and its uncertainties, perhaps ultimately constitutes an unattainable object of desire for the audience of *Twelfth Night*. But so too, possibly does the world of the fiction itself, a world of romance and foolery, of lyric and comedy. And here it is, of course, the Fool who has the last word. As *Twelfth Night*, the culminating party of the festive Christmas season, comes to an end, as the illusory realm of Illyria, constructed primarily out of language's imaginary transparency, recedes, the Fool, alone on the stage, sings a sad song about time and winter. Here in the margins of the fiction, a figure from the world made of words that is already lost to the audience defines an alternative world of wind and rain.

But that world is also made of words. Is it, we might wonder, more, or less, substantial than the realm of desire identified as Illyria?

––––––––

1. This essay took shape in the course of conversations with Kent Cartwright, Barbara Mowat, Lena

Orlin, and Elihu Pearlman. It owes much to their insights.

2. "I believe we can say that Shakspere knew *Eunuchus,* and that of Terence's plays it was his favorite," writes T. W. Baldwin, who cites a number of allusions to *The Eunuch* in Shakespeare's work, but does not mention *Twelfth Night.* See *Shakspere's Five-Act Structure* (Urbana: University of Illinois Press, 1947), pp. 544–78, esp. p. 576.

3. Julia Kristeva, *Tales of Love,* trans. Leon S. Roudiez (New York: Columbia University Press, 1987), p. 277.

Further Reading

Twelfth Night,
or,
What You Will

In addition to the following books and articles,
see www.folger.edu/Shakespeare and
www.folger.edu/online-resources.

Abbreviations: *Ado = Much Ado About Nothing;*
AWW = All's Well That Ends Well; AYLI = As You Like
It; Err. = The Comedy of Errors; 1 and *2H4 = Henry IV,*
Parts 1 and *2; Ham. = Hamlet; Lear = King Lear;*
MM = Measure for Measure; MND = A Midsummer
Night's Dream; MV = The Merchant of Venice;
Oth. = Othello; Per. = Pericles; Shr. = The Taming of
the Shrew; Temp. = The Tempest; TN = Twelfth Night;
Tro. = Troilus and Cressida; WT = The Winter's Tale

Barber, C. L. "Testing Courtesy and Humanity in
Twelfth Night." Chapter 10 in *Shakespeare's Festive
Comedy: A Study of Dramatic Form and Its Relation to
Social Custom,* pp. 240–61. Princeton: Princeton University Press, 1959. (Reprinted, with a foreword by Stephen Greenblatt, 2011.)

Barber's well-known essay treats the festive spirit
implied in the play's title. He examines *TN*'s different
groups of characters in light of a structural formula
that moves "through release" (the revels that separate
holiday "misrule" from the restrictions of everyday life)
"to clarification" ("a heightened awareness of the relation between man and 'nature'—the nature celebrated

213

on holiday"). Barber argues that *TN* explores the powers in human nature that make good the risks of social courtesy and liberty displayed in Viola/Cesario. In the world of Illyria, the presence of Malvolio, the play's refuser of festivity, is appropriate, for he acts as a foreign body that must be expelled by laughter. The chapter has four parts: (1) " 'A most extracting frenzy' " (which focuses on "madness" as a key word in *TN*); (2) " 'You are betroth'd both to a maid and man' " (wherein Barber discusses Shakespeare's use of Viola's disguise as a boy to exploit the play's emphasis on sexual difference); (3) "Liberty Testing Courtesy" (which explores the folly of misrule in *TN*'s "exhibition of the use and abuse of social liberty"); and (4) "Outside the Garden Gate." This final section attends briefly to the plays that follow *TN*: namely, the problem comedies *MM* and *AWW* (wherein release leads not to folly but to "the vicious or contemptible") and the tragedy *Ham.* (which "moves into regions where the distinction between madness and sanity begins to break down, to be recovered only through violence," not laughter. After *TN*, comedy "is always used in [a] subordinate way: saturnalian moments, comic counterstatements, continue to be important resources of [Shakespeare's] art, but their meaning is determined by their place in a larger movement." Feste may suggest that he "has been over the garden wall into some such world as the Vienna of *MM*," but *TN* remains "merry in a deep enough way" to justify its classification as a "festive comedy." [Stephen Greenblatt's foreword to the 2011 reprint of Barber's prize-winning book emphasizes the enduring legacy of *Shakespeare's Festive Comedy*.]

Belsey, Catherine. "Disrupting Sexual Difference: Meaning and Gender in the Comedies." In *Alternative Shakespeares*, edited by John Drakakis, pp. 166–90. London: Methuen, 1985.

Belsey draws on poststructuralist and feminist criticism to argue for meaning in Shakespeare's comedies
as relational, "as unfixed, always in process, always plural." By disrupting sexual difference—that is, by "calling
in question that set of relations between terms which
proposes as inevitable an antithesis between masculine
and feminine"—the romantic comedies radically challenge patriarchal values. Belsey discusses this disruption in the context of two distinct meanings of "family"
in the sixteenth and seventeenth centuries: family as
dynasty and family as "private realm of warmth and
virtue." The gap between the two provides a glimpse of
"a mode of being, which is not a-sexual, nor bisexual,
but which disrupts the system of differences on which
sexual stereotyping depends." Pursuing the way *TN*
unfixes gender distinctions of the period toward comic,
romantic ends, Belsey looks closely at the exchange
between Orsino and Viola/Cesario in 2.4.114–33. The
passage demonstrates how female transvestism, so
popular in Shakespeare's romantic comedies, "can, on
the surface, appear to reaffirm patriarchal values, but,
on closer reading, can also challenge them by unsettling the categories which legitimate [patriarchy]." In
the passage in question, Viola's male disguise indicates
that "it is possible, at least in fiction, to speak from a
position which is not that of a full, unified, gendered
subject." In other words, plays like *TN* can be read "as
posing at certain critical moments the simple, but in
comedy unexpected, question, 'Who is speaking?'" As
to "who tells the blank history of Viola's father's pin-
ing daughter . . . [t]he answer is neither Viola nor
Cesario, but a speaker who at this moment occupies
a place which is not precisely masculine or feminine,
where the notion of identity itself is disrupted to display a difference within subjectivity, and the singularity which resides in *this* difference." Belsey contends

that of all Shakespeare's comedies "it is perhaps *TN* which takes the most remarkable risks with the identity of its central figure," for it is only in *TN* that the protagonist specifically says, "I am not what I am" (3.1.148), "where 'seem' would have scanned just as well and preserved the unity of the subject." This disruption of sexual polarities, however, cannot be sustained: "With the heroine abandoning her disguise and dwindl[ing] into a wife[,] . . . closure depends on closing off the glimpsed transgression and reinstating a clearly defined sexual difference. But the plays are more than their endings, and the heroines become wives only after they have been shown to be something altogether more singular—because more plural." [The essay is frequently referenced in *TN* scholarship. For a contrasting view of gender difference in *TN,* one that underscores fixity, see Barber, above; for a reading of the cross-dressed Viola as less liberating and therefore less challenging of the patriarchal order, see Howard, below.]

Findlay, Alison, and Liz Oakley-Brown, eds. *Twelfth Night: A Critical Reader.* London: Bloomsbury Arden, 2014.

This collection consists of an introduction and eight new essays: (1) "The Critical Backstory" (R. S. White), (2) "Performance and Adaptation" (Linda Anderson), (3) "The State of the Art" (William C. Carroll), (4) " 'Ready to distrust mine eyes': Optics and Graphics in *Twelfth Night*" (Keir Elam), (5) "Shipwreck and the Hermeneutics of Transience in *Twelfth Night*" (Randall Martin), (6) "'Let them use their talents': *Twelfth Night* and the Professional Comedian" (Andrew McConnell Stott), (7) "Inverted Commas around the 'Fun': Music in *Twelfth Night*" (Tiffany Stern), and (8) "Learning and Teaching Resources" (Peter Kirwan). In their intro-

duction, Findlay and Oakley-Brown consider ways
in which the "poised indeterminacy" of *TN* "speaks
to its own period of production and to twenty-first-
century English political and pedagogical discourses
in striking ways." White's "critical backstory" moves
from John Manningham's contemporary eyewitness
account in 1602 through subsequent commentary in
the seventeenth and eighteenth centuries, the romantic era (1789–1836), and the Victorian period (1837–
1901) to the twentieth century's interest in new and
old historicism, psychoanalytic studies, and feminist
and gender analyses. Complementing White's essay is
Carroll's detailed overview of criticism from 2000 to
2014 arranged under the following headings: "Gender/
Sexuality Studies," "Geography," "Madness, Malvolio
and Puritanism," "Feste, Festivity and Fooling," "Inter-
textuality," "Social and Economic Contexts," and
"Words and Music." Carroll singles out Keir Elam's
Arden 3 edition of the play as exerting the dominant
influence over post-millennial criticism. Anderson's
survey of stage productions, film and television treatments, and adaptations (theatrical, cinematic, and
novelistic) leads her to suggest that *TN* "may be the
Shakespearean play most often rearranged in performance." She concludes that our discomfort with *TN*'s
focus on "service and class in Shakespeare's world" has
led to our turning "the play's 'balance' upside down,"
with directors giving "the tough-minded Elizabethan
social comedy" an "autumnal" or "Chekhovian" tone
"somewhere between melancholy and despair." Elam's
essay, the first of four heralding "New Directions" in
analysis, examines *TN*'s "dazzling display of optical illu-
sions and allusions to the processes of visual percep-
tion" in light of the early seventeenth century's interest
in optical and graphical phenomena; for Elam, *TN*
("probably Shakespeare's most intensely visual play")

is a large-scale "iconotext [that] strategically places the verbal and the visual [in] an often difficult and dangerous intercourse." Martin's essay probes the significance of two conflicting concepts of time—eschatological and diachronic—for our understanding of holiday and shipwreck in the play, while Stern's focuses on the role of music in adding melancholy to the generally festive themes of *TN*, and Stott's considers both Feste's status as a professional (i.e., paid) comedian and the professional context for comedy not only in *TN* but in early modern England in general. Finally, Kirwan's pedagogically oriented guide to readings and materials for researching and teaching the play finds its "proximity" to other Shakespeare texts a useful tool for better understanding *TN*; his guide gives special attention to "recent theoretical and popular interest in corporeality and spatiality."

Forman, Valerie. "Stasis and Insularity in *The Merchant of Venice* and *Twelfth Night*." Chapter 1 in *Tragicomic Redemptions: Global Economics and the Early Modern English Stage*, pp. 27–63, esp. 47–63. Philadelphia: University of Pennsylvania Press, 2008.

Forman's book deals with the tension between profit and loss as it was negotiated in early modern economic theory and on the early modern English stage at a time (the final decades of the sixteenth century and the early decades of the seventeenth) when England's economy was becoming increasingly global. The author discerns a parallel between new economic practices that "required the English to reconceptualize loss itself as something productive" and the genre of tragicomedy, a dramatic classification caught up in the opposition of two genres—one "that foregrounds [redemptive] loss, and the other [static] resolution." In the chapter on *TN*, which appears in Part I under the heading "Tragicomedy and Generic Expansion," Forman focuses her socioeconomic reading on two actions that involve the flow of money: Viola's investment of a bounteous payment to the sea captain for the purchase of new clothing (1.2.55–67) and the migrations of Antonio's purse, which "has a history" (3.3.28–30, 35–39; 3.4.345, 351, 356; 5.1.47–55, 56–59, 65, 88): it "represents what was stolen from Orsino—stolen, the play repeatedly suggests, in an act of piracy." The initial shipwreck and exchange of female apparel for male garments in conjunction "with a purse filled with money taken outside of Illyria's boundaries and then brought back within them . . . materialize the concerns surrounding England's economy of foreign trade." Chief among those concerns were "piracy's potential to inhibit trade" and the depletion of national resources by emptying English coffers in the pursuit of (uncertain) profits. Forman contends that *TN* "suppresses its material contexts and those of its literary sources" to create a "safely insular" and "static" economy. Whereas tragicomic plays like *Per.* and *WT* imagine the possibility of rematerializing losses as gains, *TN* "disavows the very conflicts that are at its center; the play thus loses the opportunity to imagine that profits can be made out of the losses the play earlier sustains." Calling the play a "stepping-stone to tragicomedy," Forman concedes that part of what is lost may be found again at the end of Act 5, but "what is found does not exceed what is lost": "Antonio's purse is never returned; the Captain who saved Viola is imprisoned; Malvolio's fantasy of social mobility is refused; and Viola's wedding to Orsino is deferred" (her female attire yet to be recovered). Forman's approach to *TN* suggests "the exceptional place of dramatic form as a participant in the newly emerging, public discourse of economic theory." [The chapter incorporates part of "Material Dispossessions and Counterfeit Investments: The Economies of *Twelfth Night*," in *Money and the Age of Shakespeare: Essays in New Economic Criticism*, edited by Linda Woodbridge (New York: Palgrave Macmillan, 2003), pp. 113–27.]

Gay, Penny. "*Twelfth Night*: Desire and Its Discontents." In *As She Likes It: Shakespeare's Unruly Women*, pp. 17–47. London: Routledge, 1994.

Gay's discussion of major postwar English stage productions focuses on the various ways in which the "unruly women" at the center of five Shakespeare comedies (*TN*, *AYLI*, *Shr.*, *MM*, and *Ado*) have been "embodied" in performance. Central to this feminist study are two questions: (1) How do gender politics affect the staging of the plays in question? and (2) How is gender "represented, both in the text and on the stage?" While Gay's focus is on the portrayals of Viola and Olivia, she also notes choices in the performances of Orsino and changes in the representation of Malvolio (who shifts from the "traditional puritanical killjoy" into "a disturbing image of the madman who cannot reconcile his sexual fantasies and the realities of his class position"). In *TN*, gender "becomes an ever more unstable mask": Viola "always exists in the margins between genders," and Orsino and Olivia play against male and female stereotypical conventions. The biological impossibility that Viola and Sebastian are identical twins enables a fantasy of sexual indeterminacy, i.e., that one can be both male and female, man and maid. Using theater reviews, promptbooks, directorial notes, and the recollections of actors and directors, Gay explores this "fluid sexuality" in Stratford-upon-Avon productions spanning the years 1955 to 1987: John Gielgud's (1955), Peter Hall's (1958), Clifford Williams's (1966), John Barton's (1969), Peter Gill's (1974), Terry

Hands's (1979), John Caird's (1983), and Bill Alexander's (1987). She argues that the play's many images of "the mobility of desire" became a prominent theme on the stage "in response to the 'sexual revolution' of the 1960s and 1970s" (e.g., the *"frisson* of unorthodox sexual play" in the relation between Olivia and Viola in Hall, and the "barely controlled eroticism" between Orsino and Viola in Williams). In the more conservative atmosphere of the 1980s, stagings of *TN* became darker, with desire being repressed (sometimes, as in Alexander, even "corrupted into sadism"); in these productions (as foreshadowed by Hands's "exploration of masculinity"), "love [was] difficult, . . . sex [was] egotistic greed, laughter . . . cruel, and any beauty [was] fraught with melancholy or danger." Gay concludes that in the latter half of the twentieth century, audiences were "invited to contemplate a changing image of 'woman', for whom a refusal of the codes of femininity offer[ed] exciting possibilities for the liberation of physical, psychic and erotic energy. But whether the heroines' transvestism or other disguise . . . is protective, evasive, empowering, or simply a game depends on the perceived relation between women and the patriarchy at the moment of the play's embodiment."

Greenblatt, Stephen. "Fiction and Friction." In *Shakespearean Negotiations*, pp. 66–93. Berkeley: University of California Press, 1988.

Representing "a quantum leap in complexity from earlier thematic readings" of the play (see William Carroll's essay in the Findlay and Oakley-Brown collection annotated above, pp. 73–74), Greenblatt's new historicist study made *TN* a key text in subsequent criticism relating to embodiment, gender fluidity, transvestism, and boy actors in the roles of women. The author begins with a Montaigne travel anecdote that Shakespeare "almost, but not quite, retells"; the account of several young girls who in late sixteenth-century France decided to dress as males and continue their lives newly gendered becomes one of those "shadow stories that haunt Shakespeare's plays." Greenblatt singles out the bowling image ("bias") in Sebastian's words of assurance to Olivia at 5.1.271–75 to focus his argument that "swerving" is not random in *TN* but central to its structural design and its "spectacle of homoerotic desire." ("Bias" is the curve that brings the ball to its desired goal in the game of bowls; see gloss to 5.1.272 and picture on page 182 in this edition.) In *TN*, success "lies in a strategic, happy swerving" that enables Olivia to take comfort in knowing that she is "betrothed both to a maid and a man." Exploring his sense that *TN* forever skirts illicit, homosexual desire, Greenblatt traces the course of the "swerving" necessary to avert social, theological, and legal disaster. By historicizing the sexual nature of Shakespeare's work within other social discourses of the body (such as medical tracts and marriage manuals), Greenblatt establishes that since women were understood "to be inverted mirror images of men in their very genital structure," there would be an inherent homoeroticism in all sexuality, although consummation of desire could be licitly figured only in the love of a man and a woman. It is this "mobility of desire" upon which the "delicious confusions of [*TN*] depend." The open secret of identity—"that within differentiated individuals is a single structure, identifiably male"—is presented literally in the all-male cast, empowering "the transvestite performances" of the boy actors. Greenblatt deliberately writes "presented" and not "represented," for the play "cannot continue without the fictive existence of two distinct genders and the friction between them." In the course of his essay, Greenblatt specifically relates

Shakespeare's "erotically charged sparring that is the heart of the lovers' experience" to the sexual friction or "chafing" discussed in contemporary anatomical theories. [The essay, which first appeared in *Reconstructing Individualism: Autonomy, Individuality, and the Self in Western Thought*, edited by Thomas C. Helle, Morton Sosner, and David E. Wellerby (Stanford: Stanford University Press, 1986, pp. 30–52), is reprinted in R. S. White's collection, below.] [For related studies see Belsey, above, and Howard, Johnston, and Maslen, below.]

Howard, Jean E. "Crossdressing, the Theatre, and Gender Struggle in Early Modern England." *Shakespeare Quarterly* 39 (1988): 418–40.

In the first part of this materialist-feminist study, which remains a groundbreaking contribution to the play's scholarship, Howard discusses how preachers' and polemicists' attacks on cross-dressing during the 1580–1620 period signaled a sex-gender system under pressure. Because it blurred gender differences, the practice was seen as a threat to the norms of male power at the core of early modern England's patriarchal society. In the second half of the essay, Howard turns to the theaters, where, collectively, cross-dressing texts "play a role in producing and managing anxieties about women . . . who are not 'in their places,' . . . and in managing anxieties about the fragility of male authority." The plays she examines—Shakespeare's *TN*, *MV*, and *AYLI*, along with Jonson's *Epicoene* and Middleton and Dekker's *The Roaring Girl*—emerge as "sites of social struggle conducted through discourse, and they were produced in a cultural institution that was itself controversial and ideologically volatile." Cross-dressing, as Howard observes, functioned with more variety on the stage than in the world at large, not always serving as a vehicle of hierarchical interrogation. *TN* is a good example of this variety, as it is Olivia, not the cross-dressed Viola, who powerfully challenges the patriarchal social order (see, e.g., her rejection of marriage in general and Orsino in particular in Act 1, her aggressive pursuit of Cesario and later Sebastian, and her efficient and authoritative management of her household [4.3.16–21]). Far less subversive is Viola, who assumes the male disguise of Cesario as a psychological "holding place," not as a political act of protest "against gender inequities." Moreover, the driving force of the plot is to liberate Viola from a disguise she views as a "wickedness" (2.2.27), so that by the end of Act 5 she may "return to her proper and natural position as wife," when "her biological identity, her gender identity, and the semiotics of dress will coincide." Howard reads Olivia as "the real threat" to the hierarchical gender system in *TN*; Viola, whose female subjectivity is never in doubt, is "but an *apparent* threat." [For different readings of the cross-dressed Viola, see Belsey and Greenblatt, above. Howard's frequently cited article is incorporated into the chapter titled "Power and Eros: Crossdressing in Dramatic Representation and Theatrical Practice" in her book *The Stage and Social Struggle in Early Modern England* (London: Routledge, 1994), pp. 94–128.].

Hurworth, Angela. "Gulls, Cony-Catchers and Cozeners: *Twelfth Night* and the Elizabethan Underworld." *Shakespeare Survey* 52 (1999): 120–32.

Unlike Ben Jonson, who was the period's principal exponent of cozenage in dramatic texts, Shakespeare rarely makes use of gulling on a grand scale in his plays. A major exception is *TN*, a text "replete with gullings, albeit of different degrees and durations." Even the word "gull," so infrequent in the canon, is applied to two characters (Malvolio, 3.2.67; 5.1.365;

and Sir Andrew Aguecheek, 5.1.217), and another is a "noble gull-catcher" (Maria, 2.5.191). Hurworth's focus is the gulling of Malvolio, which, though technically the subplot, has become over the centuries the "comic highlight, if not the center, of the play." She reads *TN* in the context of contemporary narratives of rogue/underworld literature, "where such deception known as cony-catching, cozenage or gulling, receives its fullest treatment." Common to this body of literature is the treatment of gulling as "an essentially ludic activity, and, as such, rule-bound." Hurworth focuses on similarities in diction, syntax, imagery, and theatricality to show "how the definition of gulling as a game with rules influences the configuration of the gulling in [*TN*]." Commonalities include the following: references to trickery as sport (2.3.170; 2.5.184, 201; 5.1.388); the cony-catching model of three or four tricksters tasked with luring the victim to the bait and setting him on (Maria, Sir Toby, Andrew, and Feste/ Fabian); the feature of the gamer being gamed by his own stratagems (see Toby's desire to end the matter quickly at 4.2.70–74 and his injuries at the hands of Sebastian [5.1.185–218]); and, perhaps most important, the figurative transformation of the victim into an animal species (see Malvolio's "metamorphosis into a whole range of native woodland animals" in 2.5). Hurworth concludes by noting how the trajectory of Malvolio's gulling takes a grimmer turn when it moves from the hilarity and initial harmlessness of the yellow stockings sequence (2.3.134; 2.5; 3.4.17–90) to the "savage, vengeful" cozenage of the dark house scene (4.2). By the time Malvolio issues his call for revenge, we see that "gulling has taken comedy to its limit." Shakespeare will explore the tragic potential of gulling in *Othello*, which Hurworth views as a "difference of emphasis, not essence."

Jensen, Phebe. "Falstaff in Illyria: The Second Henriad and *Twelfth Night*." Chapter 4 in *Religion and Revelry in Shakespeare's Festive World*, pp. 149–93, esp. 165–93. Cambridge: Cambridge University Press, 2008.

In her study of the relationship between traditional festive pastimes (e.g., Midsummer pageants, May games, and Whitsuntide celebrations) and Shakespeare's plays, Jensen argues for Shakespeare as "a festive traditionalist who not only acknowledges the relationship between traditional pastimes, stage plays, and religious controversy, but also aligns his own work"—"on aesthetic though not theological grounds"—"with festive energies identified with the old religion." Whereas Barber's pioneering work on Shakespeare and festive comedy stressed the political and social meanings of early modern festivity (see the Barber item above), Jensen "seeks to restore a sense of the devotional issues surrounding festivity" to our understanding of early modern culture. Reading *TN* in the context of "recent controversies over the role of religion in Shakespeare's theater, as well as the particular place of Catholicism in Shakespeare's work and world," she argues that Falstaff "haunts" the play, the Henriad's Lord of Misrule reconfigured as both Sir Toby and Feste: "[*TN*'s] consideration of Puritan satire, Catholic satire, the history of festivity and theater, and alehouse revelry, represents a return to the not-quite-dead Oldcastle controversy, spinning into a new configuration issues raised both in *1H4* and in the Admiral's Men's rewriting of Falstaff in their own Oldcastle play." Jensen discusses at length *TN*'s two mock exorcisms of Malvolio: the first is presided over by Sir Toby (3.4.91–134), the second by Feste (4.2). Taken together, they "merge the energies of 'stage' and 'pastime' with religion"; as "sham performances," however, they produce "hilarity and humiliation, not spiritual enlightenment." The chapter also considers how *TN* provides "meta-theatrical commentary" on Shakespeare's new (and more courtly) clown, Robert Armin, placing him in a "lineage of the stage fool" that extends back through Will Kemp to Richard Tarlton. *TN* "insists on continuity" not only between those three actors but also "between the professional theater and the tradition of raucous festive misrule and improvisation that they continued and transformed." In its embrace of old-fashioned ideas about festivity that lived "by the church" (3.1.3–7), *TN* "rejects the association of festive revelry with Catholic corruption promoted" in many contemporary celebrations of Friar Tuck–like figures; instead, the Shakespeare text presents "a complex vision of 'cakes and ale' that is at once nostalgic and contemporary, and that explores the unfolding of devotionally based festivity in the context of the largely secular professional theater of early modern England." For Jensen, *TN* is further evidence of her overall thesis: "[T]hematically, generically, ideologically, and above all theatrically, Shakespeare's festive world registered the ongoing disputes set in motion by the English Reformation."

Johnston, Mark Albert. "Shakespeare's *Twelfth Night* and the Fertile Infertility of Eroticized Early Modern Boys." *Modern Philology* 114 (2017): 573–600.

Viola's initial plan of seeking employment as a eunuch in Orsino's household, a plan that is subsequently modified to the position of page, leads Johnston to ask two questions: (1) Why does Orsino find the eunuch/page Cesario an appropriate emissary of love to Olivia? and (2) What is the basis for the "boy's" great appeal to both Olivia and Orsino? To answer these questions, Johnston investigates early modern adult sexual relations and attitudes toward servile boys and eunuchs as found in the discourse of the period: songs, ballads, poems, medical treatises, trial records, and plays. What he discovers is "an underestimated early modern discursive tradition augmenting the history of eroticism: the sexual pursuit of subordinate, sterile boys by powerful, libidinous women." A subordinate boy—"in early modern English parlance, 'boy' signaled male inferiority"—might be found "erotically appealing precisely because of his sexual availability, inferiority, and impotence—his mimicking, in effect, an . . . infertile dildo" (i.e., an artificial phallus). Among the texts Johnston cites are Shakespeare's *Venus and Adonis*, in which the "lovesick queen" pursues the "tender," "young," and "gentle boy" like "a bold-faced suitor" (lines 175, 32, 187, 403, 6), and Shakespeare's Sonnet 20, "which ultimately suggests that the beloved boy's erotic value inheres not in his regenerative promise" but in "his tantalizing ability to provoke and gratify female lust." Turning specifically to *TN*, Johnston argues that "Viola's eunuch-cum-page boy disguise does not undo [as Stephen Orgel suggests in *Impersonations* (Cambridge: Cambridge University Press, 1996), p. 54] but ironically proliferates her sex appeal, thereby positioning her at the center, rather than the margins of the world of love and wooing." In Malvolio's description of the unbearded (i.e., reproductively impotent) Cesario (1.5.155–61), images of immature fruits and vegetables, the inversion of "codpiece" in "peascod," the diminutive "codling," and the final figuring of the page as "filled with milk rather than fertile fluid . . . construe Cesario as boy, dildo, and eunuch simultaneously." Such a "nexus of association" makes it credible that Orsino deems Cesario the ideal emissary for awakening Olivia's sexual desires (1.4.28–30), and that Olivia "subsequently reacts not as if Cesario's lack presents any impediment to erotic union but rather as if his insufficiencies offer irresistible enticement thereto." Neither Olivia (1.5.302–4) nor Orsino (1.4.33–39) perceives Cesario's "unripe status" an imperfection; for both it is viewed as "aptness." Orsino's plan backfires, however, because he fails to foresee that Olivia will view the "boy/eunuch" not as a "mere supplement" to Orsino himself but as the perfect substitute for him. Johnston suggests that if we are to expand our understanding of the history of eroticism, topics like the one he discusses require further critical attention.

Maslen, R. W. "*Twelfth Night,* Gender, and Comedy." In *Early Modern English Drama: A Critical Companion,* edited by Garrett A. Sullivan Jr., Patrick Cheney, and Andrew Hadfield, pp. 130–39. New York: Oxford University Press, 2006.

In this overview of *TN*, Maslen examines the play's "unsettling emphasis on time, change, and confusion [specifically in relation to self-identity]." Addressing the "uncertainties associated with [early modern] constructions of masculinity, femininity, and erotic attraction of all kinds"—particularly as manifest in the plot device of cross-dressing and the theatrical practice of boy actors in female roles—Maslen demonstrates the illusory nature of normalcy in a play wherein "women are mistaken for men, men . . . for women disguised as men, and definitions of manhood and womanhood themselves called into question." The play's "trio of articulate women" exploits the patriarchal fantasy of submissive, quiet, and patient womanhood for their own purposes, none of them content to have her "history" become the "blank" of Viola/Cesario's fictive sister (2.4.122–27). If we understand *TN* as dramatizing the stalemate that occurs when male-female relationships are understood in terms of male fantasies (of ideal womanhood, ideal manhood, and ideal male friendship), then "interaction between the genders depends on the discovery of a third way, to which the boy/girl Viola/Cesario offers a beguiling key": "Neither male nor female, neither man nor boy, and in the end neither servant nor master, [Cesario] is a kind of riddle, a pun . . . in human form, testifying to the power of comedy as a means of disrupting settled notions and complicating illusory certainties." The boy actor playing the part of Viola/Cesario further demonstrates that identity need not be "fixed or trapped in a single mode of being." By having Orsino continue to call Viola "Cesario" after the revelations in 5.1, Shakespeare "preserv[es] our sense of their relationship as a love affair between men as well as between man and woman." Declaring *TN* "a paean to change," with Viola as "its presiding spirit, embodying the transitions that are always in process in the human body and mind," Maslen concludes that *TN*'s "golden time" (5.1.405) "makes it possible to believe that there is no such thing as a stable normality where gender is concerned, either in Elizabethan times or in our own."

Massai, Sonia, ed. *William Shakespeare's Twelfth Night: A Sourcebook*. Routledge Guides to Literature. New York: Routledge, 2007.

Massai divides this sourcebook into four sections: Contexts, Interpretations, Key Passages, and Further Reading. Following a brief contextual overview of "marriage and fantasies of social mobility," the first section provides snippets from contemporary documents relating to friendship, marriage, gender and clothing, androgyny and homoeroticism, and Petrarchan conventions. The section on interpretations deals with both critical views and performance history. Here Massai includes excerpts from critical accounts spanning the years 1753–1996 and covering such topics as language and myth, the "darkening of Shakespeare's festive comedy," and "power, class and carnivalesque disorder"; she follows a concise survey of the play's stage and screen life with excerpts from performance-related studies of particular issues (e.g., men in women's clothing, performance editions, and Malvolio's "metamorphosis . . . from comic butt to tragic gull") and commentary on specific productions from 1602 to 2002. In section 3, Massai selects certain passages for brief analysis: 1.1 (Orsino in love), 1.3.1–14 (Quaffing and drinking I), 1.4 (Viola in love), 1.5.137–305 (Olivia in love); 2.1 (Antonio in love), 2.2.17–41 (Knots, tangles, and love triangles), 2.3.1–123 (Quaffing and drinking II), 2.4.15–47 and 80–137 (Viola/Cesario's sister in love), 2.5.1–190 (Malvolio in love); 3.1.1–69 (Folly and foolery); and 5.1.56–134, 219–94, and 367–431 ("This most happy wreck"). Further reading suggestions are grouped under the following headings: recommended editions, collections of essays and casebooks, contexts, recent critical interpretations, and production history.

Novy, Marianne. "Outsiders and the Festive Community in *Twelfth Night*." Chapter 2 in *Shakespeare and Outsiders*, pp. 47–68. Oxford Shakespeare Topics. Oxford: Oxford University Press, 2013.

In contrast to the mythic/psychoanalytic approach of Leslie Fiedler in *The Stranger in Shakespeare* (1972), Novy draws on social, economic, and political history to examine representations of difference and exclusion in *MV*, *TN*, *Oth.*, *Lear*, and (briefly) *Temp*. In *TN*, she concentrates on Malvolio and Antonio as the play's two central outsiders and, in a section titled "Whirligigs and Mirrors," addresses the comedy's elaborate network of parallels that link the two figures to others in the play, thus rendering the "outsider" label ambiguous. Unlike Shylock's in *MV*, Malvolio's isolation is rooted not in his religious difference—"the ambiguity about whether [Malvolio] is a puritan [2.3.139, 145–46] is partly because of the ambiguity" surrounding the concept of puritan for an early modern audience—but in his hostility to the festive spirit of comedy embodied in Sir Toby, Sir Andrew Aguecheek, Maria, and Feste. Factors obscuring Malvolio's status as an outsider include explicit suggestions that the punishment is not only excessive but has gone on for too long (Toby's 4.2.70–75); Olivia's expression of emotional kinship with her steward (3.4.6–8; 5.1.294–96) and voiced sympathy for him (3.4.67–69; 5.1.373–77, 392, 402); and Orsino's desire to placate him so that he will return and thus expedite their wedding plans (5.1.403–7). For all the "seeming scapegoating" of Olivia's steward, the community needs him back. Among the mirror images of Malvolio that qualify his classification as an outsider are Orsino and Olivia (both guilty of self love), Sir Andrew (another ridiculous suitor), and Feste ("as a dependent in a court, and as one the play most clearly shows [to be] a solitary character"). With respect to Antonio, Novy links him to the feelings of Orsino and Olivia for Viola/Cesario, thus placing him firmly "inside the [play's] strong homoerotic temper." Novy suggests that there could even be a place for Antonio in Olivia's household given Sebastian's warm rediscovery of his loyal friend at 5.1.228–30. As the play concludes, Aguecheek may be the only undisputed outsider; his dashed hopes for winning Olivia, coupled with Sir Toby's tirade, isolate him from the concluding bliss. "While some theorists . . . maintain that comedy needs outsiders because a society needs [them] to define itself against by laughing at them, some theatre practitioners are staging plays to encourage identification with more outsiders, even if, as with Andrew, the audience may laugh a lot at them before they sympa-

thize." Novy reminds her reader that Malvolio's ulti-
mate revenge may lie in his "becoming for centuries
the most popular role in the play."

Paster, Gail Kern. *Humoring the Body: Emotions and
the Shakespearean Stage*. Chicago: University of Chicago Press, 2004.
    Paster draws on the second-century physician
Galen's theory of the four humors—blood, choler,
melancholy, and phlegm—to present "a new way of
interpreting the emotions of the early modern stage."
She uses moral treatises, medical texts, natural histories, and early modern drama (primarily plays from
the Shakespeare canon) to identify "a historical phe-
nomenology in the language of affect by underscoring
the significance of the four humors as the language of
embodied emotion." These humors and "their attri-
butes of hot, cold, wet, and dry carried enormous emotional, psychological, and . . . ecological significance."
(By *ecological*, Paster means the "psychophysiological
reciprocity between the experiencing subject and his
or her relation to the world.") In chapter 4, "Belching
Quarrels: Male Passions and the Problem of Individu-
ation," Paster focuses on the "vexed relation" between
early modern social and emotional hierarchies in such
plays as *MV*, *Err.*, and *TN*. (While there are references
to *TN* throughout the volume, the play receives its
most detailed treatment in this chapter; see especially
pp. 212–17.) In *TN*, "tensions [are] generated by the
combination of female rule, stewardly class-jumping,
and the thermal inadequacies of other men and near-
men." Paster claims that the social role of humors—
along with the rhetoric associated with them—hovers
around both upper-class figures such as Sir Toby and
Sir Andrew, who "claim humoral privilege as a matter
of birthright and dispute encroachment on their emo-

tional autonomy," and figures of comic aspiration like Malvolio, whose "humoral thinking is the basis for self-understanding and self-justification in a hostile world." Noting how "humoral inflection in the discourse of subjectivity is . . . a matter of . . . hot and cold, wet and dry," Paster cites Sir Andrew's lack of the proper warmth expected in the wooing of a noble lady by a man of his elite status (see 3.2.17–29). By contrast with the "thermally deficient Andrew," Malvolio "is almost literally too full of himself, too full of radical heat and moisture, and the prepossessing behaviors associated with them." In 2.5, as he imagines quenching his smile and extending his hand to the increasingly outraged Sir Toby (lines 51–54, 64–66), the steward exemplifies "the humoral triumphalism of the new man on top." Tricked into "committing a particularly egregious form of humoral insubordination—the failure to suit one's own humor and behaviors to those of one's social superiors"—the cross-gartered Malvolio in 3.4 is punished physically in humoral terms "by the imposition of 'obstruction in the blood' " (lines 21–23, 28–29). *TN*, like the other plays examined in the book, reveals the early modern world as one "in which no distinction existed between physiology and psychology": therein lies a key difference "between early modern behavioral theory and the models of mind-body relations dominant in post-Enlightenment thought."

Pennington, Michael. *Twelfth Night: A User's Guide.* London: Hern, 2000.

　　Drawing on his dual experience as both actor and director, Pennington provides a scene-by-scene analysis of the play that covers themes, characters, linkages, analysis of the verse structure, and commentary on individual lines. At the beginning, middle, and end of the volume are chapters dealing with productions

of *TN* that the author directed for the English Shakespeare Company (1991), the Haiyuza Company in
Tokyo (1993), and the Chicago Shakespeare Theater
(1995). This hands-on experience with the "delicate
balances and subtle shadings" of the play enables him
to offer a "practical account of the way [*TN*] actually works on stage." In the course of the book, Pennington addresses such issues as the first recorded
performance of *TN* (February 2, 1602, the Middle
Temple Hall of the Inns of Court), the significance of
the title (the thematic hint of topsyturvydom associated with the medieval "Feast of Fools" tradition "is
more fruitful" than seasonal and circumstantial theories), and *TN*'s "evasive grace," "deluded eroticism,"
and "profound sense of fugue." Costumes, set design,
casting, and blocking receive considerable attention.
After directing three different revivals within a five-
year period for audiences around the globe, Pennington concludes that (1) "the nuclear structure of *TN* is
like a daisy-chain, ghosted by an alternative one . . .
[with] the links [being] a series of highly charged
duologues[,] . . . each character circumstantially linked
to another . . . but [having] a deeper need for someone
else"; (2) the play "defies any single image imposed
across its grain," although one "should never forget
the sea in [*TN*]"; (3) the comedy has "no bright surface . . . without a shadow running alongside it"; and
(4) *TN* is "untypical" of Shakespeare with respect to its
ensemble of leading roles, all "carefully balanced" and
dependent on each other—even Fabian is "absolutely
central." (Pennington claims that only *Tro.*, *1* and *2H4*,
and *MND* offer a similar "range of leading parts.") The
one "uncompromised desire running through" the five
acts is the reunion of Viola and Sebastian, a fulfillment
that renders the concluding marriages "perfunctory":
"If the play could be said to hold any final meaning,

it would lie somewhere between [Malvolio] and the twins—between relationship and isolation, between the natural responses of blood and the barren imaginings of the solitary."

Schalkwyk, David. "Love and Service in *Twelfth Night* and the Sonnets." *Shakespeare Quarterly* 56 (2005): 76–100, esp. 86–97.

   Reacting to the replacement in recent Shakespeare criticism of *love* with *power* and *desire*—words that Shakespeare "seldom uses and whose theoretical inflections he would have found strange"—Schalkwyk examines the use of love in *TN* and Sonnets 26, 57, 58, and 120 to explore "ways in which love is . . . connected to social concerns," particularly service, which rather than functioning as a "class concept" determines "the fundamental conditions of identity across the whole society." The author is especially interested in demonstrating how "the intimacy and reciprocity inherent in love may be borrowed from relationships, such as those between master and servant, that appear at first sight to be wholly unerotic." Reading service as experience "rather than as a literary trope," Schalkwyk observes that the "relationships and tensions between love and service found in Sonnets 57 and 58 are clearly discernible in the play's manifold variations on Eros and duty," wherein every instance of desire is "intertwined with service": see, e.g., Viola's pursuit of Orsino in the guise of a page/eunuch; Orsino's playing the Petrarchan servant in his "dotage" on Olivia; Malvolio's aspirations of social mobility through "erotic conquest"; Antonio's homoerotic affection for Sebastian (2.1.34–35); and, finally, Sir Toby's "reciprocal service" in marrying Maria (5.1.385–87). The article focuses on three relationships—servant-poet and master friend (in Sonnets 26, 57, and 58), Viola and Orsino, and Antonio and Sebastian—to reveal how "literal service, sexual desire, and loving devotion intersect in complex ways." Schalkwyk concludes by drawing a link between the shift from a poetics of praise to one of blame or revenge in Sonnet 120, Malvolio's shockingly direct letter to Olivia (5.1), and Antonio's harsh rebuke to Viola/Cesario (3.4). In all three, a speaker is cast in the role of a servant who becomes "spokesman for the reciprocal obligations of service as a relationship of mutual respect and care." Each case also provides a powerful expression of "moral outrage at the aristocracy's perceived failure to reciprocate love and service." For Schalkwyk, *TN* "is as much a study of service and master-servant relations as it is a comedy of romantic love." [A revision of the article is incorporated in " 'More than a steward': The Sonnets, *Twelfth Night*, and *Timon of Athens*," chapter 4 in Schalkwyk's *Shakespeare, Love and Service* (Cambridge: Cambridge University Press, 2008), esp. pp. 122–43.]

Summers, Joseph. "The Masks of *Twelfth Night*." In *Shakespeare: Modern Essays in Criticism*, edited by Leonard F. Dean, pp. 134–43. Rev. ed. New York: Oxford University Press, 1967.

Summers begins by noting a key difference between *TN* and other romantic comedies: namely, the absence of a "responsible older generation," the usual Shakespearean barrier to romantic fulfillment. This absence leads him to ask why the inhabitants of Illyria appear anything but free. The answer, he suggests, lies in the characters' ignorance of self, of others, and of their social world—an ignorance that results in self-created barriers. "Every character has his mask, for the assumption of the play is that no one is without a mask in the serio-comic business of the pursuit of happiness." Sometimes the masking is conscious (e.g., Viola's male disguise and Feste's role as court jester); at other times, unconscious (e.g., Orsino's posture as the literary lover,

Olivia's as the model of the grief-stricken lady, and the deluded Malvolio's and Aguecheek's "mistaken notions of the proper role of an upper-class gentleman"). Summers claims that generally within comedy "we laugh with [those] who know the role they are playing [e.g., Viola and Feste] and we laugh at those who do not [e.g., Orsino, Olivia, Malvolio, Toby, and Aguecheek]." In *TN*, however, where "roles have a way of shifting," such a neatly schematic division requires qualification since characters from time to time reveal the self behind the mask, thereby moving from "butt" of our laughter to "master" of it: see, for instance, Olivia in the catechism scene with Feste (1.5), wherein she shows her natural preference for life and humor. Andrew may be the only butt who does not enjoy a moment in which he is the master of our laughter. On the other side, Viola, whose mask is assumed only for self-preservation and which she becomes increasingly weary of, appears as the butt of laughter in the dueling match (3.4). Only two characters wear no mask: Antonio, whose failure to do so exposes him to capture; and Sebastian, who has no need of a mask since he is the "reality of which Cesario is the artful imitation." Among Illyria's maskers, Feste, as the "one professional among a crowd of amateurs . . . never makes the amateur's mistake of confusing his personality with his mask." As the play concludes, all except Feste are unmasked: "However burdensome, masking is his career, and romantic love provides no end for it." Perhaps, Summers suggests, the play's alternative title (*What You Will*) "may hint that what 'we' collectively 'will' creates all the comic masks—that society determines the forms of comedy more directly than it determines those of any other literary genre." [The essay originally appeared in *The University Review* 22 (Autumn 1955): 25–32 (University of Missouri at Kansas City).]

Walsh, Brian. "'O Just But Severe Law!': Weighing Puritanism in *Twelfth Night* and *Measure for Measure*." Chapter 3 in *Unsettled Toleration: Religious Difference on the Shakespearean Stage*, pp. 86–128, esp. 92–113. Oxford: Oxford University Press, 2016.

In an effort to "historicize . . . and scrutinize . . . the unstable concept of toleration" as it emerges in Elizabethan and Jacobean drama, Walsh examines *TN* as representative of "the cracked religious consensus of post-Reformation England," when "intra-Christian conflict between mainstream believers and various minorities" was widespread. He begins the chapter with a brief survey of Shakespeare and the Puritans and then turns specifically to *TN*, subtitling the section "Belch vs. Olivia: *Twelfth Night* and the War Over Malvolio." He argues that close analysis of Malvolio's actual words, actions, and societal role as steward of a fine house "forces us to refine" the usual reading of the Malvolio subplot "as a fairly clear-cut instance of anti-Puritan sentiment," a view that "confidently claim[s] Shakespeare for the side of the festive merriment that Malvolio would seek to repress." Walsh claims that *TN* offers two perspectives on Malvolio: that of the anti-Puritan contingent (Toby, Feste, Andrew, Maria, and Fabian) and that of Olivia (whose benevolence and sympathy toward her "notoriously abused" steward seem unlimited [see 3.4.65–69; 5.1.293–97, 373–77, 392, 402]). As presented in *TN*, both views are "possible responses to a Puritan presence in its imagined setting of Illyria": "The real contest the play enacts as far as Olivia's steward goes is not between Malvolio *qua* Puritan and the forces of traditional joviality [but] . . . between those characters that despise him for his supposed Puritanism, and Olivia, the powerful patron who values him because of it." The context of 2.3, for instance, demonstrates that in the role of his mistress's mouthpiece, Olivia's steward is reasonable and responsible, taking issue not with revelry per se but only with its timing and volume (see lines 87–93). "By foregrounding the fact that the conflict over Malvolio's worth is unresolved when he leaves the stage unforgiving and unforgiven[,] . . . Shakespeare enacts a fundamental hesitation in response to the problem of religious differentiation": whether or how Puritans and conformists can coexist is uncertain "as long as the question of what, exactly, is objectionable about Puritanism remains unsettled."

White, R. S., ed. *Twelfth Night: New Casebooks*. New York: St. Martin's, 1996.

White's collection excerpts and reprints eight "postmodern" studies spanning the years 1979–93: Geoffrey H. Hartman's "Shakespeare's Poetical Character in *Twelfth Night*," Elliot Krieger's "*Twelfth Night*: 'The morality of indulgence,'" Michael Bristol's "The Festive Agon: The Politics of Carnival," Leonard Tennenhouse's "Power on Display: The Politics of Shakespeare's Genres," Stephen Greenblatt's "Fiction and Friction" (see above), Dympna Callaghan's "'And all is semblative a woman's part': Body Politics and *Twelfth Night*," Cristina Malcolmson's "'What You Will': Social Mobility and Gender in *Twelfth Night*," and Barbara Everett's "Or What You Will." In his analysis of the ways Shakespeare's language, especially punning and wordplay, relates to character, Hartman examines the flux of language between real consequence—as in Malvolio's desperate pleas for release—and mere quibbling; for Hartman, *TN* hints at moments of clarification ("Good madam, let me see your face") but defers pure revelation because the text, sustained by wit, keeps turning, and "[t]here is always more to say." Following the tenets of Marxist criticism and its terms of class warfare, Krieger argues that *TN* dramatizes a "privileged social class's access to the morality of indulgence" while other characters "either work to make indulgence possible for their superiors or else, indulging themselves, sicken and so die." Building on the work of C. L. Barber (see above) and Mikhail Bakhtin, Bristol views *TN* as representing the struggle between the "festive agon [misrule]" of Carnival battling against "Lenten tendencies" toward seriousness, with the battle being over the issue of "political succession." In contrast to Bristol's concern with folk tradition, Tennenhouse's focus on "high politics" reminds us that Shakespeare's representations of "vital women such as Viola" were composed and performed when the English monarch was a queen, a time when one could "imagine patriarchal power embodied in a female." Both Callaghan and Malcolmson offer feminist readings of *TN*'s presentation of gender struggles. For Callaghan, the play "re-enact[s] the oppression, marginalizing and sexual humiliation of women" (see, e.g., the ridicule of female genitals in the letter scene [2.5.88–92] and "the use of the apparently playful, but in reality demeaning, vehicle of male actors playing females"). Malcolmson's more sympathetic reading suggests that the rigid structures of the traditional patriarchal order are "destabilized, deconstructed even, by the willful confusion of gender stereotypes"; the comedy's female triumphs, generally speaking, "come at the expense of male inadequacies." Everett's essay explores musicality, characterization, verbal style, the significance of the play's subtitle, and the role of Feste in response to what, for Everett, is the primary question posed by *TN* and Shakespeare's earlier comedies: "Why do we take them seriously? Or how, rather, best to explore the ways in which it is hard *not* to take them seriously—the sense that at their best they achieve a lightness as far as possible from triviality." In his introduction, White notes how the essays gathered here reflect the movement of criticism in the last third of the twentieth century "in the direction of reader response theories." He further observes that the improbable fictions of *TN* give "a new meaning" to its alternative title, *What You Will*: *TN* "refuses to be constrained by critical or directorial authority of any kind, and in this sense is always postmodern, if not beyond."

Zucker, Adam. "*Twelfth Night* and the Philology of Nonsense." *Renaissance Studies* 30 (2016): 88–101.

Zucker discusses the social ramifications of miscomprehension or false interpretations of nonsense words in *TN* and other early modern English comedies for the imagined characters on stage as well as for scholars, editors, teachers, students, and audience members. Noting that nonsense words tease readers by suggesting meaning where there is none, Zucker writes that *TN* is a play that "imagines a universe of people getting things wrong . . . [in] an atmosphere of astonished befuddlement." Zucker locates the key to this "elaborate depiction of error" in Olivia's response to Malvolio at 5.1.392—"Alas, poor fool, how have they baffled thee"—where the modern meaning of *baffled* as "confused"/"perplexed" comes immediately to mind. Zucker's focus, however, is not on the narrative befuddlement in *TN* but on the linguistic kind found in its jokes, puns, and nonsense words that defy comprehension. Sir Andrew Aguecheek is particularly baffled by even the simplest French words: "What is '*pourquoi*'? Do, or not do?" (1.3.91). Zucker suggests that Aguecheek "serves as a kind of avatar for the philologically minded critic faced with nonsensical expressions in [*TN*]." A striking example of such nonsense is Sir Toby's untranslatable exclamation "*Castiliano vulgo*" (1.3.42), for which countless glosses have been written over the centuries in a futile effort to find meaning where none is to be found, and where, most likely, none ever existed. The phrase's comic significance, Zucker argues, has nothing to do with semantics: "In some very simple, ordinary sense, the exact translation of these words is entirely irrelevant for the action of the play, especially in performance. . . . They serve their point simply in their explosive, meaningful noise [and] need not be clarified in any way to do their job." Citing gibberish in other late Tudor and early Stuart comedies, Zucker claims that nonsense phrases involving terms from made-up languages reflect "a very real part of multilingual London" at a time when its cosmopolitan residents were "struggling to understand one another." Zucker concludes that the more "we struggle to explicate these words," thinking we are members of an elite circle of the "knowing," the "more brightly and clearly these blind spots of knowledge mirror our own ignorance back at us." *TN* stages this problem of studiously explicating nonsense in Malvolio's efforts to "crush" the "empty acrostic" of "M.O.I.A." into a meaning that suits his purposes (2.5.124–45), much like textual scholars who spend "lifetimes quibbling over words that very likely mean nothing at all." The author, who feels both insulted and embarrassed by this portrayal of literary scholars, nevertheless suggests that the play's nonsense words "can help us think more clearly about our attempts to explicate difficult language." Returning to the word *baffle* with which he began—only now in its primary early modern sense of "humiliate"/"shame"—Zucker declares that although we may be "rendered silent, or stupefied" by *TN*'s "linguistic black holes," we need not be "baffled" by our efforts to determine the "historical, material contexts of our bafflement."

Shakespeare's Language

Abbott, E. A. *A Shakespearian Grammar*. New York: Haskell House, 1972.

This compact reference book, first published in 1870, helps with many difficulties in Shakespeare's language, especially with respect to syntax, grammar, and prosody. Abbott systematically accounts for a host of differences between Shakespeare's usage and sentence structure and our own. As he observes, Shakespearean English "presents the English language in a transitional . . . condition, rejecting and inventing much that the verdict of posterity has retained and discarded. It was an age of experiments, and the experiments were not always successful." For more than a century, Abbott's book was the chief resource for questions of grammar; see Jonathan Hope (below) for a twenty-first-century approach to the subject.

Adamson, Sylvia, Lynette Hunter, Lynne Magnusson, Ann Thompson, and Katie Wales, eds. *Reading Shakespeare's Dramatic Language: A Guide*. London: Arden Shakespeare, 2001.

This interdisciplinary collection draws on literary criticism, performance, and the history of language to explore both the similarities and differences between "the writing and language use" of Shakespeare's time and our own. The first part of the book, "The Language of Shakespeare's Plays," consists of twelve essays that bring together "an understanding of Renaissance rhetoric and modern conversation theory, with some issues of reading, writing, and staging": Ann Thompson, "Heightened Language"; Lynne Magnusson, "Style, Rhetoric and Decorum"; Sylvia Adamson, "The Grand Style"; George T. Wright, "Shakespeare's Metre

Scanned"; Walter Nash, "Puns and Parody"; William C. Carroll, "Description"; David Scott Kastan, "Narrative"; Lynette Hunter, "Persuasion"; Lynne Magnusson, "Dialogue"; Pamela Mason, "Characters in Order of Appearance"; Peter Lichtenfels, "Shakespeare's Language in the Theatre"; and Keir Elam, "Language and the Body." The second part, "Reading Shakespeare's English," contains four essays that examine Shakespeare's sounds, grammar, and word-making strategies, in addition to his "rich repertoire of regional and social varieties": Katie Wales, "Varieties and Variation"; Sylvia Adamson, "Understanding Shakespeare's Grammar: Studies in Small Words"; Terttu Nevalainen, "Shakespeare's New Words"; and Roger Lass, "Shakespeare's Sounds." The volume also includes a list of rhetorical terms and an annotated bibliography.

Crystal, David. *"Think on my words": Exploring Shakespeare's Language*. Cambridge: Cambridge University Press, 2008.

Crystal's introduction to the linguistic nuts and bolts of Shakespeare's language is governed by the principle that "one should never examine a linguistic nut or bolt without asking 'what does it do?' And 'what does it do?' means two things: how does it help us understand the meaning of what is said (a semantic explanation), and how does it help us appreciate the dramatic or poetic effect of what is said (a pragmatic explanation)?" The book's chapters cover Shakespearean graphology, punctuation, phonology, pronunciation, grammar, vocabulary, and conversational style. The epilogue, "'Your daring tongue,'" locates the hallmark of Shakespearean linguistic creativity not in the words and expressions that Shakespeare coined but in an "economy of expression" that trades on the "relationship between lexicon and grammar" in "service of the poetic imagination." The appendix, "An A-to-Z of Shakespeare's False Friends," considers words that seem familiar but are not because their meanings have changed since Shakespeare's time (examples include "awful," "belch," "dainty," "ecstasy," "fancy," "honest," and "jog"). Two tables deal, respectively, with (1) shared lines in relation to the number of verse lines in the plays, and (2) the proportions of verse and prose in the plays. Notes, references, and suggested further reading conclude the study.

Crystal, David, and Ben Crystal. *Shakespeare's Words: A Glossary and Language Companion.* London: Penguin, 2002.

In this comprehensive compilation of Early Modern English vocabulary found in Shakespeare, the authors provide definitions of nearly 14,000 words along with treatments of selected language topics (e.g., frequently encountered words, archaisms, greetings, currency terms, and swearwords). To be included in the glossary, a word must "present . . . the reader with a difficulty arising out of the differences between Elizabethan and Modern English." Following the glossary is a series of "Shakespearean Circles" for each play, diagramming the family, social, and occupational relationships entered into by the characters; lines of connection between circles "identify important points of contact between different groups." Several appendices "collate . . . the way characters are named, the names of the people and places they talk about, and the foreign languages that some of them use." The editors also provide information on figures of classical mythology and nonclassical legend, religious beings and personalities, historical personages, and contemporary figures (factual and fictitious). The glossary is one part of the Crystals' larger digital project bringing computer-based

Shakespeare resources into the Internet age. See their *Shakespeare's Words*, http://www.shakespeareswords.com/, which provides a list of all the definitions associated with a word. When one clicks on a particular definition, the user is directed to other instances in the canon where the same meaning applies. A concordance accompanies the *Shakespeare's Words* website.

Hope, Jonathan. *Shakespeare's Grammar.* London: Arden Shakespeare, 2003.

Commissioned as a replacement for E. A. Abbott's *Shakespearian Grammar* (see above), Hope's book is organized in terms of the two basic parts of speech, the noun and the verb. After extensive analysis of the noun phrase and the verb phrase come briefer discussions of subjects and agents, objects, complements, and adverbials. The book targets three different audiences: Shakespeare specialists who will utilize it as a reference grammar, general readers/beginners who will benefit from the descriptive grammar provided, and literary critics who potentially will put the volume's stylistic overviews to good use in their analysis, explication, and interpretation of Shakespeare's plays and poems. Hope aims "to present Shakespeare's idiolect (that is, his particular version of Early Modern English) within a coherent linguistic structure" that will enable readers "to get a sense of the interrelatedness of many of the features of Early Modern English."

Houston, John. *Shakespearean Sentences: A Study in Style and Syntax.* Baton Rouge: Louisiana State University Press, 1988.

Houston studies Shakespeare's stylistic choices, considering matters such as sentence length, treatment of subordinate clauses, and the relative positions of subject, verb, and direct object. Examining plays throughout the canon in roughly chronological, developmental order, he analyzes how sentence structure is used in setting tone, in characterization, and for other dramatic purposes. Houston pays extensive attention to the effects of certain rhetorical devices—e.g., asyndeton, syndeton, polysyndeton, parataxis, and hypotaxis—on sentence construction.

Johnson, Keith. *Shakespeare's English: A Practical Linguistic Guide.* Harlow: Pearson, 2013.

With chapters on phonetics, grammar, vocabulary, word usage, pragmatics, rhetoric, the printed word, and prosody, this guide examines Shakespeare's early modern English within the history of the English language as a whole. In addition to discussing rhyme, meter, and pronunciation, Johnson specifically explores declensions, pronouns, compounds, speech acts (such as curses, insults, and commands), archaic word choices and forms, word clusters, word order, wordplay, spelling, punctuation, and Shakespeare's use of Anglo-Saxon, French, and Latinate vocabulary. Along with the pervasive influence of Cicero's *De inventione* and the pseudo-Ciceronian *Ad Herennium* on the writing practices of Shakespeare and his contemporaries, Johnson considers the importance of such humanist works as Thomas Wilson's *The Arte of Rhetorique* (1553) and George Puttenham's *The Arte of English Poesie* (1589). Although criticism is not the author's purpose, he does on occasion offer readings to illustrate how Shakespeare's linguistic and rhetorical choices chart changes in a character's trajectory. Throughout the book Johnson reminds the reader of shifts in lexical meaning over the centuries.

Robinson, Randal. *Unlocking Shakespeare's Language: Help for the Teacher and Student.* Urbana, Ill.: National

Council of Teachers of English and the ERIC Clearing-house on Reading and Communication Skills, 1989.

Specifically designed for the high-school and under-graduate college teacher and student, Robinson's book addresses the problems that most often hinder present-day readers of Shakespeare. Through work with his own students, Robinson found that many readers today are particularly puzzled by such stylistic characteristics as subject-verb inversion, interrupted structures, and compression. He shows how our own colloquial language contains comparable structures, and thus helps students recognize such structures when they find them in Shakespeare's plays. This book supplies worksheets—with examples from major plays—to illuminate and remedy such problems as unusual sequences of words and the separation of related parts of sentences.

Williams, Gordon. *A Dictionary of Sexual Language and Imagery in Shakespearean and Stuart Literature.* 3 vols. London: Athlone Press, 1994.

Drawing on theatrical works, broadside ballads, newsbooks, jestbooks, and pamphlets, Williams provides a comprehensive list of words and expressions to which Shakespeare, his contemporaries, and later Stuart writers gave sexual meanings. He supports his identification of these meanings by extensive quotations, which, taken together, reveal how the language and imagery of sexuality reflect both linguistic development and sociocultural change across the early modern period.

Wright, George T. *Shakespeare's Metrical Art.* Berkeley: University of California Press, 1988. (Reissued as a paperback in 1991.)

Wright examines "the basic forms of Shakespeare's iambic pentameter line, its relation to other patterns (such as short lines, long lines, and prose), its changes over his career, and, most of all, the expressive gestures and powers this system provides for Shakespeare and his dramatis personae." To better understand Shakespeare's achievement (the primary focus of chapters 5 to 16), the author historicizes it in the "context of the decasyllabic line [Shakespeare] inherited and strongly influenced." For Wright, Shakespeare's metrical art is the culmination of a metrical chain that "runs back to Chaucer," through the verse of Thomas Wyatt, George Gascoigne, Henry Howard (Earl of Surrey), Philip Sidney, Edmund Spenser, and Christopher Marlowe. Chapter 17 considers the "extravagant turns" the pentameter line would take in John Donne and John Milton. Chapter 14, "The Play of Phrase and Line," explores the "creative equilibrium" Shakespeare maintains between "the continually recurring metrical pattern and the rhythmic phrase," a balance he achieves by varying the placement of the line break from the traditional fourth syllable slot of earlier poets to any position in the line, thereby yielding "phrases of three, five, or seven syllables as readily as phrases of four or six." The result of such freedom, especially in Shakespeare's later plays, is a more flexible and "sinuous" iambic pentameter line. For Wright, "the drama of Shakespeare is played out not only through a dialogue of characters but also through a dialogue of differently formed and framed verse lines, which speak to each other and to us of the variety, grace, and plenitude of human speech and trouble." Three appendices conclude the volume: (1) "Percentage Distribution of Prose in Shakespeare's Plays," (2) "Main Types of Deviant Lines in Shakespeare's Plays," and (3) "Short and Shared Lines." (Chapter 14 first appeared in *Shakespeare Quarterly* 34 [1983]: 147–58.)

Shakespeare's Life

Baldwin, T. W. *William Shakspere's Petty School*. Urbana: University of Illinois Press, 1943.

Baldwin here investigates the theory and practice of the petty school, the first level of education in Elizabethan England, where boys from the ages of four or five until the age of seven would learn the rudiments of reading and writing, with the aid of a hornbook (a leaf of paper framed in wood and covered with a thin layer of translucent horn) that contained the letters of the alphabet (preceded by a cross), combinations of vowels, and the Lord's Prayer. Students also mastered ABC books (introductory books to a subject, usually in question and answer form), the Catechism from the Book of Common Prayer, and the Primer (a fuller version of the catechism with additional prayers and psalms). As Baldwin states, the goal of the petty school was "to teach to read and write always, and to cast accounts [numbers] frequently," but, more importantly, the "predominantly religious" curriculum aimed at providing children with the fundamentals (in both theory and practice) of their orthodox Protestant religion. Baldwin focuses on the petty school educational system primarily as it is reflected in Shakespeare's art; see, for example, references to the life of a typical schoolboy in *As You Like It* (2.7.152–54), to the hornbook in *Love's Labors Lost* (5.1.46–49) and *Richard III* (1.1.58–63), and to the ABC book in *King John* (1.1.202).

Baldwin, T. W. *William Shakspere's Small Latine and Lesse Greeke*. 2 vols. Urbana: University of Illinois Press, 1944.

Baldwin refutes the view that Shakespeare was an uneducated genius—a view that had been dominant among Shakespeareans since the eighteenth century. Instead, Baldwin shows, the educational system of Shakespeare's time would have given the playwright a strong background in the classics, and there is much in the plays that shows how Shakespeare benefited from such an education. Volume 1 deals with the evolution of the grammar school curriculum in the sixteenth century from 1509 to 1600: Baldwin devotes chapters to the work of Erasmus; the education of royalty; specific models such as the Winchester, Eton, Westminster, and Paul's systems under Queen Elizabeth; the King's Free Grammar School at Stratford; and the Latin curriculum of the lower grammar school. Turning in volume 2 to the curriculum of the upper school (primarily Latin and, to a lesser degree, Greek), Baldwin considers the emphasis on rhetorical training (by way of the key texts of Cicero, Erasmus, Susenbrotus, and Quintilian), prose and verse composition, Latin poets (namely, Ovid, Virgil, Horace, Juvenal, Catullus, and Seneca), moral history, and moral philosophy. As Baldwin concludes, "If William Shakspere had the grammar school training of his day—or its equivalent—he had as good a formal literary training as had any of his contemporaries. At least, no miracles are required to account for such knowledge and techniques from the classics as he exhibits. Stratford grammar school will furnish all that is required. The miracle lies elsewhere; it is the world-old miracle of genius."

Beier, A. L., and Roger Finlay, eds. *London 1500–1700: The Making of the Metropolis*. New York: Longman, 1986.

Focusing on the economic and social history of early modern London, the nine essays in this collection probe aspects of metropolitan life under the headings "Population and Disease," "Commerce and Manufacture," and "Society and Change." The essays are as follows: Roger Finlay and Beatrice Shearer, "Population Growth and Suburban Expansion"; Paul Slack, "Metropolitan Government in Crisis: The Response to Plague"; Margaret Pelling, "Appearance and Reality: Barber-Surgeons, the Body and Disease"; A. L. Beier, "Engines of Manufacture: The Trades of London"; John Chartres, "Food Consumption and International Trade"; Brian Dietz, "Overseas Trade and Metropolitan Growth"; M. J. Kitch, "Capital and Kingdom: Migration to Later Stuart London"; M. J. Power, "The Social Topography of Restoration London"; and Stephen MacFarlane, "Social Policy and the Poor in the Later Seventeenth Century." The collection reveals a London caught up in the redistribution of socioeconomic and political power, the result of developments in capitalism and changes in class structure.

Callaghan, Dympna. *Who Was William Shakespeare? An Introduction to the Life and Works*. Oxford: Wiley-Blackwell, 2013.

Callaghan devotes the first part of her study to an examination of Shakespeare's life in the context of the social, cultural (particularly theatrical), political, intellectual, and religious climate of early modern England. She carries this focus on period and context into the second half of the volume in short essays on twenty-four plays, grouped under the following headings: "Comedies: Shakespeare's Social Life," "English and Roman Histories: Shakespeare's Politics," "Tragedies: Shakespeare in Love and Loss," and "Romances: Shakespeare and Theatrical Magic." The strictly biographical portion of the book considers "three of the most significant issues that shaped Shakespeare's identity": education (chapter 2), religion (chapter 3), and social status (chapter 4). Callaghan contends that Shakespeare's grammar school education was "the most important factor in allowing him as a gifted individual to become a writer." Religion furnished more than the backdrop for Shakespeare's canon, forming instead "the crucible in which his secular drama was generated." Callaghan is not concerned with Shakespeare's religious affiliation ("staunch Protestant, devout crypto-Catholic, furtive nonbeliever, or the holder of any one of a range of positions in between"), but rather with the impact of the Reformation and religious persecution on his theatrical practice and "identity as a professional writer." Before turning to specific plays, Callaghan discusses the nature of theater as a new urban institution with a fixed location, the pressures of censorship on both performance and print, "the social and professional conditions that molded Shakespeare's theatrical career in London," and the "competitive environment of early modern theatre." Callaghan acknowledges that Shakespeare's life "cannot explain his works, but it can help us to understand them."

Cressy, David. *Education in Tudor and Stuart England.* London: Edward Arnold, 1975.

Cressy collects over 150 sixteenth-, seventeenth-, and early eighteenth-century documents detailing aspects of formal education that reflect "the efforts of governments, philanthropists, religious writers, social critics and other leaders of opinion, as well as schoolmasters themselves, to direct the educational enterprise" of early modern England. Cressy groups the items under eight categories: perspectives on education, control of education, the organization of schools, schoolmasters, the curriculum, educational opportunity, education of women, and the universities. The selected documents "illustrate some of the social and political pressures bearing on education in the period."

Duncan-Jones, Katherine. *Shakespeare: An Ungentle Life*. London: Arden Shakespeare, 2010.

This biography, first published in a slightly different version in 2001 under the title *Ungentle Shakespeare: Scenes from His Life*, sets out to look into the documents from Shakespeare's personal life—especially legal and financial records—and it finds there a man very different from the one portrayed in more traditional biographies. He is "ungentle" in being born to a lower social class and in being a bit ruthless and more than a bit stingy. As the author notes, "three topics were formerly taboo both in polite society and in Shakespearean biography: social class, sex and money. I have been indelicate enough to give a good deal of attention to all three." She examines "Shakespeare's uphill struggle to achieve, or purchase, 'gentle' status." She finds that "Shakespeare was strongly interested in intense relationships with well-born young men." And she shows that he was "reluctant to divert much, if any, of his considerable wealth towards charitable, neighbourly, or altruistic ends." She insists that his plays and poems are "great, and enduring," and that it is in them "that the best of him is to be found."

Enterline, Lynn. *Shakespeare's Schoolroom: Rhetoric, Discipline, Emotion*. Philadelphia: University of Pennsylvania Press, 2012.

Two questions inform Enterline's study of Shakespeare's "career-long fascination" with the classical curriculum and humanist pedagogy of the early modern grammar school: "How did [such] training influence what counted as genteel masculinity in the period?" and "How did early modern pedagogy affect experiences of sexuality and desire?" Throughout the book, Enterline underscores "the significant difference between what humanists claimed their [pedagogical] methods would achieve [the formation of proper English gentlemen who would benefit the commonwealth] and what the texts of at least one former schoolboy reveal about the institution's unintended literary and social consequences"—namely, the undercutting of the patriarchal social order that the educational system was meant to reproduce. By assuming female roles in the classroom, the boys learned to "identify with women as they learned to voice the emotions needed for a persuasive oratorical performance." The introduction and first two chapters focus on Shakespeare's grammar school curriculum and Enterline's overall thesis concerning "gender instability" in the pedagogical tradition of the time. The remaining chapters illustrate the author's argument by way of particular poems or plays: Chapter 3 deals with *Venus and Adonis*; chapter 4, with *The Taming of the Shrew*; and chapter 5, with aspects of *Hamlet*, *Lucrece*, and *The Winter's Tale*.

Evans, Robert C. *Culture and Society in Shakespeare's Day*. New York: Chelsea House, 2012.

Part of a three-part series titled *Backgrounds to Shakespeare* (the other two volumes are *Shakespeare's Life* and *Literature and the Theater in Shakespeare's Day*), Evans's illustrated overview gives historical and social-political context to the period 1564 to 1616, describing daily life as it was lived in three major centers of English existence: the countryside, London, and the royal court. Citing contemporaneous reports and comments, Evans sheds light on a diversity of topics: education; the enclosure movement and its impact on agricultural life; industries such as fishing, mining, and bricklaying; the rural poor, the rural aristocracy, and the rural parson as lawyer and doctor; courtier life, royal progresses, and the royal palaces of Whitehall, Hampton Court, and Greenwich; the road system to London, English inns, and livery companies; and meals, domestic furnishings, and "sumptuary laws" specifying the proper attire for people of different ranks and occupations. Evans also includes "special features" on the rituals and customs associated with birth, marriage, and death; religious conflict in Shakespeare's England, folklore, superstition, and witchcraft; disease and medicine; and major events of the period (such as explorations of the New World, the Spanish Armada, and the Gunpowder Plot). Frequent quotation from the plays underscores connections between topics discussed by Evans and their treatment in the Shakespeare canon.

Manley, Lawrence. *Literature and Culture in Early Modern London*. Cambridge: Cambridge University Press, 1995.

Spanning the years 1475 to 1675, Manley's study of the image of London in and the city's influence on literature in the early modern period examines a variety of writings: lyrics, ballads, epics, satires, praises, plays, chronicles, treatises, sermons, official documents, pageants, and mayoral shows. Within two hundred years London was transformed from "a late medieval commune" of 35,000 inhabitants into a "rapidly changing metropolis of nearly half a million, the engine of an evolving early modern society, a capital . . . that would soon become the most populous in Europe," and a major European trading center. These changes brought "[n]ew possibilities . . . for cultural exchange and combination, social and political order, and literary expression." Among the many factors that led to making early modern London "the largest and most widely experienced human creation in Britain" were the rise of humanist learning and the impact of a print culture; "the emergence of . . . a national conscious-ness" that coincided with transformations of late medi-eval aristocracy; changes in the rural economy; the development of new class functions, "tied especially to commerce, bureaucracy, and law"; and "new types of religious . . . association." The volume's illustrations include representations of royal and civic ceremonies, emblematic images of personified early modern Lon-don, and contemporary maps of the city as a whole and of individual streets, processional routes, and areas such as Cheapside.

Manley, Lawrence, ed. *London in the Age of Shake-speare: An Anthology.* University Park: Penn State Uni-versity Press, 1986.

A useful companion to Manley's later study (see above), this anthology seeks to "reflect the experience of London" during Shakespeare's time. The book's sixteen chapters excerpt writings published between 1485 and 1660; these include prose descriptions of the city, verse encomia, sermons, jestbooks, broadside ballads, satires and complaints, official records, civic myths, epigrams, poems of transit, erotica, and portrayals of London as found in stage comedy, character writing, and official pageantry. Challenges to social order—crime, disease, poor harvests, unemployment, and a growing and an increasingly diverse population—"animate the materi-als" gathered, underscoring how the literature of the period "amounts to a kind of city in itself, a polemi-cal space in which competing visions and voices exert a productive influence on each other. . . . Emerging from the varied strands and forms of London life, and integrated with them, the London that was performed, imagined and sung was, in many ways, the London that was lived." As the items collected attest, Tudor-

Stuart descriptions of London "reveal that a major corollary of the Renaissance discovery of man was the discovery of the city."

Potter, Lois. *The Life of William Shakespeare: A Critical Biography*. Malden, Mass.: Wiley-Blackwell, 2012.

This critical biography of Shakespeare takes the playwright from cradle to grave, paying primary attention to his literary and theatrical milieu. The chapters "follow a chronological sequence," each focusing on a handful of years in the playwright's life. In the chapters that cover his playwriting years (5–17), Potter considers events in Stratford-upon-Avon and in London (especially in the commercial theaters) while giving equal space to discussions of the plays and poems Shakespeare wrote during those years. Filled with information from Shakespeare's literary and theatrical worlds, the biography also shares frequent insights into how modern productions of a given play can shed light on the play, especially in scenes that Shakespeare's text presents ambiguously.

Schoenbaum, S. *William Shakespeare: A Compact Documentary Life*. New York: Oxford University Press, 1977.

Schoenbaum's evidence-based biography of Shakespeare is a compact version of his magisterial folio-size *Shakespeare: A Documentary Life* (New York: Oxford University Press, 1975). Schoenbaum structures his readable "compact" narrative around the documents that still exist which chronicle Shakespeare's theatrical, legal, and financial existence. These documents, along with those discovered since the 1970s, form the basis of almost all Shakespeare biographies written since Schoenbaum's books appeared. For Schoenbaum, "The story of William Shakespeare's life is a tale of two towns. Stratford bred him; London gave him, literally and figuratively, a stage for his fortune."

Shapiro, James. *Contested Will: Who Wrote Shakespeare?* New York: Simon & Schuster, 2010.

This historical investigation of the authorship controversy and its history explains "what it means, why it matters, and how it has persisted despite abundant evidence that William Shakespeare of Stratford wrote the plays attributed to him." Shapiro is able to date the onset of the controversy to the middle of the nineteenth century; he exposes as forgery documents purporting to backdate it to the eighteenth century. What gave rise to the controversy were the combination of "the presumption that Shakespeare could only write about what he had felt or done rather than heard about, read about, borrowed from other writers, or imagined" and the coincident deification of Shakespeare. So great was Shakespeare's reputation and so rich his presumed experience as it was abstracted from his writings that it became impossible for some to persist in associating him with the Stratfordian Shakespeare whose documented life consisted only of narrow legal and commercial interests. Once skepticism about Shakespeare's claim to have written his plays arose, more and more candidates for authorship began to be proposed—an activity that continues right up to the present. Shapiro acknowledges such contenders as Christopher Marlowe, Mary Sidney, the Earl of Derby, the Earl of Rutland, Sir Walter Ralegh, and Queen Elizabeth; his emphasis, however, falls on only two candidates, each of whom is the subject of a full chapter: Francis Bacon and the Earl of Oxford. For Shapiro, their candidacies are "the best documented[,] . . . most consequential [and] representative." The epilogue explains why the author thinks William Shakespeare wrote the plays and poems attributed to him.

Wolfe, Heather, curator. *Shakespeare Documented.* Digital Project. 2016. The Folger Shakespeare Library. Washington, D.C. See http://www.shakespearedocu mented.org.

Assembled by the Folger Shakespeare Library to commemorate the 400th anniversary of Shakespeare's death, this multi-institutional collaboration brings together the resources of the Folger, the Bodleian Library of Oxford University, the Shakespeare Birth-place Trust, the National Archives, and the British Library to provide the "largest and most authoritative" collection of primary source materials documenting the life of William Shakespeare. Materials include all known manuscripts and print references relating to the poet-playwright, his works, and family, including a letter addressed to him, manuscripts signed by him, and references to his coat of arms. Dating from his lifetime and shortly thereafter, the documents reveal a portrait of Shakespeare as a professional playwright, actor, poet, businessman, and family man who lived in both London and Stratford-upon-Avon. They trace his path "to becoming a household name," from the earliest reference to his father in Stratford (1552) through the publication of the First Folio in 1623 to the gossiping about him in the following decades. Images, descriptions, and transcriptions of 107 manuscripts that refer to Shakespeare by name, ninety-five printed books and manuscripts that mention or quote his plays or poems, and eighty-four printed editions of his plays and poems up to and including the First Folio point to "a remarkable legacy for someone of his socio-economic status and profession."

Shakespeare's Theater

Astington, John H. *Actors and Acting in Shakespeare's Time: The Art of Stage Playing*. Cambridge: Cambridge University Press, 2010.

Astington describes and analyzes the "cultural context of stage playing, the critical language used about it, and the kinds of training and professional practice employed" by actors on the early modern English stage from Richard Tarlton to Thomas Betterton. Drawing on recent discoveries "about actors and their social networks, about apprenticeship and company affiliations, and about playing [venues] outside" the theatrical center of London, this study compares "the educational tradition of playing in schools, universities, legal inns and choral communities . . . to the work of the professional players." In addition to portraying the early modern actor's versatility in playing many parts, Astington attends closely to the study of oratory in the grammar school curriculum and to the use of dramatic performance as a pedagogic tool, even at the university level, thereby underscoring the connection between "the performative arts of the stage and the select and remote realm of contemporary formal education." In the chapter "Players at Work," he uses Shackerley Marmion's *Holland's Leaguer* (1631) and Philip Massinger's *The Roman Actor* (1626) "to approach some of the pragmatics of a particular moment of theatrical production in the earlier seventeenth century." Astington concludes with commentary on changes in acting styles and the "social place" of actors: neither descendants from gentry nor university graduates, leading actors were, nevertheless, "of a social rank equal to the respectable citizens of London"; journeymen actors, however, lived "on the margins of poverty." An appendix provides a comprehensive biographical dictionary of all major professional actors in the years 1558 to 1660.

Berry, Herbert. *Shakespeare's Playhouses.* New York: AMS Press, 1987.

    With illustrations by Walter Hodges, Berry's six essays collected here discuss varying aspects of the four playhouses in which Shakespeare had a financial stake: the Theatre of 1576 in Shoreditch (the subject of two essays), the Blackfriars of 1596, the Globe of 1599, and the Globe of 1614. The final essay, "A New Lawsuit about the Globe," addresses the legal action brought by the King's Men in their efforts to seek an extension of their lease on the Globe property, which was due to expire in 1635. The four theaters at the core of Berry's study "embrace and virtually define the whole of the most remarkable period in English theatrical history."

Berry, Herbert, William Ingram, and Glynne Wickham, eds. *English Professional Theatre, 1530–1660.* Cambridge: Cambridge University Press, 2000.

    This study of the English professional theater in the years designated consists of three parts: "documents of control," "players and playing," and "playhouses," each part divided into chapters with their own subdivisions. Wickham presents the government documents designed to control professional players, their plays, and playing places. Ingram handles the professional actors, giving as representative a life of the actor Augustine Phillips, and discussing among other topics patrons, acting companies, costumes, props, playbooks, provincial playing, and child actors. Berry treats the twenty-three different London playhouses from 1560 to 1660 for which there are records, including four inns. As he reminds us, "Probably nothing of the kind had happened in any other city on earth." The documents supporting the third part are primarily legal.

Cook, Ann Jennalie. *The Privileged Playgoers of Shakespeare's London.* Princeton: Princeton University Press, 1981.

Cook sets out to answer the question, "Who were the people for whom Shakespeare, Marlowe, Jonson, Webster, and their fellow dramatists wrote plays?" Were they "ignorant or intelligent, riotous or refined, libertine or law abiding, plebeian or privileged?" In contrast to Alfred Harbage (see below), Cook argues, on the basis of sociological, economic, and documentary evidence, that Shakespeare's audience—and the audience for English Renaissance drama generally—consisted mainly of the "privileged," a group that ranged "from the threadbare scholar or the prospering landholder, newly risen from the yeomanry, all the way up to nobility and royalty itself." Such an audience was ready-made, given the fact that the "privileged had long fostered the drama as schoolboys, as patrons, and even as playwrights themselves." To claim that the "privileged" dominated the "plebeians" as playgoers is not to say that they did so exclusively: "Ordinary people who could afford the price of a ticket made their way to attend a play on any given day, especially on holidays, but not (as the economic and social pressures affecting them demonstrate) in the numbers or frequency previously thought."

Dutton, Richard, ed. *The Oxford Handbook of Early Modern Theatre.* Oxford: Oxford University Press, 2011.

Dutton divides his study of the theatrical industry of Shakespeare's time into the following sections: "Theatre Companies," "London Playhouses," "Other Playing Spaces," "Social Practices," and "Evidence of

Theatrical Practices." Each of these sections is further subdivided, with subdivisions assigned to individual experts. W. R. Streitberger treats the "Adult Playing Companies to 1583"; Sally-Beth MacLean, those from 1583 to 1593; Roslyn L. Knutson, 1593–1603; Tom Rutter, 1603 to 1613; James J. Marino, 1613–1625; and Martin Butler, the "Adult and Boy Playing Companies 1625 to 1642." Michael Shapiro is responsible for the "Early (Pre-1590) Boy Companies and Their Acting Venues," while Mary Bly writes of "The Boy Companies 1599–1613." David Kathman handles "Inn-Yard Playhouses"; Gabriel Egan, "The Theatre in Shoreditch 1576–1599"; Andrew Gurr, "Why the Globe Is Famous"; Ralph Alan Cohen, "The Most Convenient Place: The Second Blackfriars Theater and Its Appeal"; Mark Bayer, "The Red Bull Playhouse"; and Frances Teague, "The Phoenix and the Cockpit-in-Court Playhouses." Turning to "Other Playing Spaces," Suzanne Westfall describes how " 'He who pays the piper calls the tune': Household Entertainments"; Alan H. Nelson, "The Universities and the Inns of Court"; Peter Greenfield, "Touring"; John H. Astington, "Court Theatre"; and Anne Lancashire, "London Street Theater." For "Social Practices," Alan Somerset writes of "Not Just Sir Oliver Owlet: From Patrons to 'Patronage' of Early Modern Theatre," Dutton himself of "The Court, the Master of the Revels, and the Players," S. P. Cerasano of "Theater Entrepreneurs and Theatrical Economics," Ian W. Archer of "The City of London and the Theatre," David Kathman of "Players, Livery Companies, and Apprentices," Kathleen E. McLuskie of "Materiality and the Market: The Lady Elizabeth's Men and the Challenge of Theatre History," Heather Hirschfield of " 'For the author's credit': Issues of Authorship in English Renaissance Drama," and Natasha Korda of "Women in the Theater." On "Theatrical Practices," Jacalyn Royce discusses "Early Modern Naturalistic Acting: The Role of the Globe in the Development of Personation"; Tiffany Stern, "Actors' Parts"; Alan Dessen, "Stage Directions and the Theater Historian"; R. B. Graves, "Lighting"; Lucy Munro, "Music and Sound"; Dutton himself, "Properties"; Thomas Postlewait, "Eyewitnesses to History: Visual Evidence for Theater in Early Modern England"; and Eva Griffith, "Christopher Beeston: His Property and Properties."

Greg, W. W. *Dramatic Documents from the Elizabethan Playhouses*. 2 vols. Oxford: Clarendon Press, 1931.

Greg claims that "generally speaking it may be said that for every piece in the repertory of an Elizabethan theatre company there must have existed three play-house documents or sets of documents. First . . . was the Book, or authorized prompt copy. . . . Next there were the Parts of the several characters, written out for actors on long scrolls of paper. . . . Last there were the Plots, skeleton outlines of plays scene by scene, written on large boards for the use of actors and others in the playhouse." In the first volume, Greg itemizes and briefly describes almost all the play manuscripts that survive from the period 1590 to around 1660, including so-called prompt copies, players' parts, and plots. His second volume offers facsimiles and transcriptions of selected manuscripts associated with the playhouses. (For some other kinds of playhouse documents, see the books by Stern and by Werstine, below.)

Harbage, Alfred. *Shakespeare's Audience*. New York: Columbia University Press, 1941.

Harbage investigates the fragmentary surviving evidence to interpret the size, social composition, behavior, and aesthetic and intellectual capacity of Shakespeare's audience. He concludes that common-ers, the plebeians, and not the privileged were the mainstay of Shakespeare's audience. In contrast to public theaters like the Globe, private theaters such as the Blackfriars were the domain of the upper levels of the social order. The book's seven chapters are titled "The Evidence," "How Many People," "What Kind of People," "Behaviour," "Quality: Elizabethan Appraisals," "Quality: Modern Appraisals," and "Our Shakespeares and Our Audiences." Two appendices provide, respectively, estimates of attendance and attendance charts. Harbage's view remained uncontested until Ann Jennalie Cook's argument for the privileged (see Cook, above).

Keenan, Siobhan. *Acting Companies and Their Plays in Shakespeare's London.* London: Bloomsbury Arden Shakespeare, 2014.
   Keenan "explores how the needs, practices, resources and pressures on acting companies and playwrights informed not only the performance and publication of contemporary dramas but playwrights' writing practices." Each chapter focuses on one important factor that shaped Renaissance playwrights and players. The initial focus is on how "the nature and composition of the acting companies" influenced the playwrights who wrote for them. Then, using "the Diary of theatre manager Philip Henslowe and manuscript playbooks showing signs of theatrical use," Keenan examines the relations between acting companies and playwrights. Other influences include "the physical design and facilities of London's outdoor and indoor theatrical spaces" and the diverse audiences for plays, including royal and noble patrons.

Stern, Tiffany. *Documents of Performance in Early Modern England.* Cambridge: Cambridge University Press, 2009.

Stern interrogates "two competing current schools of thought on playscripts: whether surviving playbooks are ever fully representative of plays as they were performed ('performance texts') and whether playbooks are ever fully stripped of the theatre to become plays in an ideal literary form ('literary texts')." Singling out the label "play-patcher," one of several used to identify playwrights in Shakespeare's time, she argues that despite its pejorative connotation, the term accurately depicts the patchwork nature of dramatic texts "made from separate documents." Stern's extensive examination of early modern playscripts allows her to consider the many papers created by authors and theaters before the actual opening performance of a play. These documents, each treated in its own chapter, are as follows: plot scenarios; playbills and title pages; "arguments" as programs and as "paratext"; prologues and epilogues (often drawn up on pieces of paper separate from the play they flanked and not necessarily by the author(s) of the rest of the text); songs ("completed and sometimes written by composers, and disseminated to be learned separately"); scrolls (including such property documents as letters, proclamations, bills, and verses that were to be read aloud during a performance); backstage plots ("profoundly theatrical document[s]" that hung in the tiring-house and that provided detailed stage entrances, including the properties needed by actors when onstage); and, finally, actors' parts. What lies behind a theatrical production in the early modern English theater, then, was not "any single unified [and authorized] book" but rather a "patch-work" of parts "easily lost, relegated or reused," always open to continual revision and to new configurations for subsequent performances. Taken together, the performance documents explored by Stern were "the play," a conclusion that not only "redefin[es] what a play actually is" but also redefines "what a playwright is"—namely, a "play-patcher." Unlike the "whole artworks [that] poems" were considered to be, "plays had the bit, the fragment, the patch in their very natures." (For accounts of extant playhouse manuscript books and quartos used as playbooks in the theaters, see Greg, above, and Werstine, below.)

The Publication of Shakespeare's Plays

Blayney, Peter W. M. *The First Folio of Shakespeare.* Hanover, Md.: Folger, 1991.

Blayney's accessible account of the printing and later life of the First Folio—an amply illustrated catalogue to a 1991 Folger Shakespeare Library exhibition that showcased twenty-four of the Folger's First Folios—analyzes the mechanical production of the First Folio, describing how it was made, by whom and for whom, how much it cost (probably a retail price of 15s for an unbound copy), and its ups and downs (or, rather, downs and ups) since its printing in 1623. Blayney contends that probably no more than 750 copies were printed. Among the topics discussed are the order of the pages, the importance of casting off (the process of setting a Folio quire by first estimating just what text would fit in the first six pages), stop press corrections, the portrait of Shakespeare, the belated inclusion of *Troilus*, and the activities of Henry Clay and Emily Jordan Folger, the founders of the Folger Shakespeare Library, as collectors.

Hinman, Charlton. *The Norton Facsimile: The First Folio of Shakespeare.* 2nd ed. New York: W. W. Norton, 1996.

This facsimile presents a photographic reproduction of an "ideal" copy of the First Folio of Shakespeare; Hinman attempts to represent each page in its most fully corrected state. The second edition includes an important new introduction by Peter W. M. Blayney, which consists of four sections: "The First Folio and Its Publishers," "The Players and Their Manuscripts," "The Proofreading," and "The Printing" (which includes a table listing the pages of each play in the order in which they were set and the "more reliable compositorial reattributions that have been offered since 1963"). A significant feature of the Hinman facsimile is its "through line numbering" system (TLN), based on the lines printed in 1623 rather than on the acts, scenes, and lines of a modern edition.

Hinman, Charlton. *The Printing and Proof-Reading of the First Folio of Shakespeare.* 2 vols. Oxford: Clarendon Press, 1963.

Prior to the 2012 publication of Eric Rasmussen and Anthony James West's descriptive catalogue of the Shakespeare First Folios (see Rasmussen and West, below), Hinman's attempt to reconstruct how the Shakespeare First Folio of 1623 was set into type and run off the press, sheet by sheet, was the most arduous study of a single book ever undertaken. This two-volume celebration of the 1623 collection—based on a thorough examination of many of the eighty-two copies of the First Folio in the Folger Shakespeare Library—also identifies individual compositors and provides almost all of the variations in readings from copy to copy; it was thus a seminal work for future editors and bibliographical scholars.

Murphy, Andrew. *Shakespeare in Print: A History and Chronology of Shakespeare Publishing.* Cambridge: Cambridge University Press, 2003.

Murphy's comprehensive account of Shakespeare

publishing provides a discursive history of the most editorially significant texts of Shakespeare's poems and plays (both single and collected editions) published in Britain and America between the years 1593 and 2002. Focusing on the circumstances surrounding the publication and the reception of these printed texts, the eleven-chapter history begins with coverage of the early quartos and the early collected editions—Folios 1 (1623), 2 (1632), 3 (1663–64), and 4 (1685). Murphy then moves on to the "emergence of a theoretically self-conscious tradition of Shakespeare editing" in the eighteenth century (with its "market-leading 'celebrity-edited'" collected works), followed by chapters on nineteenth-century popular and scholarly editions, the New Bibliography of the early twentieth century (established by W. W. Greg, R. B. McKerrow, A. W. Pollard, and John Dover Wilson in his Cambridge New Shakespeare), and, turning to the later twentieth century, such publications as the selectively modernized *Riverside Shakespeare* and the "bold . . . and experimental" Oxford Shakespeare. The history section of the volume concludes with an examination of the electronic and hypertext editions of the twenty-first century, which reveal technology to be as important as textual theory. An annotated chronology of more than 1,700 editions constitutes the second part of the book, with five helpful indexes organizing the annotated editions by play/poem title, series title, editor, publisher, and place of publication (excluding London).

Rasmussen, Eric, and Anthony James West, eds. *The Shakespeare First Folios: A Descriptive Catalogue.* Basingstoke: Palgrave Macmillan, 2012.

While biographies of Shakespeare, performance studies of the plays, and accounts of the Folio's prepublication history abound, "little has been offered on the relationship of the First Folio's post-publication history to Shakespeare's reception and recognition over the centuries." The editors of this catalog—the result of twenty years of research during which 232 surviving copies of the First Folio were located and carefully examined—seek to remedy this situation by providing "full bibliographic descriptions of each extant copy, including accounts of press variants, watermarks, damage or repair, leaves in facsimile, annotations, bindings, end-papers, bookplates, and provenance [including lists of ownership]." Praising the editors' meticulous description of each copy, Paul Werstine writes in the catalog's preface that Rasmussen and West take their place beside the monumental efforts of Charlton Hinman (see above). Werstine singles out as the editors' "greatest gift to Shakespeareans[:] . . . their significant expansion of our knowledge of the extent to which press corrections have interposed themselves between manuscript printer's copy . . . and the early printed texts of the plays." Because of their labors in producing a complete record of press variants in all accessible volumes, future editors "can provide Shakespeare's readers with editions of the [eighteen] Folio plays based on fully informed decisions about which printed variant has the highest probability of reflecting the manuscript from which the text was printed."

Werstine, Paul. *Early Modern Playhouse Manuscripts and the Editing of Shakespeare.* Cambridge: Cambridge University Press, 2012.

Werstine examines in detail nearly two dozen texts associated with the playhouses in and around Shakespeare's time, conducting the examination against the background of the two idealized forms of manuscript that have governed the editing of Shakespeare from the twentieth into the twenty-first century—Shakespeare's so-called foul papers and the so-called promptbooks of his plays. By comparing the two extant texts of John Fletcher's *Bonduca*, one in manuscript and the other printed in 1647, Werstine shows that the term "foul papers" that is found in a note in the *Bonduca* manuscript does not refer, as editors have believed, to a species of messy authorial manuscript but is instead simply a designation for a manuscript, whatever its features, that has served as the copy from which another manuscript has been made. By surveying twenty-one texts with theatrical markup, he demonstrates that the playhouses used a wide variety of different kinds of manuscripts and printed texts but did not use the highly regularized promptbooks of the eighteenth-century theaters and later. His presentation of the peculiarities of playhouse texts provides an empirical basis for inferring the nature of the manuscripts that lie behind printed Shakespeare plays.

Key to
Famous Lines and Phrases

If music be the food of love, play on.   [*Orsino*—1.1.1]

And what should I do in Illyria?   [*Viola*—1.2.3]

O, you are sick of self-love, Malvolio, and taste with a distempered appetite.   [*Olivia*—1.5.89–90]

Make me a willow cabin at your gate
And call upon my soul within the house,
Write loyal cantons of contemnèd love
And sing them loud even in the dead of night . . .
      [*Viola*—1.5.271–74]

. . . she bore a mind that envy could not but call fair.
      [*Sebastian*—2.1.28–29]

O Time, thou must untangle this, not I.
It is too hard a knot for me t' untie.
      [*Viola*—2.2.40–41]

Not to be abed after midnight is to be up betimes . . .
      [*Toby*—2.3.1–2]

O mistress mine, where are you roaming?
      [*Fool*—2.3.40]

Am not I consanguineous?   [*Toby*—2.3.78]

Dost thou think, because thou art virtuous, there shall be no more cakes and ale?   [*Toby*—2.3.114–15]

I have no exquisite reason for 't, but I have reason
good enough.   [*Andrew*—2.3.143–44]

The spinsters and the knitters in the sun
And the free maids that weave their thread with bones
Do use to chant it.   [*Orsino*—2.4.50–53]

Come away, come away, death . . .

                                          [*Fool*—2.4.58]

 She never told her love,
But let concealment, like a worm i' th' bud,
Feed on her damask cheek.   [*Viola*—2.4.122–24]

. . . like Patience on a monument . . .   [*Viola*—2.4.126]

Some are born great, some achieve greatness, and
some have greatness thrust upon 'em.

                              [*Malvolio*—2.5.149–50]

 When that I was and a little tiny boy . . .

                                          [*Fool*—5.1.412]

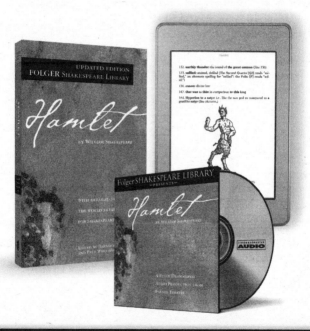

The Folger Shakespeare Editions combine expertly edited texts with illuminating explanatory notes and images to help you discover the works of William Shakespeare in exciting new ways.

ALL PLAYS NOW AVAILABLE